Hospitality & Construction Disputes Post-COVID

International and Comparative Business Law and Public Policy

VOLUME 6

The titles published in this series are listed at *brill.com/blpp*

Hospitality & Construction Disputes Post-COVID

Edited by

Steven G. Shapiro, Shaheeza Lalani, and Derek Heath

BRILL | NIJHOFF

LEIDEN | BOSTON

The Library of Congress Cataloging-in-Publication Data is available online at https://catalog.loc.gov
LC record available at https://lccn.loc.gov/2023039995

Typeface for the Latin, Greek, and Cyrillic scripts: "Brill". See and download: brill.com/brill-typeface.

ISSN 2667-3495
ISBN 978-90-04-51486-7 (hardback)
ISBN 978-90-04-51487-4 (e-book)
DOI 10.1163/9789004514874

This book is printed on acid-free paper and produced in a sustainable manner.

Contents

PART 2

Foreword

Hospitality and Construction – Two Candidates for Legal Harmonization

Legal harmonization projects often tackle big issues – the law governing insolvency, marriages, or the recognition and enforcement of judgments in civil and commercial matters illustrate the point. With hindsight, the more limited and pinpointed projects are often more successful, however. The prime illustration of this phenomenon is, of course, the Hague Convention on Child Abduction, which succeeded in changing state practice in large parts of the world on a very specific but crucial issue forever. There are scores of other examples as well, ranging from the Geneva Conventions on bills of exchange and cheques to the Hague Service Convention or the Cape Town Convention on Mobile Equipment. It seems the more limited the issue is, the easier it is for states to find consensus on its international regulation, provided an evident need for action can be demonstrated.

Hospitality and construction may just be two such issues which lend themselves to international harmonization. They are comparatively limited in the sense that they represent only a particular sector of the economy. But they are the source of specific cross-border problems which may well deserve the attention of international lawmakers. By deciding to act in these fields, the impact they will be making is likely to outsize the necessary effort.

In the case of hospitality, the promised benefits are relatively easy to demonstrate. Staying in short-term accommodation is a common experience, and frequently so in a transnational context. If problems arise, this will often be the first time for a citizen to get into contact with a foreign legal system, facing a dazzling multitude of issues, from the identification of the applicable law to the exploration of its content, to the determination of the competent tribunal and the enforcement of the judgment it has rendered. In addition, the information on the legal issues is mostly distributed asymmetrically, with airlines, hotel chains, booking platforms and travel agents as repeat players knowing perfectly their game, against the guest as an ignorant novice. The amount in dispute, though certainly important from the individual's perspective, is often not worth hiring a specialized lawyer. A short but precise international legal tool, for instance on security for cost requirements, the enforceability of settlements or an information database, might be a game changer.

In the case of construction, the setting is quite different. The parties involved in cross-border construction cases are typically professionals. They often have sophisticated knowledge and equal bargaining power. The stakes are also much higher than in hospitality. But very specific problems exist that may well be addressed by international law. They concern, for instance, the distribution of tasks in a consortium, the liability of its members as well as the liability of suppliers and contractors, the applicable health and safety standards, or the length of the statute of limitations. While these issues are so far exclusively dominated by national law, uniform conflicts rules may provide some tangible benefits for the global construction market.

One may think the link made here between hospitality and construction to be fortuitous. However, what binds them together, besides the obvious point that hospitality requires accommodation that needs to be constructed, is that both the hospitality and the construction industries have faced particular challenges during the COVID-19 pandemic. Lockdowns have negatively affected the activity in both sectors, often leading to complete and long closures and standstills. The different national vaccination certificates and the different virus test standards have made production more costly and created bureaucratic obstacles for a swift rebound. Some degree of harmonization will be instrumental in managing the next pandemic in a better way.

Whether the abundant legal diversity is to be handled or steps towards uniform law are to be made, well-trained lawyers in the particular area are needed. Despite their economic heft, specialization in the fields of hospitality and construction law is relatively rare. More targeted education is necessary. The University of Vienna has taken a step in this direction by creating a new Master of Laws program dedicated to "Tourism and Law" (*Tourismus und Recht*). It provides, *inter alia*, an introduction to conflict-of-laws and conflict-of-jurisdiction issues, as well as general government regulations and specific travel and hospitality rules on a national and international basis. The communication of these complex legal and economic issues is essential for the tourism industry and the persons entrusted with management and law enforcement. According to the broad field of the tourism industry the range of content taught in the Master of Laws program ranges from hotel and hospitality law, travel and aviation law to tax and fee law. In addition, the courses also cover the relevant aspects from real estate law and general tort law to business management and tourism marketing.

But specialization also requires research. Excellent examples are provided in this book. It is to be hoped they will help to raise the awareness of the specific issues of these two important sectors.

Matthias Lehmann and Helmut Ofner
Vienna, 6 May 2022

Figures and Tables

Figures

Tables

Notes on Contributors

Hadrian Beltrametti Walker
is the General Counsel and Company Secretary for Kempinski Hotels, Europe's oldest luxury hotel brand. He speaks four languages and delivers business-oriented legal services. He began his career in hospitality at Hilton Worldwide, and joined Kempinski Hotels in 2012. He is a solicitor of England & Wales, and holds an LL.B. in English and European Laws (Hons) from the University of Essex, an LL.M. in European Business Law (Hons) from the Pallas Consortium of Universities, and the LPC from the College of Law London (Moorgate). With a true passion for luxury, hospitality and sustainability, he also chairs the Kempinski group's Sustainability Committee. Additionally, he is on the Advisory Board of the Luxury Law Alliance, and is a member of the Energy and Environment Alliance's General Counsels Committee.

Jamey Collidge
is an Associate in the Construction Group with Troutman Pepper Hamilton Sanders LLP, based out of the Philadelphia, Pennsylvania office. He focuses on construction and government contract matters throughout the United States and represents clients in both state and federal court litigation as well as alternative dispute resolution proceedings. He also provides pre-dispute project counseling. He has been recognized in the "Ones to Watch" list published by The Best Lawyers in America. He completed his BA at Wake Forest University and his JD at Villanova University.

Yasaschandra Devarakonda
is a graduate of the B.A.-LLB. (Hons.) degree from National Law University Odisha, India in 2022, and practices in the dispute resolution and arbitration space in India. His practice primarily focuses on complex commercial and construction arbitrations, commercial litigation and insolvency matters.

Olivia Flasch
is a Legal Consultant in public international law. She regularly works on projects commissioned by the United Nations and other international organizations. Before becoming a consultant, Olivia was a litigation and arbitration associate at Signature Litigation. She holds a Bachelor's Degree in Public International Law and EU Law from The Hague University of Applied Sciences and a Master's Degree in Law from the University of Oxford.

Pierre Yves Gunter
is a Partner and the founder of Gunter Arbitration, a boutique law firm in Geneva that focuses on arbitration and dispute resolution. Prior to founding his own firm, he was a Partner and co-head of the arbitration practice at Bär & Karrer, a leading Swiss law firm with offices in Zurich, Geneva, Lugano, Zug, and Basel. He has been acting since 1991 in the field of international commercial arbitration and has extensive experience as counsel and arbitrator in the fields of construction and complex projects, joint-venture, oil & gas, telecommunications and IT, pharmaceutical, commodity and international trade as well as corporate and post M&A. He also regularly acts before state courts for litigation cases. He is currently a member of the Board of Directors of the Swiss Arbitration Centre and was previously a member of the Board of Directors at the Singapore International Arbitration Centre and co-chair of the International Arbitration Committee of the American Bar Association (Section of International Law and Practice).

Kang He
is a litigator with McGuireWoods in Northern Virginia. He focuses his litigation practice on contract disputes, real estate and zoning matters, franchise disputes, and eminent domain. He has been recognized as a "Legal Elite: Young Lawyer" by the Virginia Business Magazine, and a "Virginia Rising Star" by Thomson Reuters. As a trial lawyer, he also teaches trial tactics and evidentiary rules to local high schools and colleges. Before joining McGuireWoods, he clerked for Judge John M. Tran at the Fairfax County Circuit Court and served as an editor for the William & Mary Law Review.

Derek Heath
is a New York-licensed attorney who recently graduated summa cum laude with an LL.M. in International Business Law, where he specialized in International Business Disputes. He is now an Associate at CMS CEE in Budapest, Hungary, where he works as a foreign legal advisor, handling managed legal services for international corporations and assisting in their day-to-day legal operations. In the past, he has researched and studied a wide variety of subjects, such as US administrative law, data protection in arbitration, US cybersecurity regulations in the energy sector, and eConsent in clinical trials.

Eckhard Hellbeck
is counsel at White & Case in Washington, DC. He is qualified in Germany, New York and Washington, DC. For more than 23 years, he has represented parties in international commercial arbitration, as well as states and foreign

investors in investment treaty arbitration. He also regularly advises on issues of public international law. He has for many years judged student moot court competitions, in particular the annual Jessup Competition and various international arbitration moots. He also publishes regularly on issues of international arbitration and international law.

Richard D. Holzheimer, Jr.
is a partner with McGuire Woods. He is a first-chair trial attorney with extensive courtroom experience. His litigation practice focuses on construction, commercial litigation, government contracting, financial services, and real estate. He also serves as the President of the Asian Pacific American Bar Association of Virginia. He completed his B.A. at the University of Virginia and his J.D. at Notre Dame, where he served as the Notes Editor of the Journal of College and University Law.

Shaheeza Lalani
is the Executive Director of the LL.M. Programme at the University of Lausanne. She holds degrees from Queen's University and McGill University (Canada), the London School of Economics and the University of Lausanne. Her PhD thesis in Private International Law was awarded the UNIL Faculty Prize. She is a barrister & solicitor, admitted to the Law Society of British Columbia, has taught courses at the Universities of Fribourg, Bern, and Paris, and was the Founding Director of two other postgraduate programs in Switzerland. Previously Senior Legal Counsel with the Swiss Chambers' Arbitration Institution and Legal Counsel to the Swiss Institute of Comparative Law, Dr. Lalani has worked as an Assistant Legal Officer with The Hague Conference on Private International Law and has authored and edited several publications on international law and arbitration.

Cindy Lee
is an Associate in the Construction Group with Troutman Pepper Hamilton Sanders LLP, based out of the Los Angeles, California office. Her practice focuses on representing contractors, design professionals, and owners in construction disputes in the private and public context. She also advises clients on various contractor licensing issues and pre-litigation contractual disputes.

Matthias Lehmann
is a Full Professor at the University of Vienna, where he holds the Chair for Private Law, Private International and Comparative Law, and a Rotating Professor of European and Comparative Business Law at Radboud University

Nijmegen. Previously, he was a full professor at the Universities of Halle-Wittenberg and Bonn. He holds doctoral degrees from the University of Jena and Columbia University as well as a *Habilitation* (professorial thesis in Germany) from the University of Bayreuth. His main interest is in private international law, comparative law and dispute resolution. He is a member of the International Academy of Comparative Law, of the Council of the European Law Institute (ELI), of the American Law Institute (ALI), of the Academia Europaea (AE), and of the Academic Board of the European Banking Institute (EBI). Prof. Lehmann has been a visiting scholar at the London School of Economics and Political Science, Oxford University and Stanford University. He is regularly teaching as a guest professor at the Sorbonne Université, the Université de Fribourg, the Université de Lausanne, and the Universidad Pablo de Olavide in Spain.

Giacomo Lorenzo
is currently working as senior legal counsel at Deminor, an international litigation funder leader in Europe. Based in Brussels, he is in charge of identifying, assessing, and managing the funding of international and domestic disputes. Before joining Deminor, he worked as lawyer with the litigation and arbitration department of the leading Italian law firm, Gianni & Origoni. Giacomo has obtained a Master of Law (LL.M.) degree from the University of Lausanne, with a specialization in International Business Disputes. He is actively engaged in conferences regarding litigation funding and gives his contribution by regularly publishing articles on the subject.

Martina Magnarelli
is an Italian-qualified lawyer and a member of the Munich Bar, with working experience in five jurisdictions across Europe. She has acted as counsel and administrative secretary in several international arbitration proceedings under the ICC, DIS, and Swiss Rules of International Arbitration in a diverse range of sectors, including energy and natural resources, aviation and defence, construction, manufacturing, and private equity. Before joining 7SA in January 2019, she worked as legal counsel for Siemens in Paris and gained experience in international arbitration at the ICC International Court of Arbitration in Paris and the international arbitration group of Freshfields Bruckhaus Deringer LLP in Vienna. A graduate from LUISS Guido Carli University, Rome, she holds LL.M. and Ph.D. degrees from the University of Lausanne. She is the author of *Privity of Contract in International Investment Arbitration* (Kluwer Law International 2020) and regularly publishes and speaks on international commercial and

investment arbitration. She is an active member of AIA-ArbIt-40 – the Italian Below-40 arbitration association.

Bernhard Maier
is a Counsel in the London office of Signature Litigation LLP, a leading disputes boutique. He practices commercial and investment treaty arbitration, focusing on the natural resources, technology and infrastructure sectors. He also advises sovereign States and private clients on matters of general public international law, including before domestic courts. He is also a member of the UK Attorney General's C Panel of Public International Law Counsel to the Crown and an adjunct professor at Kings College London, where he co-convenes an LLM course on cyber law.

Anya Marinkovich
is Counsel at the boutique arbitration and dispute resolution firm Gunter Arbitration in Geneva. She has acted as counsel, arbitrator and arbitral secretary in a number of international commercial arbitrations concerning construction, oil & gas, sales, and corporate and post-M&A disputes. She is admitted to the California Bar and has training and practical experience in both common and civil law systems, as well as in the field of public international law. In 2023, she was appointed for a second term as member of the board of ICDR Young & International.

Gautam Mohanty
is an Assistant Professor at Jindal Global Law School (JGLS), Sonipat, India. He is also a PhD candidate in international economic law at Kozminski University, Warsaw, Poland. He is also an advocate enrolled at the bar in India and is also serving as a Fellow with JGLS Centre of Alternate Dispute Resolution (CADR).

Amadeu Blasco Muñoz
is Head of Legal at Copernicus Servicing. Before Copernicus, he was the Head of Litigation at the Spanish "bad bank", SAREB. He has more than 20 years of experience in debt workouts and insolvencies. He has participated in the largest insolvencies and debt restructurings of the last decade in Spain, including Martinsa Fadesa or Reyal Urbis, among others. Amadeu holds a *Licenciado en Derecho* from the *Universitat de Barcelona*, a Juris Doctor from the University of Puerto Rico Law School, an LL.M. from American University, Washington College of Law and an MBA from IESE Business School.

Helmut Ofner

is a Professor of Comparative Law, International Private Law and Civil Law at the University of Vienna where he completed his doctorate in law. He holds an LL.M. from the University of Trier and wrote his *Habilitation* (professorial thesis) in the field of Private Law. He is a member of the Scientific Advisory Board of the LL.M. program "European and International Business Law" at the University of Vienna, Deputy Chairman of the Arbitration Commission of the University of Vienna, Vice Leader of the Study Program at the Faculty of Law, Head of the Institute for European, International and Comparative Law, and Member of the Scientific Advisory Board of the LL.M. Program "Information and Media Law" at the University of Vienna. He also holds functions and memberships in scientific societies and journals.

Oluwaseun Oloruntimehin

is a dual-licensed lawyer in New York, USA and Nigeria with a Master of Laws (LL.M.) from the University College London, an arbitrator, negotiator, chartered secretary and governance professional qualified in the UK and Nigeria. She is a dispute resolution specialist focused on international commercial arbitration with a successful track record of strategically advising and representing clients across a wide range of industries, in domestic and cross border disputes. She also sits as an arbitrator and is a member of the Panel of Neutrals for arbitral institutions including LCA and CIArb-LCA MSME Scheme. She teaches arbitration courses and is a fellow of the ciarbas well as an editor for the lca. She is a global legal consultant providing corporate and dispute resolution services in multiple regions including North America, Asia Pacific, Europe and Africa. She is the founding partner of S. O. Oloruntimehin & Co and sits on the advisory board of multiple organizations including Axiom (International Legal Talent) in Switzerland. She enjoys teaching, writing and speaking on diverse arbitration topics.

Fernando Ortega

is a partner and Head of Arbitration at IAA Law Firm based in Dubai. He holds a Bachelor of Arts in History from the University of California Los Angeles and a J.D. from American University, Washington College of Law. He has led arbitration programs at multiple firms in the Middle East and has become a figurehead of international arbitration and enforcement.

Steven G. Shapiro

teaches, writes, and speaks on topics in complex hospitality issues and construction law at the American University Washington College of Law, blending his career in law firm practice, construction engineering, and academics. Recognized for innovation in bringing the realities and economics of commercial practice into the classroom and in service to the law school, he imagined and proposed the idea of the Hospitality & Tourism Law program. In addition, he brings a distinct experience in the interplay of commercial transactions in law school courses in contract drafting, real estate and hotel development, construction law, and externship studies. He received his undergraduate degree from Georgetown University in 1984, a law degree from the Georgetown University Law Center in 1987, and a Masters of Law degree from Georgetown Law Center in 1991. In 2001, he made a mid-career move from the practice of law to construction, and in 2004, he received a Masters of Engineering Degree from the University of Maryland.

Katherine Simpson
is an arbitrator and mediator with Simpson Dispute Resolution (US) and 33 Bedford Row Chambers (UK). She is a Fellow of the College of Commercial Arbitrators and the Chartered Institute of Arbitrators and is a Member of the National Academy of Distinguished Neutrals. Her ADR practice includes commercial, international, investor-state, consumer, employment, and labor arbitration. She is an attorney admitted in Maryland and New Jersey in the United States. She is well known for her work to increase diversity among appointed neutrals, and she currently serves as Vice Chair of the Ray Corollary Initiative and as Chair of the Women in Dispute Resolution (WIDR) Committee of the American Bar Association (ABA) Dispute Resolution Section. She is a Postdoctoral Associate at the Scheinman Institute on Conflict Resolution at the School of Industrial and Labor Relations at Cornell University. She serves the CPR's Panels of Distinguished Neutrals and the American Arbitration Association's icdr, Employment, Consumer, and Commercial Panels.

Thomas R. Snider
is a Partner and the Head of International Arbitration at Charles Russell Speechlys LLP in Dubai. He is experienced in international commercial arbitration, international investment disputes, state-to-state arbitration, and foreign sovereign immunity issues. He is on the panel of arbitrators of several arbitral institutions around the world, and is a member of the Board of Directors of the Dubai International Arbitration Centre, the Court of Arbitration of the Singapore International Arbitration Centre, the Arbitration Committee of the Lagos Court of Arbitration, and the International Arbitration Committee of KCAB International (an independent division of the Korean Commercial Arbitration Board).

Greig Taylor
is a managing director in AlixPartners' New York office. His practice focuses on the assessment of damages and related quantum issues, and the provision of expert testimony, in the context of disputes, domestic and international. He completed a B.A. (Hons) in Modern History at the University of Manchester in England and is a fellow of the Institute of Chartered Accountants of England and Wales. In 2004–2005, he spent 10 months at sea racing a 72-foot yacht around the world.

R. Zachary Torres-Fowler
is a Partner in Troutman Pepper's Construction Practice Group based in the firm's Philadelphia and New York offices. His practice focuses on construction-related disputes, including complex domestic and international arbitration proceedings. He has experience before arbitral panels and tribunals under a wide variety of U.S. domestic and international arbitration rules including the AAA, JAMS, ICDR, ICC, LCIA, and ICSID. His experience includes advising clients in connection with construction and infrastructure projects in the U.S., Africa, the Middle East, and Latin America. He has significant experience representing owners, contractors, and suppliers/subcontractors in connection with disputes arising from a wide variety of construction projects including power plants, airports, commercial buildings, and other civil infrastructure works.

John D. Wilburn
a partner with McGuire Woods, is an experienced first-chair trial lawyer. His practice focuses on construction, land use, and eminent domain litigation around the country. He has been invited to join numerous panels on land use and development as a well-known speaker, including many events hosted by his Firm or outside groups, such as the Southern Gas Association.

PART 1

Introduction: Hospitality Disputes

Hadrian Beltrametti-Walker

It was March 2020. The hospitality and tourism industry had been growing steadily for decades, reaching its peak at around 10% of global GDP[1] and generating US$ 550 B in global rooms revenue.[2] Then, as COVID-19 spread around the world, the industry all but came to a complete standstill. Governments imposed lockdowns, borders closed, people were confined to their homes.

In the wake of such a catastrophe, businesses worldwide sought ways to mitigate their losses. Whilst some industries thrived, others were left destitute. Few were hit as hard as hospitality and tourism.

In many ways, the industry found ways to adapt. Hotels hosted people being repatriated or in quarantine; restaurants delivered food and prepared meals for healthcare workers; bed linens were donated to repurpose them into face masks; hotel rooms were temporarily turned into hospital rooms. It is a huge testimony to the resilience and kindness of hospitality industry professionals to dedicate their time to such endeavours whilst dealing with a crisis of this magnitude. On the corporate side, an evolving business and legal landscape also arose, requiring legal practitioners to stay on top of insurance claims, government regulations, travel restrictions, *force majeure*, and contracts disputes.

What this also illustrates is two important things: the ability to adapt to changing circumstances, and to find solutions to emerging problems. These two characteristics are also relevant in dispute resolution, and have been ever more so since the beginning of the pandemic.

Indeed, among the many challenges of the global health crisis, not least the humanitarian aspect, has been the allocation of risk and loss in business transactions arising from the pandemic. As creditors sought payment from their debtors, and contractual counterparties sought performance by their obligors, disputes arose around the world, invoking negotiations, mediation, arbitration, and litigation.

1 "50+ Hospitality Statistics You Should Know (2023)," Hotel Tech Report, November 2, 2022, https://hoteltechreport.com/news/hospitality-statistics. It is now 75+ Hospitality Statistics You Should Know (2023), last updated August 9, 2023, https://hoteltechreport.com/news/hospitality-statistics.

2 Natalie Weisz, Denise DeGirolamo, and Gary Stringer, "2019 Global Hotel Study: An unprecedented, worldwide view of the hospitality industry," STR, accessed December 23, 2022, https://str.com/sites/default/files/global-hotel-study-report-2019-2020.pdf.

 | DOI:10.1163/9789004514874_002

The pandemic was not without its challenges for dispute resolution, which would normally take place in person. In many cases, the resolution of disputes had to be postponed, held via video conference, or in hybrid form. As an in-house legal practitioner myself, one of my goals is to guide the business to avoid disputes, but in pandemic times where disputes are more likely to arise, we are deprived of one of our most powerful weapons: hospitality! We must not underestimate the importance of meeting people face to face, body language, and informal discussions.

The UNIL International Conference on Hospitality and Construction Disputes Post-COVID was a great example of adapting to the "new normal." Gathering subject-matter experts from around the world, some were able to attend in person, whilst others joined via video link. The result of this conference is the present book, composed of articles written by these experts, which include in-house counsel, private practitioners, advisors and consultants from Europe, Asia, the Middle East, Africa, and the Americas. With its global, comparative nature, Hospitality and Construction Disputes Post-COVID offers the reader an in-depth specialist perspective into dispute resolution in the hospitality and construction sectors around the world.

As a lawyer working in-house for a global business, I have found the content useful and insightful. Hotel brands, owners and operators will find the paper on Disputes under Hotel Management Agreements (Chapter 4) particularly interesting, as it discusses rights, remedies, termination rights, *force majeure*, and fee calculations. Also anyone working in or with hospitality will recognise that funding disputes will be ever more relevant as the economic effect of the pandemic continues to leave its mark – a topic discussed in Chapter 1, which discusses the third-party funding of hospitality disputes in the UAE. Unfortunately, and linked to this, a very relevant topic to read about is the possibility of lender foreclosure on hospitality assets. The author approaches this from an innovative game theory approach in Chapter 2.

At the time of writing this introduction, thinking back on the pandemic, we are living a moment of relative normality compared to the past two years; and with the vaccine there is hope that we will not suffer future waves of the coronavirus as much as the first few. But we are not yet out of the woods: there is talk of another wave: What to take away from this is not a loss of hope, but awareness that the "new normal" is here to stay a little while longer, and I hope that this book will help guide the reader along the way.

CHAPTER 1

Funding Construction and Hospitality Disputes after COVID

Fernando Ortega and Giacomo Lorenzo

1 Introduction

COVID-19 has altered the world in many ways, changing how we conduct business, interact with one another, and how we resolve disputes. The virus has also impacted the use of Third-Party Funding (hereinafter "TPF") to finance disputes, in the Middle East and elsewhere.

Prior to COVID-19, third party funders (hereinafter "funders") were selective in the types of claims they funded. However, because of COVID-19, the funders have become even more selective, increasing their rates and adding additional terms to funding arrangements. These additional terms include adding interest on the money paid for the arbitration and litigation costs, because these funders are aware of market conditions and potential claimants' lack of financial resources during the pandemic and beyond.

This chapter focuses on how funders look at construction and hospitality claims when determining whether to fund the claim. It provides background on TPF, and an overview of how COVID-19 impacted the construction and hospitality sectors. It also explores what funders look for when considering a claim, and what a claimant will need to consider if it wishes to have its claim funded.

2 An Introduction to TPF

2.1 *Definition of TPF*

TPF is the financing method for funding litigation or arbitration proceedings by a specialized funder, which is not involved in the dispute and whose interest is to gain potential profit in return for providing financial support.[1] This mechanism consists of an agreement, by which the funder is obliged to cover a

1 Gian Marco Solas, *Third-Party Funding* (Cambridge University Press, 2019), 2.

 | DOI:10.1163/9789004514874_003

party's legal costs and expenses of a legal claim in exchange for a share in any future compensation arising from the litigation or arbitration proceedings.[2]

2.2 *Origin and Developments of TPF*

The first cases in which a third party funded a lawsuit date back to medieval England: at that time, English nobles funded the lawsuits of their subjects, who acted as proxies that filed lawsuits on their nobles' behalf.[3]

Historically, in many common law jurisdictions, TPF was prohibited according to principles of champerty[4] and maintenance.[5] According to these doctrines, it was unethical, and therefore prohibited, to support the lawsuit of a third party.[6] On the other hand, in many civil law legal systems, this practice has never constituted an unlawful act.

Although TPF has its roots in the past, it represents a relatively new phenomenon for some countries where this financing method is less known. However, unpredictable times have accelerated innovation, and, in the last year, a renewed interest has led to the development of TPF at a global level, causing it to once again become one of the major topics in the legal world. This special attention is undoubtedly due to the financial impact of the COVID-19, the increase of disputes arising from contract breaches, and sovereign measures in response to the pandemic. In addition, investors, who have increased their search for alternative investments, especially during the pandemic, are now even more attracted by this new asset class, given its potential high returns and its uncorrelated nature to the traditional equity market.[7]

2 "Report of the ICCA-Queen Mary Task Force on Third-Party Funding in International Arbitration," ICCA, accessed December 23, 2022, 50, https://cdn.arbitration-icca.org/s3fs-public/document/media_document/Third-Party-Funding-Report%20.pdf.

3 "Litigation Funders: Champions or Champertous?," Omni Bridgeway, December 1, 2017, https://omnibridgeway.com/insights/blog/blog-posts/global/2017/11/30/litigation-funding-champions-or-champerty.

4 Champerty is the financial support, by a party not naturally concerned in the suit, of a plaintiff that allows them to prosecute a lawsuit on condition that, if it be brought to a successful issue, the plaintiff will repay them with a share of the proceed from the suit. See *Oxford English Dictionary* (Oxford University Press, 2022), available at www.oed.com.

5 Maintenance is the intermeddling of a disinterested party to encourage a lawsuit See L.B. Curzon, Dictionary of Law, 6th ed. (London: Longman, 2001).

6 Valentina Frignati, "Ethical implications of third-party funding in international arbitration," *Arbitration International* 32, no. 3 (September 2016): 505.

7 Elad Smadja, "Courting success: litigation funding a fresh alternative to stock market," BusinessDay, March 31, 2021, https://www.businesslive.co.za/bd/opinion/2021-03-31-courting-success-litigation-funding-a-fresh-alternative-to-stock-market/.

TPF has traditionally been considered an important tool that guarantees access to justice for "impecunious claimants," who could potentially be at a disadvantage when pursuing a case due to their financial situation.[8] Through recourse to the TPF, the risk of losing the money invested pursuing the arbitration or litigation is transferred from the impecunious claimant to the funder.[9]

However, the pandemic has shown that TPF may also benefit large companies and even public entities looking for cost-risk externalization. Indeed, TPF offers the possibility of managing risk, reducing legal expenses, taking the litigation costs off balance sheets, and monetizing existing claims and/or decisions and awards. In this way, claimants can utilize their own funds for other business priorities rather than allocating resources to legal proceedings, or they can use part of the TPF funds for their other business needs.

3 How TPF Works

3.1 *Main Provisions of Litigation Funding Agreements*

The litigation funding agreement is not qualified and is often not regulated by the laws governing contracts in the different jurisdiction and is referred to as an atypical contract.

In this regard, it is important to clarify that a litigation funding agreement cannot be qualified as a loan. Indeed, one of the essential elements of such a contract, namely the obligation to return the financed sums to the lender, is missing. As stated above, the obligation of the funded party to pay the funder arises only if the funded party effectively recovers the sums claimed in the legal action.[10]

The litigation funding agreement cannot be qualified as an insurance contract either. Indeed, even in this case, one of the essential elements that characterizes insurance contracts, namely, the payment of the insurance premium is missing.[11]

8 Solas, *supra* note 1, at 175.

9 Jérôme Saulnier, Klaus Müller, and Ivona Koronthalyova, "Responsible Private Funding Litigation: European added value assessment," European Parliamentary Research Service, accessed December 23, 2022, https://www.europarl.europa.eu/RegData/etudes/STUD/2021/662612/EPRS_STU(2021)662612_EN.pdf.

10 Giorgio De Nova, "Il Finanziamento della Lite," conference organized by the Milan Chamber of Arbitration, filmed October 21, 2021, Milan, Italy, video, https://www.youtube.com/watch?v=ViSApojYGt4.

11 *Id.*

Although it is not possible to give an internationally recognized qualification of the litigation funding agreement, it is possible to highlight the most important provisions characterizing this type of contract:

- *costs covered by the funder*: in order to avoid misunderstandings, it is necessary to specify which costs of the legal action will be borne by the funder;
- *investment cap*: the investor will set a cap on its investment, beyond which it will not pay further disputes-related costs;
- *counterclaims*: in the litigation funding agreement will be determined whether the funder is obliged to pay the costs of legal action concerning any counterclaim. In some cases, the funder may also decide to bear the risk of paying the amounts claimed as counterclaim. Thus, in the event of an adverse judgment, the funder will bear the costs of the dispute including the legal costs related to the counterclaim;
- *funder's remuneration*: litigation funding agreement specifies how the funder will be compensated in case of a favorable outcome of the proceedings. It can be a percentage of the proceeds or a multiple of the invested capital in the dispute or a combination of both;
- *control over the dispute*: it is essential to determine how the key decisions will be taken and also who is entitled to take those decisions (*e.g.*, settle the case, propose an appeal against the judgment and legal strategy);
- *termination right*: besides cases where one of the parties breaches the agreement, the litigation funding agreement may also provide for the funder's right to terminate the contract if an event has occurred which has irremediably jeopardized the outcome of the proceedings. Moreover, it is commonly provided that, in the event of a disagreement between the funder and the funded party, the funder may decide to terminate the contract.[12]

3.2 *The Benefits of TPF*

When a party decides to pursue a dispute, it decides to take a financial risk. This is because no matter how meritorious a claim may be, there will always be the risk of losing the case. Therefore, the major benefit parties find in TPF is that the risk of losing the money of the legal costs is transferred from the litigant to the funder.

TPF can be used by different entities to meet different needs.

Historically, the TPF has been qualified as a tool that provides access to justice to so-called "impecunious claimants," *i.e.*, those who cannot afford to cover

12 Jens Benoot, "The Third Party Litigation Funding Law Review: Belgium," The Law Reviews, November 22, 2021, https://thelawreviews.co.uk/title/the-third-party-litigation-funding-law-review/belgium.

the costs associated with a dispute. Therefore, thanks to the TPF, companies or individuals that are in a financial predicament can still pursue their claims. Without the TPF, such litigants would have to waive their rights or, in any case, accept disadvantageous settlement agreement. In addition, some funders offer the opportunity to receive monies as an upfront: if the party is in a difficult financial circumstance, the funder, besides covering the costs of the dispute, can pay in advance a portion of the proceeds that the funded party can use to run its business. This arrangement can be vital for the company, which, without such support, would go bankrupt.

Another scenario where the TPF represents added value is when there is a significant financial gap between the two litigants, (*i.e.* when a small/medium-sized company is involved in an international dispute against a large multinational). Even if the small/medium-sized company is financially sound, it may not have the necessary resources and experience to deal with international arbitration, which is generally complex and costly. In such a scenario, TPF levels the playing field, allowing the funded party to be assisted by experienced lawyers and experts without incurring in any costs. Therefore, thanks to the TPF, the small/medium-sized company will be allowed to engage highly qualified practitioners and therefore have a better chance of winning the case. Furthermore, in working with a professional, experienced litigation funder with a global presence, the company sends a powerful message to the opposing party that they will pursue the case to its logical conclusion, as money, time and resources are no longer obstacles.

In addition, TPF is also utilized by large corporations that want to optimize the legal costs. Every year, large corporations allocate a budget to be used for legal costs. However, it is possible that the corporation may face extra legal costs that were not foreseen at the beginning of the year, due, for example, to the start of new dispute. In such a case, without asking for an increase in the legal budget, the general counsel may choose recourse to TPF in order to optimize costs and externalize risk. Thanks to TPF, therefore, large corporations avoid wasting money on time-consuming and costly disputes and give priority to the development of their core business.

Considering the above, it is clear that from a financial point of view, that TPF represents a solution to several problems. These benefits are even more appreciable in times of financial crisis or great economic uncertainty, during which costs and risk reduction become essential for companies.[13]

13 Jane Croft, "Litigation Finance Follows Credit Crunch," Financial Times, January 27, 2010, http://www.ft.com/cms/s/0/7c98c38a-0ab1-11df-b35f-00144feabdc0.html; Maya Steinitz,

3.3 *What Types of Disputes Can Be Funded?*

All types of disputes can be funded. Indeed, funders generally choose to fund several cases involving different legal matters and belonging to different areas of law to diversify their risk.[14]

The issues that count in assessing the fundability of a case can be divided into legal and economic aspects. The first thing the funder will assess is the economics of the investment. In particular, there must be a good proportion between the investment (the costs that the funder will have to bear) and the total value of the claim. Generally speaking, this proportion should be at least 1 to 10. In other words, if the value of the case is 100 million euros, the funder's total investment must not exceed 10 million euros. This allows the guarantee that, in the event of a positive outcome of the proceedings, the funder can have its percentage and at the same time the funded party obtains a reasonable portion of the proceeds.[15]

Once this first aspect has been assessed, the funder will assess the merits of the case. The risk of losing the case should not be particularly high (in general, no more than 30%). This assessment is not easy and funders, after an internal analysis of the case, often engage specialized law firms for further legal opinions on the risk of losing the case.

Subsequently, other features of the proceedings will be assessed, such as the expected duration of the proceedings, the competent court and all aspects of the enforcement phase. An essential element is that the other party is solvent, otherwise even if the outcome of the proceedings and the enforcement phase are successful, it will not be possible to recover the amount claimed.

Notwithstanding the above, it is important to clarify that even if, in general, all the types of disputes are financeable, some type of disputes are particularly suited to TPF.

As it will be explained in the next paragraphs, litigation funders are particularly interested in funding arbitration. Indeed, from the litigants perspective, arbitration is usually very costly and complex and, on the other hand, from the funders' perspective, it constitutes a more "secure" investment, since it allows the funder to foresee certain essential aspects of the procedure (duration, who will decide the dispute, expected costs, *etc.*).

"Whose Claim Is This Anyway? Third Party Litigation Funding," *Minnesota Law Review* 95, no. 4 (April 7, 2010): 1268, 1283.

14 "Transform commercial litigation and arbitration claims into financial assets," Deminor, accessed April 15, 2022, 13, https://drs.deminor.com/en/deminor-litigation-funding-ebook.

15 *Id.*

In conclusion on this matter, usually the cases excluded from TPF are the following: when prospects for success are particularly low; when it is not possible to quantify the success expected; when the total amount of the legal budget is too high in comparison with the total value of the claim.[16]

3.4 *Remuneration of the Funder*

3.4.1 Plaintiff

As mentioned at the very beginning of this chapter, the fundamental principle of litigation funding is "no cure, no pay." Therefore, the funder will be entitled to receive a profit only if and when the funded party recovers the amount claimed. If the outcome of the proceedings is unfavorable, the funded party will not have to pay anything to the funder, who will lose the entire investment.

It is important to clarify that the positive outcome of the proceedings does not entitle the funders to ask for remuneration. The funder has the right to obtain its remuneration only when the funded party recovers the sums claimed. For this reason, one of the key aspects subject to review during the due diligence phase is the enforceability of the award and the existence/location of enforceable assets.

Once the funded party has recovered sums claimed, the funder will be entitled to a remuneration that can be calculated in the following ways: it may be a percentage of the sums recovered by the party; it may be a multiple of the initial investment; it may be a combination of the multiple of the investment and a percentage of the sums recovered by the funded party at the outcome of the judgment.[17]

The type of remuneration is decided as part of the negotiations of the litigation funding agreement. The percentage or multiple of the investment is proposed by the funder based on certain criteria that take into account the risk of the investment and the expected timing of any return on the investment.[18]

3.4.2 Defendant

Historically, TPF is used by plaintiffs. This feature of the TPF market is explained by the fact that, in this way, it is "easier" to structure the litigation funding agreement as well as to agree on the eventual remuneration of the funder.

That said, however, in recent years we are witnessing an increased interest in defense-side funding.

16 See De Nova, *supra* note 10.

17 Deminor, *supra* note 14.

18 *Id.*

However, in this case it is essential that the funder and the funded defendant properly structure the financing agreement, in particular, define what is to be understood by "success" of the case.[19]

Indeed, it is more complicated to decide what is meant by "success" of the case in a defense-side funding and on what basis the funder's percentage will be calculated.

In general, the success of the case from the defendant's perspective occurs in different scenarios. The first is when the defendant is successful and, therefore, does not have to pay anything to the plaintiff. Nevertheless, it may happen that the defendant is ordered to pay a lower amount of money compared to what the plaintiff claimed in court and this may in some cases represent a "success."[20]

As an example, if the value of the plaintiff's claim is EUR 10 million and, at the end of the proceedings, the defendant is condemned to pay EUR 3 million, the funder may be entitled to a percentage calculated on EUR 7 million. Thus, in such a case the funder's profit will be calculated on the basis of the amounts that was spared by the defendant.[21]

3.5 *When Can the Funder Intervene in the Proceedings?*

TPF can be utilized by the funded parties in any phase of the dispute. Indeed, depending on the specific case, it may make sense to seek the assistance of a funder at different stages of the proceedings.

Before commencing legal action, it can certainly make sense to turn to a funder. In this way, the litigant can obtain an independent third-party opinion at no cost. The funder's assessment of the case is extremely thorough and considers several aspects that the parties do not usually take in consideration. This preliminary assessment may help the litigant to decide whether it is worth going to court.

Applying for funding may also make sense during the proceedings. It is common that the litigant no longer wants to invest money in a dispute. Very often, what happens is that the litigant, exhausted by the length of the proceedings, gives up and accepts an unprofitable settlement. The involvement of a funder, in such a case, can give new strength to the litigant who, no longer having to bear the costs of litigation, will decide to continue until the end of the proceedings.

---

19 Emily Samra, "The Business of Defense: Defense-Side Litigation Financing," *University of Chicago Law Review* 83, no. 4 (October 2016): 2299–2341.

20 *Id.*

21 *Id.*

Even if the party has obtained an enforceable title, such as a final judgment, arbitration award or settlement agreement, it may make sense to have recourse to TPF. Indeed, having obtained an enforceable title is very often not the end of the dispute. If the counterparty does not wish to pay, the enforcement phase must be carried out, which can be complicated if the location of the assets is not known or the assets are located abroad. In those cases, it is advisable to turn to a funder that is present in several jurisdictions: it will be able to conduct asset tracing and to hire the qualified lawyers and experts who can proceed with the enforcement.

Finally, being supported by a funder in the negotiation of a settlement agreement can be decisive. Indeed, the counterparty will understand that the case is strong on the merits and that time and money are no longer an obstacle for the party, who will therefore not be inclined to give up recovering the sums due.

3.6 *Who Will Manage the Dispute Taking the Most Important Decisions?*

One of the most important issues related to TPF concerns the management of the proceedings: who will take the relevant decisions in the course of the proceedings? Who will give instructions to the lawyers? What happens in case of divergent positions between the funder and the funded party?

To answer these questions, a distinction must first be made between the so-called "active" and "passive" TPF.

In the first case, the funded party decides to rely completely on the funder and generally grants it the management of the legal action.[22] However, it must be borne in mind that the funder will not be part of the dispute. Indeed, the TPF mechanism differs from the purchase of the claim where the purchaser becomes the owner of the rights of action and a part of the proceeding. With an active TPF mechanism, the funder will have a broad decision-making power and will be able to propose to the party the lawyers to be appointed, taking in consideration the type of dispute.[23] Moreover, it can also discuss the strategy directly with the lawyers. Notwithstanding the above, all the important decisions will be taken by the clients.

In the case of passive TPF the funder will only assess the case and, if the criteria for funding are met, it will cover the cost of the legal action on behalf of the funded party. In this case, the funder will not be involved in the decisions related to the legal strategy and it will only be informed of the most important developments in the proceedings.[24]

---

22 Deminor, *supra* note 14, at 8.

23 *Id.*

24 *Id.*

As mentioned above, in both scenarios, the most important decisions are taken by the client, who always remains a party to the proceedings. What happens then if the funded party makes a decision that is not approved by the funder? The most common case is when the counterparty makes a settlement proposal. In such a case, there may be an interest for the funded party to accept, while the funder may not consider the proposal adequate in the light of the investment that has been made to cover all legal costs. To protect the interests of both parties, it is appropriate to determine what will happen in such cases in the litigation funding agreement.

Generally, the litigation funding agreement contains a clause that allows the funder to withdraw from the agreement: if the funder believes that it is not worth pursuing an appeal against an unfavorable decision and, on the other hand, the funded party is determined to pursue the case, the litigation funder has the right to withdraw from the litigation funding agreement. In this case, the funded party will be able to pursue its legal action, however, the costs of the legal action will no longer be borne by the funder but by the party itself.

3.7 *Increasing Recourse to TPF in Arbitration*

There are several advantages that stem from the use of TPF in arbitration and this is the reason why we are advocating an increased use of TPF by parties involved in arbitration proceedings.

First, it is well known that, despite the objective pros of arbitration, many companies and individuals prefer to entrust the resolution of their disputes to state courts. The reason is that they cannot afford the costs of arbitration, which are higher than those of state court proceedings. In this regard, TPF may represent a solution since the funder will cover all the costs of arbitration instead of the funded party and the risk of loss is also transferred to the funder.

Moreover, with TPF, the funded party can rely on the free and independent opinion of the funder, who will conduct comprehensive due diligence exercises, analyzing the documents, evaluating the risk of losing the case and the possibility of enforcing the award. In this way, the funded party can make an informed decision on whether to initiate arbitration proceedings or not.

Furthermore, specialized funders have an international team of professionals with an in-depth experience in the legal field. They usually have good connections with leading law firms all over the world and this can be an additional advantage if the party is involved in an international dispute, where the knowledge of foreign law and access to experienced lawyers can make the difference.

On the other hand, from a funder's perspective, arbitration constitutes a more "secure" investment since it offers the possibility of foreseeing several aspects of the proceedings.

Indeed, the expected duration of the proceedings constitutes an essential element in the funder's evaluation of the case. Thus, given that arbitration is characterized by shorter timeframes and predictability in the duration of proceedings, it is typically the preferred choice.

In addition, since there are limited grounds on which to appeal an arbitral award, in comparison to a court's judgment, the enforced award is usually obtained in a shorter timeframe.

Finally, another important aspect is that the dispute will be decided by one or more arbitrators, who usually have in-depth knowledge of, and extensive experience on, the subject matter in dispute. Therefore, the risk of a wrong decision for lack of experience of the decision-maker is drastically reduced.

Notwithstanding the above, it is important to mention that questions have been raised on the impact of TPF on arbitral proceedings, these include, issues relating to the transparency and disclosure obligations.

3.8 *Disclosure Obligations and Potential Conflict of Interests*

The first question to be asked is whether the TPF can lead to conflict of interests. Scholars and practitioners have reached different conclusions. Some have emphasized that TPF is one of many possible ways to receive financial support in pursuing a legal action.

According to the supporters of this theory, the issues concerning the financial aspects of the dispute would have nothing to do with the merits of the dispute and, therefore, there is no valid justification for treating a funding obtained by a litigation funder differently from a corporate loan.[25] Following this argument, similarly with a corporate loan, a TPF does not raise the issues of conflict of interest. In addition, another argument made against the disclosure obligation is that disclosure of the existence of a financing agreement could trigger frivolous challenge to arbitrators or claims for security for costs. These arguments, however, have not been accepted by the arbitration community.

The parties involved in an arbitration have the interest and the right to a fair and unbiased decision. Therefore, to safeguard the integrity of the arbitral process, arbitrators must be independent and impartial. That is the reason why arbitrators have a duty to investigate and disclose potential conflicts of interest, informing the parties of any circumstances that could affect their

25 Munir Maniruzzaman, "Third-Party Funding in International Arbitration – A Menace or Panacea?," Kluwer Arbitration Blog, December 29, 2012, http://kluwerarbitrationblog.com/2012/12/29/third-party-funding-in-international-arbitration-a-menace-or-panacea/?doing_wp_cron=1503332583.8441140651702880859375.

impartiality or independence. In order to allow the arbitrators to inform the parties of possible circumstances that may compromise their integrity, the arbitrators must be aware of the identity of the parties that have an interest (even a purely economic interest) in the arbitration.

Since the funder has an economic interest in the favorable outcome of the arbitration proceedings and since the funder very often has a decision power regarding the strategy to be adopted, it is conceivable that a conflict of interest may arise.[26] Therefore, the requirements of independence and impartiality of the arbitrators must also be investigated with respect to the funder. Indeed, funders work on regular basis with lawyers and practitioners that are usually appointed as arbitrators. Therefore, there is the possibility that arbitrators have in the past had a business relationship with the funder and this could jeopardize the validity of the arbitration proceedings and/or the arbitral award.[27]

Considering the above, to protect the interests of the parties and the investment of the funder, it is essential that the funded party discloses the identity of the funder, enabling the arbitrators and the counterpart to assess possible conflicts of interest.

Furthermore, another argument in favor of making disclosure of funding arrangements mandatory is that it permits the parties to the proceedings, especially the non-funded party, and the tribunal, to make an appropriate assessment with respect to orders for security for costs.

Security for costs is a precautionary measure, so the plaintiff must prove that the following conditions are met: the court has *prima facie* jurisdiction to decide the dispute; *fumus boni iuri; periculum in mora*; the balance of interests is in its favor.

In addition, it is required that the claimant prove the existence of an exceptional circumstance ("fundamental change") affecting the capability of the funded party to reimburse the legal costs of the counterparty.

To determine the existence of a fundamental change of circumstances, arbitration case law focuses on the content of the TPF agreement and in particular on the following questions:

- Who actually controls the defense strategy?
- Is there an *ad nutum* withdrawal clause in favor of the funder?

26 Sebastián Torres Linke, "Third-Party Litigation Funding in International Arbitration: Conflicts of Interest with Arbitrators" (L. Deg. diss., University of Münster, 2019).

27 Sahana Ramesh, "Third-Party Funding in International Arbitration: Ownership of the Claim, Consequences for Costs Orders, and Regulation," *Arbitration International* 36, no. 2 (June 2020): 275.

- Is the funder liable for adverse costs?
- What is the financial situation of the funded party?

Recourse to the TPF is not an indicator of insolvency of the funded party. However, there is a risk that the funded party is insolvent and will not pay the adverse costs. In such a case, if the litigation funder has no obligation to pay the adverse costs if the financed party loses its case, the defendant may face a real risk of not being reimbursed for its legal costs incurred. Therefore, in such a case, the tribunal will have to carefully assess the situation and decide whether an order for security of costs is appropriate.

Therefore, since the existence of a litigation funder may change the decision also on the security for costs, most practitioners believe that the intervention of a third-party funder must be regulated with respect to the disclosure obligations.

This is the approach taken by some arbitral institutions that have included new provisions in their regulations concerning the disclosure obligations for the funded party:

- *Centre for Arbitration and Mediation of the Chamber of Commerce Brazil-Canada* ("*CAM-CCBC*"): *Recommendations regarding the existence of third-party funding in arbitrations administered by CAM-CCBC, Communication*, article 4, provides a recommendation for the funded party to disclose the existence of the litigation funding agreement and avoid potential conflicts of interest "[i]n order to avoid potential conflicts of interest, CAM-CCBC recommends the parties to report the existence of third-party funding to CAM-CCBC at the earliest opportunity. The complete qualification of the funder should be included in this communication."[28]
- *China International Economic and Trade Arbitration Commission* ("*CIETAC*"): China International Economic and Trade Arbitration Commission International Investment Arbitration Rules, article 27(2), provides an obligation for the funded party to disclose the existence of a litigation funding agreement as soon as it is executed, "[a]s soon as the third party funding agreement is concluded, the party accepting the funding shall notify in writing, without delay, the other party or parties, the arbitral tribunal, and the IDSC or the CIETAC Hong Kong Arbitration Center that administers the case, of the existence and nature of the third party funding arrangement, and the name and address of the third party funder. The arbitral tribunal

28 "Recommendations regarding the existence of third-party funding in arbitrations administered by CAM-CCBC," Center for Arbitration and Mediation of the Chamber of Commerce Brazil-Canada, July 20, 2016, https://ccbc.org.br/cam-ccbc-centro-arbitragem-mediacao/en/administrative-resolutions/ar-18-2016-recommendations-regarding-the-existence-of-third-party-funding-in-arbitrations-administered-by-cam-ccbc/.

shall have the power to order the disclosure by the party accepting the funding of any relevant information of the third party funding arrangement."[29]

- *Hong Kong International Arbitration Centre* ("*HKIAC*"): Hong Kong International Arbitration Centre Administered Arbitration Rules 2018, article 44 (1), provides a disclosure obligation for the funded party "[i]f a funding agreement is made, the funded party shall communicate a written notice to all other parties, the arbitral tribunal, any emergency arbitrator and HKIAC of: (a) the fact that a funding agreement has been made; and (b) the identity of the third party funder."[30]
- *International Centre for Settlement of Investment Disputes* ("*ICSID*"), ICSID Rules, Rule 14, provides that "[a] party shall file a written notice disclosing the name and address of any non-party from which the party, directly or indirectly, has received funds for the pursuit or defense of the proceeding through a donation or grant, or in return for remuneration dependent on the outcome of the proceeding ("third-party funding"). If the non-party providing funding is a juridical person, the notice shall include the names of the persons and entities that own and control that juridical person."[31]
- *Milan Chamber of Arbitration* ("*CAM*"): Arbitration Rules, article 43, provides that "[t]he party that is funded by a third party in relation to the proceedings and its outcome shall disclose the existence of the funding and the identity of the funder."[32]
- *Singapore International Arbitration Centre* ("*SIAC*"), SIAC Investment Rules, article 24(1)(l), provides that "[u]nless otherwise agreed by the Parties, in addition to the other powers specified in these Rules, and except as prohibited by the mandatory rules of law applicable to the arbitration, the Tribunal shall have the power to ... order the disclosure of the existence of a Party's third-party funding arrangement and/or the identity of the third-party funder and, where appropriate, details of the third-party funder interest

29 "China International Economic and Trade Arbitration Commission International Investment Arbitration Rules (For Trial Implementation)," China International Economic and Trade Arbitration Commission, http://www.cietac.org/index.php?m=Page&a=index&id=390&l=en.

30 "2018 Administered Arbitration Rules," Hong Kong International Arbitration Centre, effective November 1, 2018, https://www.hkiac.org/sites/default/files/ck_filebrowser/PDF/arbitration/2018_hkiac_rules.pdf.

31 "ICSID Arbitration Rules," ICSID, accessed December 23, 2022, https://icsid.worldbank.org/sites/default/files/Arbitration_Rules.pdf.

32 "Arbitration Rules," Milan Chamber of Arbitration, effective July 1, 2020, https://www.camera-arbitrale.it/upload/documenti/arbitrato/Regolamento%20arbitrale%20CAM-luglio2020.pdf.

in the outcome of the proceedings, and/or whether or not the third-party funder has committed to undertake adverse costs liability."[33]

Furthermore, even in soft law we can find different provisions regarding the disclosure obligations:

- IBA Guidelines on Conflicts of Interest in International Arbitration, 6(b), provides that "[i]f one of the parties is a legal entity, any legal or physical person having a controlling influence on the legal entity, or a direct economic interest in, or a duty to indemnify a party for, the award to be rendered in the arbitration, may be considered to bear the identity of such party."[34]
- IBA Guidelines on Conflict of Interest in International Arbitration, 7(a), provides that "[a] party shall inform an arbitrator, the Arbitral Tribunal, the other parties and the arbitration institution or other appointing authority (if any) of any relationship, direct or indirect, between the arbitrator and the party (or another company of the same group of companies, or an individual having a controlling influence on the party in the arbitration), or between the arbitrator and any person or entity with a direct economic interest in, or a duty to indemnify a party for, the award to be rendered in the arbitration. The party shall do so on its own initiative at the earliest opportunity."[35]

Such obligations are essential to avoid conflicts of interest that, as highlighted above, may jeopardize the validity and enforcement of the award.

It is interesting to look also at the case law issued in relation to the disclosure obligation concerning the existence of TPF agreement.

In the case *Muhammet Çap & Sehil In_aat Endustri ve Ticaret Ltd. Sti. v. Turkmenistan, ICSID Case No. ARB/12/6, PO 2 (giugno 2014)*, the Tribunal identifies several reasons that could justify an order against the plaintiff to disclose the existence of the litigation funding agreement:

> It seems to the Tribunal that the following factors may be relevant to justify an order for disclosure, and also depending upon the circumstances of the case:
>
> a. To avoid a conflict of interest for the arbitrator as a result of the third-party funder;

33 "SIAC Investment Rules," Singapore International Arbitration Centre, January 1, 2017, https://siac.org.sg/wp-content/uploads/2022/06/SIAC-Investment-Rules-2017.pdf.

34 "IBA Guidelines on Conflicts of Interest in International Arbitration," International Bar Association, October 23, 2014, https://www.ibanet.org/MediaHandler?id=e2fe5e72-eb14-4bba-b10d-d33dafee8918.

35 *Id.*

b. For transparency and to identify the true party to the case;
c. For the Tribunal to fairly decide how costs should be allocated at the end of any arbitration;
d. If there is an application for security for costs if requested; and
e. To ensure that confidential information which may come out during the arbitral proceedings is not disclosed to parties with ulterior motives.

However, the Tribunal rejects Turkmenistan's request for an order to the plaintiff to disclose whether it was financed by third parties, since the counterparty had not provided any arguments (not even a potential conflict of interest) to support the request.

Subsequently, Turkmenistan renewed its request after the publication of the IBA Guidelines, explicitly referring to General Standard 7(a) and arguing that disclosure of the existence of the lender is necessary to (i) verify the presence of conflicts of interest; and (ii) assess whether to claim security for expenses.

The Tribunal, therefore, granted the request on three grounds:

9. First, the importance of ensuring the integrity of the proceedings and to determine whether any of the arbitrators are affected by the existence of a third-party funder. In this respect the Tribunal considers that transparency as to the existence of a third-party funder is important in cases like this.
10. Second, although it has not yet done so, Respondent has indicated that it will be making an application for security for costs.
11. There are two additional factors which the Tribunal considers support the conclusion it has reached. Claimants have not denied that there is a third-party funder for the claims in this arbitration. It would have been straightforward to do so, just as they denied having assigned any of their rights to another party.[36]

In another case, *South American Silver Limited v. Bolivia, PCA Case No. 2013–15, PO 10*, Bolivia became aware of the existence of a TPF agreement entered into by the other party and declared its intention to file a claim for security for costs. The plaintiff had agreed to disclose the name of the funder but not the terms of the TPF agreement because they were deemed irrelevant and confidential.

---

36 *Muhammet Çap & Sehil In_aat Endustri ve Ticaret Ltd. Sti. v. Turkmenistan*, ICSID Case No. ARB/12/6, PO 3 (June 2015).

The Tribunal accepted the plaintiff's argument on the following basis:

> 79. [...] the Tribunal considers that, for purposes of transparency, and given the position of the Parties, it must accept Bolivia's request of disclosure of the name of SAS' funder.
> 80. [...] concerning the disclosure of the terms of the financing agreement entered into with the third-party funder, the Tribunal will reject such request.
> 81. Firstly, because, for the above-mentioned reasons, exceptional circumstances required to order security for costs are not present and the mere existence of the funder is not sufficient to order it.
> 82. Secondly, because no additional circumstances have been proven that, in the opinion of the Tribunal, warrant the modification of the decisions already taken concerning document production in the corresponding procedural phase.

3.9 *TPF and Reimbursement of the Legal Costs*

The fact that one of the parties has relied on the TPF to cover its legal costs does not affect the right to claim the reimbursement of legal costs. The costs incurred by the victorious party to reimburse the funder's investment and to pay the agreed fee are part of the costs directly related to the arbitration proceedings.[37] In particular, the possibility of obtaining recovery of costs related to the TPF depends on the *lex arbitri* and the applicable arbitration rules – as long as the costs are reasonable. Finally, it should be noted that arbitral tribunals have no jurisdiction to order third-party funders to reimburse litigation costs incurred by the other party.

In the *Ioannis Kardassopoulos v. Georgia, ICSID Case No. ARB/05/18, Award* the court rejected the losing party's claims regarding the non-refundability of the counterparty's legal costs. In particular, Georgia (the losing party) had argued that the costs incurred by the investor (the victorious party) were excessive and had been borne in part by a funder.

In particular, the Tribunal states that:

37 Jeremy Mash, "Recoverability of third party funding costs in arbitration: Essar v Norscot revisited," CMS, December 21, 2021, https://www.cms-lawnow.com/ealerts/2021/12/recoverability-of-third-party-funding-costs-in-arbitration-essar-v-norscot-revisited?cc_lang=en.

> 691. The Tribunal is not persuaded in the circumstances of these cases that the Claimants should not be allowed to recover their reasonable costs. The Tribunal observes that among those factors identified by the Respondent in support of its submissions on costs is the fact that the Claimants have an arrangement with a third-party concerning the financing of these proceedings. The Tribunal knows of no principle why any such third-party financing arrangement should be taken into consideration in determining the amount of recovery by the Claimants of their costs.

In another case, *Renta 4 S.V.S.A, Ahorro Corporación Emergentes F.I., Ahorro Corporación Eurofondo F.I., Rovime Inversiones SICAV S.A., Quasar de Valors SICAV S.A., Orgor de Valores SICAV S.A., GBI 9000 SICAV S.A. v. The Russian Federation, SCC No. 24/2007*, during the course of the proceedings, the Investors revealed that they had been entirely financed by former Yukos shareholders. At the end of the proceedings, the state contested the payment of the counterparty's legal costs. The court, finding the arguments brought by the state as meritorious, granted the request based on the following arguments:

> 223. The usual arguments about the recoverability of costs where a party's representation in a case has been financed by a third party are inapposite here, because such third-party financing is typically part of a legally enforceable bargain under which the prevailing party in the arbitration has given up something in return for that support. Here, it is conceded that there is no legal duty on the part of the Claimants to hand over any recovery on account of costs to Menatep [funder].
>
> 224. [Russia's] proposition must be right. On the one hand, the Claimants have neither expended money nor incurred obligations on account of the costs of pursuing their claims. On the other, Menatep, the Claimants' Good Samaritan (as it were), has no standing before this Tribunal or indeed more generally under the BIT.

Lastly, another important decision was issued by Queen's Bench Division (Commercial Court) on 15 September 2016 in the *Essar Oilfield Services Ltd v. Norscot Rig Management Pvt Ltd* case.

In the decision *Essar Oilfield Services Ltd v. Norscot Rig Management Pvt Ltd, Queen's Bench Division (Commercial Court) 15 September 2016, [2016] EWHC 2361 (Comm)* the arbitral tribunal rendered a partial award on the merits and damages in favor of the plaintiff. In addition, the tribunal included in the costs related to the arbitration USD 4 million in favor of the claimant and ordered the defendant to pay TPF costs in an amount to be determined in a second award but approximately £1.94 million. The Tribunal agued "other costs" is not limited to "legal costs" but also includes TPF costs. Subsequently, the defendant challenged the award on the ground that the arbitral tribunal had decided a matter that was not in dispute (*ultra petita*).

In particular, the Court stated that

> 47. For all of those reasons, I conclude that there was no serious irregularity within the meaning of s.68(2)(b), even if the arbitrator was wrong in his construction of "other costs."
> That disposes of this application altogether. But, in deference to arguments made on the other issues, I deal with them as well. [...]
>
> 68. [...] as a matter of language, context and logic, it seems to me that 'other costs' can include the costs of obtaining litigation funding. The expression should not be confined by some legal straightjacket imposed by reason of what a court might or might not be permitted to order. All that this conclusion entails is that such litigation funding costs falls within the arbitrator's general costs discretion. Whether and, if so, how the arbitrator exercises that discretion in any particular case is an entirely different matter. [...]
>
> 70. In my judgment, therefore, I unhesitatingly conclude that the arbitrator's interpretation of "other costs" was correct, in that it extended in principle to the costs of obtaining third party legal funding. Whether then to award it is a matter of discretion.

3.10 *Use of Artificial Intelligence in TPF*

The evolution of the legal industry is particularly slow because this sector is bound by traditions and customs that lawyers and judges are not inclined to change. However, a radical revolution could be represented by the use of artificial intelligence, an increasingly interesting tool for the growth and improvement of any business.

With specific regard to artificial intelligence applied to the field of litigation and arbitration, the use of devices that can help judges in the decision-making process and lawyers in predicting the outcome of the case is increasingly being considered.

To date, there are still many problems related to this tool and we are still a long way from the moment when a computer can decide the outcome of a case.

However, technology is moving very fast and in the next ten years we will see a radical change in the legal market.

As a preliminary issue, an important distinction should be made between weak AI programs that mimic human thinking and reasoning abilities without having them, and strong AI programs that can think or reason independently, without merely using pre-programmed ways of human thinking or reasoning.[38] Strong AI can accomplish any task, including learning new things.[39]

AI is being studied and applied in different fields and has become one of the "hot topics" even in the legal world. Indeed, these new tools can be used in legal activities by lawyers, decision makers and legislator. In practice, the AI systems are most frequently applied in advanced case-law search engines, online dispute resolution, assistance in drafting legal acts, predictive analytics systems, automated verification of legal compliance or legal aid chatbots.[40]

Therefore, a first application of artificial intelligence consists in the automatization of tasks usually carried out by lawyers and judges. In this case, artificial intelligence tools will speed up the process of analyzing and reviewing documents, help judges and lawyers to find previous decisions on similar cases more quickly and to immediately identify which is the prevailing orientation.

A second scenario, which is currently considered to be a utopia, relates to the possibility that such tools will completely take over and replace the job of lawyers and judges. In that case, everything would be automated, drastically reducing the time taken by justice and making the existence of courts and arbitration institutions unnecessary.

In addition to lawyers and judges, funders, that are a relatively new players in the legal market, will also benefit from the integration of artificial intelligence tools. Indeed, at the core of the funder's activity is the assessment of the case and the evaluation of the risk of losing the case. The use of artificial intelligence would give the funder the possibility to speed up the due diligence process, obtaining a forecast of the outcome of the case in less time.

---

38 Maxi Scherer, "International Arbitration 3.0 – How Artificial Intelligence Will Change Dispute Resolution," in *Austrian Yearbook of International Arbitration 2019*, eds. Christian Klausegger et al. (Austria: MANZ Verlag Vienna, 2019), 505.

39 Kate Baggaley, "There are two kinds of AI, and the difference is important," Popular Science, February 23, 2017, https://www.popsci.com/narrow-and-general-ai.

40 "European ethical Charter on the use of Artificial Intelligence in judicial systems and their environment," European Commission for the Efficiency of Justice, adopted December 3–4, 2018, Appendix I at 14 ("the European Charter on the Use of AI in Judicial Systems" or "the Charter").

4 TPF Market and Regulations in the United Arab Emirates

The United Arab Emirates (hereinafter "UAE") has not traditionally been an attractive jurisdiction for funders, but, in recent years, it has become an increasingly attractive venue for resolving disputes locally, regionally, and internationally.[41]

The UAE is divided into seven emirates, each with their own local courts, called "onshore" courts. The onshore system of the UAE is a civil law system; there are no impediments arising from the common law doctrines of champerty and maintenance.[42]

The UAE also has different "free zones," based on the common law legal system, including the Dubai International Financial Centre (hereinafter "DIFC")[43] and the Abu Dhabi Global Market (hereinafter "ADGM"), which have their own independent legal systems and courts.

While the traditionally civil law UAE does not currently regulate the use of TPF, the UAE Central Bank has recently considered implementing regulations on TPF. In contrast, the common law DIFC and ADGM do provide some regulations on the use of TPF in their free zones.

4.1 *TPF under Shari'ah Law*

In recent years, and especially due to the COVID-19 pandemic, TPF has been on the rise in the Middle East. To understand how TPF functions in the Middle East, it is important to understand how TPF would operate with *Shari'ah* law.

In the Middle East, Islamic *Shari'ah* plays a central role in the legal system of all Gulf states. It is the law of the Islamic religion, derived from the *Holy Qur'an* and the *Sunna,* which is the code of conduct established by the Prophet

41 Mohamed El Hawawy and Monika Humphreys-Davies, "The Third Party Litigation Funding Law Review: United Arab Emirates," The Law Reviews, November 22, 2021, 1, https://www.lexology.com/library/detail.aspx?g=5783303d-7521-49b7-a8c9-4321424fb5cf.

42 Out-Law Guide, "Jurisdiction guide to third party funding in international arbitration," Pinsent Masons, May 7, 2021, https://www.pinsentmasons.com/out-law/guides/third-party-funding-international-arbitration#United%20Arab%20Emirates.

43 The DIFC is a special economic zone in Dubai established in 2004 and a financial hub for the Middle East, Africa, and South Asia ("MEASA") markets. DIFC has its own independent, internationally regulated regulator and judicial system, common law framework, global financial exchange, tax-friendly regime, and a large business community. The district houses hundreds of financial institutions, including wealth funds and private investors, but it also hosts multinationals, retail outlets, cafés, restaurants, residential space, public green spaces, hotels, and art galleries.

Mohammed. Thus, it is important that transferring the legal risk from one party to another party is *Shari'ah* compliant.

There are several considerations for a transaction to be *Shari'ah* compliant:
- the subject matter of the transaction must be lawful in the eyes of *Shari'ah,* or "*permissible*" ("*Halal*") under Islamic Law. For example, the subject matter of the transaction cannot be in wine, swine, dead bodies of animals, or idols;
- the transaction cannot involve gambling ("*Maisir*"), because gambling is prohibited in Islam;
- the transaction must be "certain," meaning the transaction cannot be based on fraud or speculation;
- there must be a valid contract, with an offer and acceptance, the involvement of the parties, and the purpose of the contract must be identified;
- the transaction must not involve interest ("*Riba*"), which is prohibit in Islam.

The considerations for a *Shari'ah* compliant TPF transaction are satisfied, because TPF does not deal with the trade of a prohibited item such as swine or wine, thus TPF is permissible ("Halal"). TPF is also not considered as gambling since the funders share a significant risk of the case failing and losing its investment. In terms of uncertainty, TPF avoids any uncertainty since the terms of the funding arrangement between the funder and the claimant are negotiated and entered into by the parties in a funding agreement, which is a valid contract.

TPF relies on a partnership arrangement between the claimant and the funder to fund a dispute. Under Islamic *Shari'ah*, there are several structures that can be utilized for TPF. The most appropriate are *Mudarabah* and *Musharakah*: *Mudarabah* is the most-widely known Islamic contract. It is a profit-sharing contract in which one party provides funds and the other party provides the management expertise; *Musharakah* is a joint enterprise or partnership structure where the partners share in the profits and losses of the partnership. This structure allows the financier of the project to achieve a return from the profits according to an agreed percentage, but the financier will also share in any potential losses.

During COVID-19, the availability of *Shari'ah* compliant products were limited, and TPF served an as alternative asset class for Islamic investors. Under *Shari'ah* law, the arrangement between a funder and a claimant would be a partnership where the funder is entitled to a share of the money awarded to the claimant and also shares the risk of losing the claim. Since the funder and the claimant shared in the risk, this arrangement would be *Shari'ah* compliant either through a *Mudarabah* or *Musharakah* structure.

Thus, the basic structure and practice of TPF does not violate principles of Islamic *Shari'ah*; even though few Middle Eastern countries have regulated the practice of TPF, the structure of TPF arrangements in Islamic countries would nonetheless be *Shari'ah* compliant and not in violation of Islamic law.

4.2 *TPF in the Dubai International Financial Center ("DIFC")*

Historically, the DIFC Courts have recognized the existence of TPF agreements.[44] In 2017 the DIFC Courts issued the Practice Direction No. 2 of 2017 on Third Party Funding in the DIFC Courts (hereinafter "Practice Direction on TPF"). The Practice Direction on TPF does not have a retroactive effect and only applies to TPF arrangements entered on or after March 14, 2017.

The Practice Direction on TPF outlines which requirements must be met by funded parties before DIFC Courts and how they must handle their relationship with funders during the course of the proceedings.[45] In particular, funded parties have a duty to inform their counterparts that they have entered into a TPF agreement to obtain the resources to pursue their case, and they must also disclose the identity of the funder.[46] Unless the DIFC Courts order otherwise, the party does not need to disclose a copy of the funding agreement.[47]

In line with English law,[48] the Practice Direction on TPF states that the DIFC Courts have jurisdiction to make cost orders against third party funders when the Courts deem it appropriate based upon the circumstances of the case.[49]

In addition, the recourse to the TPF instrument is relevant when DIFC Courts must decide on the applications for security costs, but the fact that a party is funded is not by itself determinative.[50]

---

44 For example, in the cases of *Rafed Al Khorafi and Others v Bank Sarasin-Alpen (ME) Ltd and Bank Sarasin & Co Ltd* (DIFC Courts – 21 August 2014 – CFI 026/2009) and *Vannin Capital Pcc Plc v Mr Rafed Abdel Mohsen Bader Al Khorafi and others* (DIFC Courts – 18 April 2016 – CFI 036/2014).

45 Andrew Mackenzie and Lina Bugaighis, "Third party funding in the UAE," Global Arbitration News, April 25, 2019, https://globalarbitrationnews.com/third-party-funding-in-the-uae/#page=1.

46 "Practice Direction No. 2 of 2017 on Third Party Funding in the DIFC Courts," Dubai International Financial Centre, March 14, 2017, art. 4, https://www.difccourts.ae/rules-decisions/practice-directions/practice-direction-no-2-of-2017-on-third-party-funding-in-the-difc-courts ("Practice Direction on TPF").

47 *Id.*

48 English Civil Procedure Rules Part 25.14 (2)(b).

49 Practice Direction on TPF, *supra* note 46, at art. 9.

50 *Id.* at art. 8.

The Practice Direction on TPF seeks to balance the need for transparency with the confidentiality between the parties by expressly providing that the TPF agreement must not be disclosed unless the court expressly orders it.[51]

In September 2019, the DIFC issued DIFC Order No. 4 of 2019 (hereinafter "Order No. 4"). Order No. 4 addresses the conduct of practitioners in the DIFC and contains several provisions relevant to TPF. Order No. 4 imposes the duty to avoid conflicts of interest, which is an essential consideration when choosing a funder.[52] In order to protect the funded party, Order No. 4 provides that the lawyer for the funded party may not carry out instructions from the funder if they are in the interest of the funder and have not been approved in writing by the funded party.[53] It also imposes a duty on lawyer to advise their clients on the effect of any TPF agreements on the client's potential liability regarding legal fees and expenses.[54] The Order No. 4 prohibits practitioners from accepting referral fees or benefits from a TPF provider, unless full disclosure is made in writing to the client.[55]

4.3 *TPF in Abu Dhabi Global Market ("ADGM")*

The ADGM is a common law jurisdiction located in the Emirate of Abu Dhabi, which has incorporated several English law statutes by express reference.[56]

The ADGM Courts, Civil Evidence, Judgments, Enforcement and Judicial Appoints Regulations 2015 (hereinafter "ADGM Regulations") regulates some aspects of the litigation funding agreements in the ADGM's jurisdiction.[57]

---

51 Mackenzie and Bugaighis, *supra* note 45, at 4.

52 "DIFC Courts' Order No. 4 of 2019: Mandatory Code of Conduct for Legal Practitioners in the DIFC Courts," Dubai International Financial Centre, September 18, 2019, Part C, art. 12, lett. E, https://www.difccourts.ae/wp-content/uploads/2019/09/DIFC_Courts_Order_No._4_of_2019_Mandatory_Code_of_Conduct_for_Legal_Practitioners_in_the_DIFC%20Courts.pdf ("Order No. 4").

53 *Id.*

54 *Id.* at Part C, art. 17, lett. B.

55 *Id.* at Part C, art. 18, lett. D.

56 Mackenzie and Bugaighis, *supra* note 45, at 5.

57 Abu Dhabi Global Market ("ADGM") Regulations, art. 225 provides that the following main conditions must be satisfied for a litigation funding agreement to be valid in the ADGM "funder must be a person, or a person of a description, prescribed by the Chief Justice; the agreement must be in writing; the agreement must not relate to proceedings which cannot be the subject of an enforceable conditional fee agreement or to proceedings of any such description as may be prescribed by the Chief Justice; the agreement must comply with such requirements (if any) as may be so prescribed; the sum to be paid by the litigant must consist of any costs payable to him in respect of the proceedings to which the agreement relates together with an amount calculated by reference to the funder's anticipated

Like the DIFC Practice Direction on TPF, the ADGM Regulations provide that a party which has entered a TPF arrangement must inform all counterparties that it has entered into a litigation funding agreement.[58] Unlike the Practice Direction on TPF, there is no express requirement for a copy of the agreement to be disclosed or not.[59]

On April 16, 2019, the ADGM enacted the Litigation Funding Rules 2019 (hereinafter "ADGM Litigation Funding Rules"), the first regulation in the region specifically regulating TPF. The ADGM Litigation Funding Rules govern third-party litigation funding, such as the requirements that the funder must meet and the essential elements of the funding agreement.[60] The ADGM Litigation Funding Rules also apply to arbitration proceedings in the ADGM.

Pursuant this new regulation, funders must meet the following requirements:

- the funder's core business must be funding third-party proceedings; and
- the funder must have qualifying assets worth not less than $5 million.[61]

These requirements have been established to ensure the reliability of the funder and to ensure that the funder has the financial strength to bear the costs of the proceedings until the end.

The ADGM Litigation Funding Rules regulate the content of litigation funding agreements by stipulating minimum criteria for an agreement to be enforceable. Litigation funding agreements must be in writing and include at a minimum: 1) the scope, amount and timing of funding; 2) the funder's recovery, including the timing and manner of recovery; 3) whether the funder is liable to the funded party for adverse costs and/or the premiums when obtaining adverse costs insurance; 4) the possibility of involving the funder in potential settlements; 5) the cases in which the funder can terminate the litigation funding agreement; and 6) the confidentiality obligations on funders.[62]

---

expenditure in funding the provision of the services; and that amount must not exceed such percentage of that anticipated expenditure as may be prescribed by the Chief Justice in relation to proceedings of the description to which the agreement relates."

58 *Id.* at art. 225(6).

59 Mackenzie and Bugaighis, *supra* note 45, at 5.

60 James Abbott, Paul Coates, and Arun Visweswaran, "ADGM Litigation Funding Rules," accessed August 13, 2021, https://www.cliffordchance.com/content/dam/cliffordchance/briefings/2019/07/adgm-litigation-funding-rules.pdf.

61 "Litigation Funding Rules," ADGM Courts, April 16, 2019, Part 2, art. 4(1), https://www.adgm.com/documents/courts/legislation-and-procedures/legislation/rules/litigation-funding-rules-2019.pdf ("ADGM Litigation Funding Rules").

62 *Id.* at Part 3, art. 7.

In addition, the funder must ensure that the funded party has been adequately informed by independent counsel of the implications of entering into the funding agreement.[63]

The implementation of the rules confirms the progression of TPF in the region, offering more certainty on the enforceability of these arrangements and regulating the relationship between funders, funded parties, and lawyers.

5 The Impact of COVID-19 on Construction and Hospitality Sectors

5.1 *Overview*

The COVID-19 pandemic and government-imposed restrictions to prevent the spread of the virus had a massive impact on the international economy, including the construction sector.[64]

COVID-19 caused serious delays, and in most cases interruption, in the execution of construction projects.[65]

In the UAE, from 20, 2020, all flights were restricted[66] and stringent security measures were imposed to counter the spread of the virus.[67] Construction projects, however, were declared "vital" to the economy, and, were allowed to proceed as long as the contractors obtained special authorizations.[68]

Even though construction projects in the UAE were considered essential and were allowed to continue, the restrictions imposed on the movement of workers and transport vehicles, the mandatory social distancing, and other restrictions inevitably had a negative impact on the construction industry.[69]

These restrictions created complications that led to delays in the completion of projects and contractual breaches that gave rise to numerous disputes.

---

63 Abbott, Coates, and Visweswaran, *supra* note 60, at 2.

64 Todd Wetmore and Sam Elliot, "Chapter 12: COVID-19 and Construction Disputes," in *International Arbitration and the COVID-19 Revolution*, eds. Maxi Scherer, Niuscha Bassiri, and Mohamed S. Abdel Wahab (Kluwer Law International, 2020), 203.

65 *Id.* at 205.

66 "UAE suspends all passenger and transit flights for two weeks," The Straitstimes, March 23, 2020, https://www.straitstimes.com/world/middle-east/uae-suspends-all-passenger-and-transit-flights-for-two-weeks.

67 Wetmore and Elliot, *supra* note 64, at 209.

68 "Dubai's Supreme Committee of Crisis and Disaster Management announcement," Government of Dubai Media Office, accessed August 2, 2021, https://dxbpermit.gov.ae/assets/exempted-en.jpeg.

69 Wetmore and Elliot, *supra* note 64, at 209.

It is important to highlight that construction disputes are very complex, costly and extremely long lasting.[70] Construction disputes are characterized by the factual and technical complexity of the case, the involvement of multiple parties, the large amount of documents, the essential intervention of experts, and the large amount of money in dispute.[71]

On one hand, these issues may discourage parties from pursuing their cases, especially companies that have faced financial difficulties caused by the impact of the pandemic.[72]

On the other hand, construction disputes represent an attractive investment opportunity for funders that can alleviate the financial burden for claimants in exchange for higher rewards.[73]

The hospitality sector was also severely affected by government restrictions adopted to slow the spread of COVID-19. Specifically, the restrictions imposed on travel, the limited number of guests that could be accommodated indoors, and social distancing all drastically reduced the revenue of existing hotels and caused delays in new hotel projects.[74]

The UAE hospitality sector was also damaged from the pandemic, which suffered large losses in revenue compared to the pre-pandemic period because the number of international visitors traveling to Dubai dropped from 16.7 million in 2019 to 5.5 million in 2020.[75]

However, during the previous year, the UAE maintained a high occupancy rate by shifting focus from international to domestic tourism, called

70 Fabian Bonke and Tara Theiss, "How to Fund Construction Disputes – Relying on Third-Party Funding?," Kluwer Arbitration Blog, December 24, 2019, http://arbitrationblog.kluwerarbitration.com/2019/12/24/how-to-fund-construction-disputes-relying-on-third-party-funding/.

71 Pinsent Masons, "International Arbitration Survey: Driving Efficiency in International Construction Disputes," Queen Mary University of London, 3, 10, https://www.pinsentmasons.com/thinking/special-reports/international-arbitration-survey.

72 Frédéric Gillion, "Third party funding: a game-changer for construction disputes?," Pinsent Masons, September 11, 2019, https://www.pinsentmasons.com/out-law/analysis/third-party-funding-a-game-changer-for-construction-disputes.

73 Bonke and Theiss, *supra* note 70, at 3.

74 Wanjing Goh, "Disputes under Hotel Management Agreements in a COVID-19 World – Part I: Development Phase Disputes," Bryan Cave Leighton Paisner LLP, October 15, 2020, https://www.bclplaw.com/en-US/insights/disputes-under-hotel-management-agreements-in-a-covid-19-world-part-i-development-phase-disputes.html.

75 "Dubai Tourism Statistics: Number of International Visitors to Dubai," Dubai Online, accessed August 17, 2021, https://www.dubai-online.com/essential/tourism-statistics/.

"staycations," supported by the local governments.[76] While the arrival of international tourists decreased dramatically, the number of local tourists staying in hotels increased by 107%. Additionally, luxury resorts on the beach and in deserts surpassed business hotels in visitors.[77]

One of the strengths of the UAE was the use of new technologies to ensure the highest levels of safety and hygiene: in particular, automation was implemented to limit contact between people while still providing optimal customer service.[78]

However, the efforts to limit the negative consequences of COVID-19 were not enough to avoid disputes in the hospitality field. The highest number of disputes arise between hotel-owners and hotel-operators because of breaches of hotel management agreements. A distinction must be made between disputes that arise during the construction of the hotel and disputes that arise once the hotel has already been built.[79]

First, it should be noted that hotel management agreements provide certain obligations on behalf of the owner during the construction of the hotel, including the commencement of construction work, the termination of the work, and the opening of the hotel to the public.[80] The owners might face difficulties in obtaining the necessary licenses and permits to begin hotel activities.[81] If the owner fails to perform the above services within the time specified in the agreement, the operator has the right to request termination of the contract for non-performance and claim liquidated damages.[82] Because of COVID-19, it was almost inevitable that owners had problems meeting the timeframe set in agreements for the beginning and termination of work, and for the opening of the hotels. This increased the number of disputes initiated by operators to terminate contracts and obtain compensation for damages.[83]

Disputes in the hospitality sector can also arise even after the opening of the hotel and commencement of business activities. Specifically, some disputes may arise in relation to the annual budget, which is subject to the owner's approval, and where the owner and operator may disagree on the cost-cutting

---

76 Sidharth Mehta, "Suite Success: Dubai hospitality survey 2021," KPMG, accessed December 23, 2022, 6, https://assets.kpmg/content/dam/kpmg/ae/pdf-2021/05/dubai-hospitality-survey-2021.pdf.

77 Dubai Online, *supra* note 75, at 11.

78 Mehta, *supra* note 76, at 5.

79 Goh, *supra* note 74, at 1.

80 *Id.*

81 *Id.* at 3.

82 *Id.* at 2.

83 *Id.* at 3.

that one party might propose to reduce expenses and preserve the financial viability of the business.[84]

Before the beginning of business activities, the owner puts the operator's business plan under certain stress tests to assess both risks and possible revenues.[85] If the operator's plan fails, the owner has the right to terminate the agreement. The tests are intended to assess the operator's ability to be competitive and to manage gross revenues from the business.[86]

In this framework, the recourse to the TPF can be a valuable tool that helps operators and/or owners pursue proceedings without incurring additional costs associated with arbitration or litigation.

COVID-19 increased the need of TPF in the construction and hospitality sectors. However, in response to the COVID-19 pandemic and with knowledge of market conditions and claimants' lack of financial resources, funders became more selective, increased their rates, and included additional payment terms such as interest on the money paid for the arbitration or litigation costs.

5.2 *How Should TPF Be Seen by a Claimant?*

The biggest obstacle for a claimant in obtaining funding is their lack of knowledge of TPF and their lack of understanding of how a funder will evaluate their dispute. For many claimants, they are not aware of what it is, how it works, what is needed to obtain funding, to whom to speak, and how the process works if funding is provided. This creates a huge disadvantage for the claimant from the start, which can significantly hurt their chances of receiving TPF.

A claimant only has one opportunity to convince a funder to fund their dispute. Once a claimant receives a rejection from one funder, the likelihood of another funder funding the same claim decreases tremendously. Provided with only basic information, funders will quickly form an opinion on the dispute, because in the COVID-19 era, the number of claimants that require funding has increased tremendously, giving funders the luxury of picking and choosing what dispute they will fund. In this environment, the claimants must package their disputes in the best possible manner, which includes targeting funders who will fund their dispute in their respective jurisdiction and presenting their claim in terms favorable to a funder on why they would be interested in

84 Stephen Greyling, "Disputes under Hotel Management Agreements in a COVID-19 World – Part II: Operational Phase Disputes," Bryan Cave Leighton Paisner LLP, October 15, 2020, 1, https://www.bclplaw.com/en-US/insights/disputes-under-hotel-management-agreements-in-a-covid-19-world-part-ii-operational-phase-disputes.html.

85 *Id.* at 2.

86 *Id.*

funding the dispute. Often, the claimant is unaware that it is its responsibility to convince the funder of the merits of its claim.

This is a problem, because many claimants will approach the process with little to no knowledge of the process. They will either search on the internet to find a funder, contact a lawyer who may know a funder or that works with one or two funders (usually from the same jurisdiction), or they will contact a funder whom they met at a conference, since many funders attend conferences to promote their services.

For a claimant to be successful, they must first understand that the TPF process is not simply an online application, nor it is a process of submitting key documents to an investment manager. It is a much more complicated process. The claimant must create a strategy that considers:

- how the dispute will be presented to the funders (the information contained in a funding request memo, documents, budget, *etc.*);
- which funders to approach (for example, there are funders in the Middle East, South Africa, the United States, the UK, France, and Australia who will fund disputes around the world, but there are also local funders who will fund disputes in their own jurisdiction);
- what are the terms the claimant would consider as part of the funding arrangement (award percentages, the costs to be covered by the funder, *etc.*); and/or
- what issues will be important for the funder to consider in their decision to fund the claim.

A claimant should also keep in mind that having a TPF arrangement with a funder is about obtaining the best deal for both parties; it is not a "take it or leave it" arrangement once the funder proposes its terms. Everything in the TPF arrangement is negotiable. If a funder is interested in funding the dispute, it will do everything it can to come to an agreement with the claimant.

Even though the funder is receiving funding requests at a higher volume than normal during the COVID-19 period, it is still a business, and their business is to obtain a high return on disputes for their investors. If the funder believes it will receive a high return on the claimant's claim, and if it can obtain the return quickly, the funder will do anything to come to an agreement with the claimant to fund the dispute. This will include offering a lower-than-normal rate, making other concessions such as paying salaries of employees, paying the costs of maintaining records, and even funding other disputes that it considers risky to satisfy the claimant and fund its dispute.

Many claimants who seek funding are not aware of this from the start of the process. Many lawyers and consultants, especially in the construction sector, are not aware of how TPF works, and provide incorrect advice to the claimant, and/or approach funders who will not fund the dispute.

5.3 *What Must Be Considered when Applying for TPF?*

There are many things that a claimant must consider before making a funding request to a funder. The first and more important question is whether the dispute is fundable. In other words, will a funder fund the claimant's claim?

Many lawyers and consultants do not understand what it takes or what funders are looking for when deciding to fund a dispute. A funder does not evaluate a dispute like a lawyer advising or assessing a claim would evaluate the dispute. A funder is primarily looking at how much money the claimant is currently owed and how much the funder can make from this. A funder will evaluate a claim and determine whether the claim is supported and has legal merit; some funders will do their own due diligence without the support of legal counsel. However, the funder is concerned less about how much the claimant will recover after going through litigation or arbitration, but rather is more concerned on how to make as high of a return in as short of a time as possible. For example, if the claimant is owed large sums of money because they supplied a product to the counterparty and the claimant has the evidence to support this, a funder will view this as guaranteed money owed to the claimant, meaning a funder is almost guaranteed a return on the sums of money owed.

Another example is in the construction sector. If a contractor has payment certificates that have been certified by the counterparty (or by an engineer/consultant), in most jurisdictions, this is considered a debt owed to the contractor and is considered guaranteed money to the contractor. The funder will base its evaluation of the dispute primarily on the money owed. A funder will also consider other damage claims that will need to be established and awarded in an arbitration or litigation, such as extension of time and time-related costs; however, to the funder, these claims are not guaranteed until they are awarded at the conclusion of legal proceedings.

For example, a consultant in a construction dispute with a very large claim (over $50 million USD) that required TPF approached a funder. The consultant was convinced that the contractor had a solid case (above 70% probability of success); however, the contractor was having difficulty obtaining TPF. Upon review of the claim, the actual money owed to the contractor was only around $2 to $3 million USD, and the rest of the claims were extension of time and prolongation claims. A funder would not be interested in a claim that is valued at $2 or $3 million USD. This scenario is very common in the construction sector, where contractors will have claims for extension of time and time-related costs. A funder will not consider these claims as money owed to the contractor and they will be seen as secondary.

5.4 *Basic Criteria for a Funder*

When a funder considers a claimant's dispute for funding, the funder will have certain criteria that the funder's investment manager needs satisfied before bringing the dispute to its investment board for final approval. A funder will usually need to consider and be satisfied with the following:

- the total claim amount;
- the potential counterclaim amount;
- the legal entitlement of the claims;
- any jurisdictional issues (including, but not limited to, capacity of the signatory of the arbitration agreement and contract, preconditions to arbitration, the validity of the arbitration agreement, *etc.*);
- the potential for a security for costs award;
- the enforcement and collectability of the final award;
- the current status of the counterparty (*i.e.*, whether the counterparty is insolvent or about to become insolvent);
- the background and history of the claimant;
- the reasons the claimant requires funding;
- the potential of future claims that utilize TPF with the same claimant;
- the applicable law to the contract, the arbitration center, the seat of arbitration, and the number of arbitrators;
- the costs of the arbitration or litigation (*i.e.*, lawyer and expert fees, arbitration costs, *etc.*); and/or
- the expertise of the lawyer(s), expert(s), and/or the team put together for the dispute.

These are only a few of the factors a funder considers and needs to be satisfied before approving the funding of the case. However, each funder is different, and each funder will consider some, all, or a combination of these factors as well as other criteria. Funders do not disclose or advertise how they assess the risk level for each dispute, how they assess the terms presented by the claimant for funding, and/or on how they select which disputes they will fund and which they will reject. Lawyers and consultants who have close relationships with a funder will usually understand what is required and how best to present the claim to the funder.

Many funders will also apply a claim value and cost criteria for each dispute as part of their evaluation. Each funder has different criteria. Typically, international funders have a minimum threshold of $10 million USD as the value owed to the claimant. In other words, for many funders, if the actual claim value does not exceed $10 million USD, they will not be interested in funding the dispute, regardless of the merits of the claim and/or the probability of a quick collection. Some funders have a much higher minimum threshold for funding disputes, such as $50 million USD.

Some international funders will fund lesser claim amounts, but it depends on the circumstances of the claims (*i.e.*, who the parties are, the type of claim, the applicable law, *etc.*). There are other funders who are local to the market, and will fund disputes below $10 million USD. It is important to stress that all claim amounts have an opportunity for funding regardless of the jurisdiction; it is a matter of locating and presenting the claim to the right funder for the jurisdiction.

Many funders will also implement a dispute budget-to-claim-value ratio of 1 to 10 as a minimum criterion to fund a dispute. For example, with this ratio, if the total amount of money a funder will invest for the dispute is $1 million USD, then the minimum total claim value would have to be $10 million USD.

Another applicable ratio is a dispute budget-to-return-on-money ratio of either 1 to 3 or 1 to 4. This means that if the total amount of money a funder will invest for the dispute is $1 million USD, then the funder expects a minimum return of $3 or $4 million USD.

It is not uncommon for a funder to consider both ratio options as part of its requirement criteria before funding a claim. Funders will also have different criteria depending on the type of dispute; for example, a funder will evaluate a construction dispute differently compared to a hospitality dispute.

5.5 *Criteria for Construction and Hospitality Disputes*

For a construction dispute, a funder typically evaluates a claim by identifying what money is owed to the contractor versus claims that must be determined through legal proceedings. Funders will usually evaluate a contractor's claims by separating the claims into three (3) groups, giving priority to Group 1, with Group 3 being claims that are very speculative and that are not considered or are not given any weight to the funder's overall assessment of the claim.

The funders will focus their evaluation of a contractor's claims based on the claims identified in Group 1. A funder will give weight to and consider the claims in Group 2 as part of the overall claim; however, they will not consider the full monetary amount of the claims in Group 2, since these claims are never awarded completely in an arbitration or litigation. The funder will consider the documentary support for these claims as well as whether witness testimony will be required to establish or support the claims. Based on this evaluation, the funder will assign a claim value which will be added to the claim amount established from the Group 1 claims.

The groups and type of claims are set forth in Table 1.1.

As for Group 3, a funder will not consider these claims as part of its overall assessment of the contractor's claims. These claims stand a high chance of failing in an arbitration or litigation. If a funder decides to provide funds to the claimant, it is not uncommon for a funder to set out in its terms that it will have the final say as to which claims are brought forward in the dispute, and the funder will more than likely disregard the Group 3 claims.

Typically, when reviewing a claim for TPF, the contractor will not have had a consultant review, organize, and prepare their claims for funders and/or for arbitration or litigation. In some instances, claim consultants prepare reports that provide an overview of the claim and entitlements under the contract. However, it can be difficult to evaluate a claim for TPF with these prepared reports. Instead, this sample spreadsheet can help evaluate a contractor's

TABLE 1.1 Typical claims in construction disputes grouped in order of priority by a funder

Group 1	Group 2	Group 3
– Certified Payment Certificates – Agreed variations – Uncertified Payment Certificates (can demonstrate work performed) – Retention money – Bond wrongfully called – Interest under the contract and applicable law – Sums agreed in final settlement agreement	– Extension of time claims – Prolongation costs – Acceleration claims – Dispute claims – Bonds called – Disputed variations – Money owed under a disputed final account (excluding retention) – Other claims that will need to be established through a legal proceeding	– Claims for moral or reputational damage – Claims not supported with documentary evidence (witness testimony will be required to establish)

claims for TPF without the need of a claim consultant or law firm by quickly identifying the claims that fall under each group, as shown in Table 1.2.

A spreadsheet like this one can help a contractor organize their claims in a way to identify which claims fall under Group 1, 2, or 3.

Note that the above groups are not a complete list of claims. However, these claims are ones that are typically found in construction disputes, especially because of the COVID-19 pandemic.

Funders tend to favor funding hospitality (or commercial) disputes over construction disputes, because the cost of the arbitration/litigation is significantly less, there is less reliance on witness testimony, and the amount of evidence necessary to support any claim is considerably less than compared to a construction dispute. Additionally, the number of experts required for a hospitality dispute is usually only one (1), while a construction dispute requires usually two (2) or three (3) experts. This increases the costs for the funder, since expert costs tend to be the most expensive in an arbitration proceeding.

Many hospitality disputes arise under the Technical Services Agreement (hereinafter "TSA") or the Hotel Management Agreement (hereinafter "HMA"). Each dispute will be assessed differently based on the nature of the agreement.

By way of example, under the TSA, the dispute will focus on the initial design and development of a hotel. Under an HMA, the dispute will revolve around the hotel owner's relation with the hotel operator during the operation of the hotel. While the obligations under the TSA involve the construction and opening phases of the hotel and could be concluded shortly after the hotel is operational, the duration of the HMA can be from 10 to 20 years (and possibly even longer), which means that the claim value of a claim can be considerably higher in a dispute under an HMA.

If a dispute arises under an HMA, it will usually involve the early termination of the operator by the hotel owner. If the dispute is evaluated by a funder, they will likely require an assessment of the projected losses by the operator over the remaining period under the HMA from the date of termination, in addition to other damages caused by the early termination. The assessment will be conducted by a third-party evaluation expert who would more than likely be retained by the claimant if the claim is funded by the funder.

5.6 *Other Considerations to Obtain TPF*

For a claimant to be successful in obtaining funding with favorable terms, there are certain steps the claimant can take to enhance its chances. These include:

- *Approach more than one funder.* Not all funders are the same. A claimant should approach at least five (5) funders to consider their dispute, because some funders are less risk-averse than others and may be more willing to

TABLE 1.2 Spreadsheet to evaluate a contractor's claim for TPF

	Work applied	Work certified	Advance payment recovery	Retention	Contra charges approved	Contra charges not approved	Other deductions		VAT	Net amount paid
							Value	Reason		
Advance payment received										
PC No. 1										
PC No. 2										
PC No. 3										
PC No. 4										
PC No. 5										
Variation orders – approved										
Variation orders – not approved										

fund certain claims. Funders will compete to fund a dispute if they believe the dispute will bring a high return. By approaching several funders, a claimant will obtain several funding offers. The claimant can work and try to negotiate better terms by leveraging the offers against each other. If the funder is interested, it will work to provide better terms than the other funders. Note that some funders will not compete with other funders and will operate on a "take it or leave it" approach with their terms.

- *Use law firms with working relationships with funders.* Certain law firms have special arrangements with certain funders that can assist in obtaining favorable funding terms for the claimant. Many of these law firms will advertise this relationship. However, in practice while these lawyers will promote their arrangements with funders, it does not make a difference as to whether the claim will be funded by the funder and/or whether the claimant will receive better terms as a result. It is recommended that the claimant not be tied down to one law firm with an engagement for one funder. This will limit options for the claimant and reduce its negotiation power over its terms.
- *Work with local funders.* There are many funders from the UK, the US, Europe, and Australia reviewing and funding claims around the world. However, certain claims are better suited for local funders. Local funders will be less risk averse, since they know the market and understand the local courts. A claimant should also consider that local funders will have more flexibility in their terms and may come up with other arrangements to fund the dispute. Many of the international funders are publicly traded and have certain reporting obligations that will require them to only fund under certain conditions, while many local funders do not have these requirements. Further, local funders will be less concerned suing governmental entities in their home jurisdictions. Many of the international funders will not sue certain governmental entities in the local courts or in arbitration seated in the jurisdiction. Local funders have a better understanding of the market, which governmental entity will settle early, who will pay (or not pay) a final award, and how the local courts work for enforcement purposes.
- *Avoid law firms with no working relationships with funders.* There are many law firms in the market who will try to steer a claimant away from funding or avoid the conversation altogether. These firms usually do not have working relationships with funders and will not put in the work to obtain funding. If the firm is not supportive or does not have a working relationship with funders, it is best to seek another law firm who can provide TPF, because most claims can be funded under the right conditions.

6 Conclusion

Over the past few years, countless companies have been under financial pressure due to the COVID-19 pandemic.

In this climate of severe economic uncertainty, these companies need to allocate their financial resources to strategic areas that are more important to business development than litigation expenses.

TPF is a valuable resource for companies, which can save money on legal costs by investing those saved sums in improving their core business activities without giving up on pursuing legal action to protect their rights.

With specific regard to the current situation, at the beginning of the pandemic, it was expected that there would be an exponential increase in disputes and thus a higher demand for TPF. However, against expectations, at the beginning of 2020 listed litigation funding companies experienced a decrease in funding requests. The explanation lies in the support that states have provided to the companies which have avoided the outbreak of many disputes.

Nevertheless, to date, litigation funders activity seems to have surpassed pre-pandemic levels. The reasons are mainly related to the growth of the legal market and in particular the upsurge of litigation as well as the increased awareness of law firms and corporations about the benefits of TPF.

In addition, litigation funders have become increasingly specialized and sophisticated and can provide new optimal solutions that meet clients' different needs.

Furthermore, as explained in this chapter, the most important arbitral institutions have included provisions in their regulations governing different aspects of litigation funding such as, for example, disclosure duties. These rules give more visibility to TPF, increase confidence in its use, and prevent its misuse.

In the near future there will certainly be a regulation of TPF in all jurisdictions where its use is widespread. Such a regulation will create a safer environment for funders, lawyers and clients, contributing to the exponential growth of TPF.

With specific regard to hospitality and construction sectors, after the pandemic period disputes arising from business interruption increased. Construction and hospitality companies experienced a slowdown in work that, in some cases, even came to a complete halt. The financial pressure on these companies led hospitality and construction companies to seek external capital to cover the expenses resulting from litigation. In the future, an increasing number of disputes in this field are expected as well as an increased recourse to TPF easing the burden of costs related to complex lawsuits.

Lastly, with regard to the UAE market, even if TPF is not yet widely used, a greater attention shown in the last years confirms that the UAE has recognized the advantages of this instrument for investors as well as for local companies: many litigation funders are now entering the UAE market since it aims to become one of the major center for dispute resolution.

As the legal landscape in the UAE continues to change, we are seeing a much greater appetite for TPF funding of court litigation and arbitration cases. Such funding opportunities could be extremely beneficial to lawyers, companies and funders operating in the UAE.

CHAPTER 2

After COVID, Unintended Economic Partners and Adversaries when Banks Foreclose on Properties – a Game Theory Approach: "Coopetition"

Amadeu Blasco Muñoz

1 Introduction

While every country has been impacted by COVID-19 in some way, the economic impact of the pandemic on Spain has been worse than almost anywhere else. In 2020, 19 million foreign tourists arrived in Spain, 77.3% fewer than the 83.5 million in 2019, making 2020 the worst year in the history of the Spanish tourism sector. Tourism represented about 12.4% of the Spanish GDP, which means that this drop in tourism had a massive impact on the Spanish economy, and 2021's numbers were not better.

These tourists, foreign and nationals, stayed in one of the seventeen thousand hotels in Spain. 77% of those hotels were still closed at the beginning of 2021, and the occupancy on those that since opened was around 20% in FY21. It is clear that COVID-19 had a substantial impact on the hotel business in Spain. While the summer of 2021 saw numbers of national tourists similar to 2019, the same cannot be said regarding the number of foreign tourists, which are key for the Spanish economy,[1] with a decrease of 60% compared to 2019.

Considering the weight of the tourism sector in the Spanish economy, clearly hotel financing represents a large portion of banks' financing activities and balance sheets. The lack of tourism means that many delinquent loans turned into non-performing loans ("NPLs").

The most obvious strategy a bank follows regarding an NPL is foreclosure. That has been historically the main exit strategy. However, in general terms, foreclosure will not maximize returns, neither for the parties that are directly involved (borrowers and lenders), nor for other stakeholders, such as the hotel operators, nor for the business itself (it may even be destroyed as an ongoing

1 Hugo Gutiérrez, "Spain's tourism industry celebrates strong summer season," El País, September 2, 2021, https://english.elpais.com/economy-and-business/2021-09-02/spains-tourism-industry-celebrates-strong-summer-season.html.

 | DOI:10.1163/9789004514874_004

concern). The business of banks is lending money, not managing hotels or other businesses; therefore, their capabilities may not be aligned with the repossession and subsequent management of a hotel.

If enforcement is excluded from being the best strategy, a loan workout agreement or other consensual solution may be the best outcome, if all the parties want to maximize their position (indirectly maximizing positions of other stakeholders, such as employees or shareholders, as well). If each party considers maximizing its position independently of the other parties, intuitively, an agreement will not be the best possible outcome. This creates a zero–sum scenario, where the gain of one party is the loss of the other party. Unilateral actions taken to maximize returns for one party usually result in a lower overall return than if all parties collaborated.

Basic game theory principles apply to these loan workout and consensual solutions and can be analyzed with different outcomes for each of the three types parties, or "players," in consensual and non-consensual scenarios: the lender ("Star Bank"), the owner–borrower ("John Ltd"), who owns 80% of the hotel with his siblings owning the remaining 20% with no management control, and the hotel operator ("Roe Inc."). There are other stakeholders as well, who may not directly be part of the loan workout agreement, but they can have an impact on the outcome of litigation or a loan workout agreement through their bilateral bargaining with the three principal players.

While the focus is on the impact that COVID-19 has had on hotel loan enforcement and loan workout agreements, and how to find the best possible strategy for each of the parties involved in response to the difficulties brought by COVID-19, many other major events that bring significant uncertainty regarding the value of the hotel business in particular, and the market or the economy in general, may be substituted for COVID-19. This may be helpful when considering what to do after a material event that affects the forecasted cash flows of a business. This major event can be global or local but, either way deeply affects the forecasted cash flows of a business.

2 Assumptions

Game theory principles assume that parties will or at least will pretend to act, rationally (subjectively and/or objectively) and, some actors will act irrationally. In times of uncertainty, assuming rationality is less than ideal, especially when considering specific relationships and not the general market. In times of turbulence, human (mis)behavior may also have a compounding effect. Brinkmanship and bluffing must be considered, and it is also relevant that parties may break the law when operating under game theory, but will not necessarily be subject to criminal prosecution.

In England, the court in *Lord Ackner in Walford v. Miles*[2] held that the duty to negotiate in good faith is inherently repugnant to the adversarial position of the negotiating parties. On the other hand, under Article 7.1 of the Spanish Civil Law, and in other civil law countries, there is a duty to act on good faith. In negotiations that involve loan workout scenarios and/or business restructurings, parties may be aligned with *Lord Ackner*'s opinion.

The last assumption to make is that post-COVID-19 gross valuations and the net present values ("NPV") of investments have been drastically reduced. Market uncertainty means that investors demand a larger required rate of return ("RRR"), and because cash in-flows are now delayed, there has been a direct effect on the NPV of hotel businesses and liabilities must be renegotiated. After COVID-19, the internal rate of return ("IRR," or the discount rate that brings NPV to zero) can be lower than the RRR and can even be negative.[3]

3 Game Theory as a Conceptual Framework to Decide whether to Negotiate or to Litigate

Game theory is defined as "the study of mathematical models of conflict and cooperation between intelligent rational decision-makers." Game theory provides general mathematical techniques for analyzing situations in which two or more individuals make decisions that will influence one another's welfare.[4] Put simply, "game theory is a technique for analyzing how people, firms and governments should behave in strategic situations (in which they must interact with each other), and in deciding what to do must take into account what others are likely to do and how others might respond to what they do."[5] "Game theory provides conceptual insights that allow one to understand and predict, before others what it is likely to happen in such games."[6]

2 *Lord Ackner in Walford v. Miles* [1992] 2 AC 128.

3 An IRR lower than the RRR means that investors are not getting their expected returns. A negative IRR means that the returns are smaller than the initial investment.

4 Roger B. Myerson, *Game Theory: Analysis of Conflict* (Massachusetts: Harvard University Press, 1991), 1–36.

5 "Economics A-Z terms beginning with G," The Economist, accessed April 24, 2022, https://www.economist.com/economics-a-to-z/g#node-21529904.

6 David McAdams, *Game-Changer: Game Theory and the Art of Transforming Strategic Situations* (New York: W. W. Norton & Co., 2014), 15.

What it is paramount here is to understand the concepts and build upon them. Game theory is just that, a theory. Game theory gives a very interesting conceptual framework. However, the framework is built over several assumptions that have been proved to be correct at times, but not always. Peoples have animal spirits and rationality is overpriced, especially when a major event is disrupting the *status quo*.

There are six basic concepts to better understand the strategies that a bank, an owner-borrower, and an operator may follow. Those concepts are (1) dominant and dominated strategies, (2) the Nash equilibrium, (3) the prisoner's dilemma, (4) bluffing, (5) the Hobbesian trap, (6) the game of chicken, and (7) brinkmanship.

3.1 *Dominant and Dominated Strategies*[7]

In a game with simultaneous moves, such as a loan workout or debt enforcement over a hotel, players should look for a dominant strategy. A dominant strategy is one that outperforms the other players' strategies, no matter what they do; it is the best of all available strategies. Game theory assumes that a rational player will always choose the dominant strategy. For instance, if the best outcome for a lender is to enforce the loan no matter what the owner-borrower or the operator does, then the lender will enforce the loan. Of course, if a lender has a dominant strategy, the other players will respond with strategies developed to counter the lender's dominant strategy.

If players do not find a strategy that outperforms the rest, then each player may look for dominated strategies. A dominated strategy is a strategy that is the worst for a player. There may be more than one dominated strategy. For instance, the worst outcome for a lender is to do nothing after the owner-borrower has defaulted, or the owner-borrower handing over possession of the hotel to the operator (if there is equity or value handed over for free). Assuming there are no dominant strategies, and once all dominated strategies are ruled out, the mutual best strategy for the parties is the Nash equilibrium of that game.[8]

---

7 Avinash K. Dixit and Barry J. Nalebuff, *The Art of Strategy: A Game Theorist's Guide to Success in Business and Life* (New York: W. W. Norton & Co., 2010), 70.

8 *Id.* at 124.

3.2 *Nash Equilibrium*[9]

The Nash equilibrium is a set of strategies where each player chooses its best strategy in response to the other players' strategies. If one player has not chosen its best strategy, then there is no Nash equilibrium.

For instance, if after the COVID-19 pandemic the owner-borrower honors the financing agreement because it is the best strategy, the Nash equilibrium will exist with the lender receiving payments by the owner-borrower when the installments are due and payable. The lender's choice to receive the payments owed is a direct response to the owner-borrower's choice to pay.

In a Nash equilibrium, the player chooses its best strategy in response to the other players' best strategies. This is not the same as a dominant strategy, where players choose their best strategy independent of what the other players do. All dominant strategies are best strategies, but not all best strategies are dominant strategies.

3.3 *Prisoner's Dilemma*[10]

A prisoner's dilemma is a decision-making and game theory paradox in which two or more rational players make decisions in their own self-interest without cooperation, decisions that cannot result in the best solution for either individual,[11] with emphasis on "without cooperation."

For example, hypothetically, John and Doe are two old school real estate developers from Spain, self-made businessman, well versed in getting things done, cutting corners if necessary. They are cutthroat competitors, but from time to time, they cooperate with each other, always with a "nothing personal, just business" approach. Both built their own hotels in town. However, the town inspector believes that John and Doe did not comply with all technical specifications and zoning requirements when they constructed the buildings.

Their respective licenses to operate have not yet been granted. The town inspector has no substantial evidence of wrongdoing, only hearsay from the former ex-girlfriend of a master mason who was instructed to cut costs and might have bribed a municipal clerk. If the town inspector carries out a full

9 *Id.* at 104.

10 *Id.* at 64.

11 "Prisoner's Dilemma," CFI, accessed April 24, 2022, https://corporatefinanceinstitute.com/resources/knowledge/other/prisoners-dilemma/.

		Doe			
		Remain Silent		Blame	
	Remain Silent		1Y+ Min. Penalty		Open Now
John		1Y+ Min. Penalty		5Y+ Demol	
			5Y+ Demol		3Y+ Penalty
	Blame	Open Now		3Y+ Penalty	

FIGURE 2.1 Value pre-COVID-19

investigation of the matter, there will be a five-year delay in granting the operating licenses. If he confirms his beliefs, the hotels will have to be partially demolished and rebuilt at a very substantial cost. However, the town inspector does have evidence of a minor technical issue that would delay the opening of both hotels by one year, with a minor penalty if an investigation were to be put in place. So, keeping John and Doe in different meeting rooms, the town inspector proposes to each of them:

> If you blame your pal and he stays silent, he will be fully investigated and his hotel will be demolished, while you can open your hotel right away with minor changes. If you keep silent and he blames you, then the opposite will occur. If you both blame each other, then you will both be subject to a three-year investigation and penalties, but eventually both hotels will be opened. It's your call. If neither party says anything, the most that they will suffer is a one-year delay and minor penalty.

From the example, both parties remaining silent would produce the best outcome for both developers. However, because communication was not possible between the two parties to coordinate mutual silence and considering the risk of the other developer becoming the new best friend of the town inspector, then from their respective positions, John and Doe are incentivized to blame one another. Thus, they would choose the best strategy given the circumstances without considering what the other party would do.

3.4 *Bluffing*[12]

Any game may have a great deal of deceiving. There are mainly two kinds of deceiving: factual and tactical. Factual bluffing means that some facts are not shared or are invented. Tactical bluffing is that the facts are known but a party hides its real position.

Using an example slightly departing from the same case above, assume there is communication between the two developers through a not-so-honest municipal clerk. Also, John doubts that the former ex-girlfriend of the master mason will ever talk because she left town. He, a keen player of poker, believes that the municipal inspector is bluffing. He makes this information known to Doe and both agree to remain silent.

Bluffing is a very risky tactic. It can generate a lot of value for one of the players in a zero-sum game, but at risk of negatively impacting a possible consensual solution if the other players become aware of the bluff.

3.5 *The Hobbesian Trap (or Schelling's Dilemma)*[13]

Although cooperation between John and Doe would be the better strategy for both, mutual distrust leads to the adoption of strategies that have negative outcomes for both parties. If they trusted each other, John and Doe could have their hotels open in one year with a minimum penalty, but because they distrust one another and blamed each other, they both must open in three years with a penalty. Distrust negatively affects the strategies that each party will follow, making them choose a strategy that is not their best or dominant strategy out of fear of what the other party will do. The end of the game is a negative feedback loop that leads to mutual destruction.

Following the previous example, if Doe does not believe that John will remain silent, that John is bluffing, and as a matter-of-fact John will blame Doe, then Doe will blame John.

3.6 *Chicken Game*

Assume now a new game where John and Doe have not yet initiated the construction of their respective hotels but both have obtained the necessary permits. They decide to see which one of them is the best real estate developer by building the largest, most oversized, and expensive five-star hotel. While

---

12 Thomas C. Schelling, *The Strategy of Conflict* (Massachusetts: Harvard University Press, 1981), 23.

13 Sandeep Baliga and Tomas Sjöström, "The Hobbesian Trap," in *The Oxford Handbook of the Economics of Peace and Conflict*, eds. Michelle R. Garfinkel and Stergios Skaperdas (Massachusetts: Oxford University Press, 2012).

John \ Doe	Stop		Construct	
Stop	Tie			Win
		Tie	Lose	
Construct		Lose		Lose
	Win		Lose	

FIGURE 2.2 Value post-COVID-19

the ideal outcome is for one of them to stop building their hotel, or not even initiate construction, in a place where there is only a market for a medium sized four-star hotel, both avoid halting construction out of pride and to not look like a "chicken." John and Doe will taunt the other to increase the shame in stopping. When one player does stop, the conflict is ended and there is a winner and a loser, the "chicken." If both players stop, they would both be perceived as "chickens" by the industry. However, the best strategy for John and Doe would have been to stop the construction of the oversized and very expensive five-star hotels, because the town only has a market for one medium size four-star hotel.

Related to the game of chicken is the concept of brinkmanship.

3.7 *Brinkmanship*[14]

Brinkmanship is a hardball negotiation or diplomacy technique "in which one or both parties force the interaction between them to the threshold of confrontation in order to gain an advantageous negotiation position over the other. The technique is characterized by aggressive risk-taking policy choices that court potential disaster."[15] Former U.S. Secretary of State John Foster Dulles claimed that, in diplomacy, "[t]he ability to get to the verge without getting into the war is the necessary art (…) if you are scared to go to the brink, you are lost."[16]

---

14 Schelling, *supra* note 12, at 199.

15 "Brinkmanship: foreign policy," Britannica, accessed April 10, 2022, https://www.britannica.com/topic/brinkmanship.

16 James Shepley, "How Dulles Averted War," *LIFE Magazine* 40, no. 3 (January 16, 1956): 78.

The easiest example of brinkmanship would be the Cold War, where the West and the East continually upgraded their respective weapon arsenals with larger and more dangerous bombs to scare the other into submission. This deliberate effort to increase the risk of destruction may get out of control.

4 Other Concepts to Be Added to the Game Theory Conceptual Framework

4.1 *Net Present Value*

Net present value, or "NPV,"[17] is the value of all future cash flows (positive and negative, money coming in and going out, including the initial cost of investment) over the entire life of an investment, discounted at a specified rate (usually the required rate of return or "RRR," which is how much gain creditors and shareholders expect in consideration for the risk they undertook) to the present date. A positive NPV is considered a valid investment because it creates value, meaning there is value in the business after all the stakeholders have obtained their desired return. It is extremely difficult to consider all the required inputs to properly calculate the NPV.

Using the NPV allows players to compare its different NPV options and choose the one that generates more value, allowing each of them to choose their best strategy, whether it is a dominant strategy or not.

There are several other valuation methods, but discounting the future cash flows from a hotel indicates the capacity of the hotel to generate cash for all players and its stakeholders. Cash and time can be calculated, but it takes a lot of effort and ultimately is just a forecast of the future and not a definite fact.

However, a NPV can suffer a huge deviation from its projected values; for instance, no one knows the length and cost of one particular mortgage enforcement. Average length can be calculated; however, it is not possible to know for one specific proceeding. There are several unknown factors which cannot be predicted. For example, is the owner-borrower going to oppose the enforcement, and if it does, will the owner-borrower appeal an adverse ruling? Will the court accept the owner-borrower's opposition, only to be overruled by a higher Court?[18] The true value of a hotel or project will not be known until the

17 "Economics A-Z terms beginning with N," The Economist, accessed September 10, 2021, https://www.economist.com/economics-a-to-z/n#node-21529704.

18 There are more; for instance, the court having a very important and large case that consumes resources well beyond the average case, or the paternity or maternity leave of a court professional directly involved in the proceeding.

project is completed and the returns collected. The NPV looks into the future, but it is only an educated guess.

Because of COVID-19, the situation has become aggravated, and the exact impact of COVID-19 is not yet known. The incurred (sunk) costs are known, but it is still difficult to say what is going to happen in the short term. Uncertainty means that investors will demand a higher RRR, and the projected cash flows may be smaller and/or taken place much later than previously expected. Overall, these changes make the NPV for each player smaller.

To decide which strategy to follow, the players will have to value the NPV of the hotel, and then its own NPV. This would be the NPV of the hotel, the NPV of the loan, the NPV of the lease agreement the NPV of the equity, *etc.*

4.2 *Animal Spirits*

Animal spirits is a term John Maynard Keynes used to describe the gloom and despondence that led to the Great Depression and the changing psychology that accompanied recovery.[19] Several years later, economists George Akerlof and Robert Shiller used that term to challenge the economic wisdom that markets are perfect and are not affected by personal considerations.

Strategy and decision-making are influenced by psychological, behavioral forces, which partly explains why some decisions are considered irrational. Game theory is a system of thought that expects players to behave as unemotional, rational beings, but this is probably the biggest flaw of the theory. People act "irrationally" on a day-to-day basis, and organizations are no more than the sum of its constituent people and their psychological, behavioral forces. Irrational actors, in addition to COVID-19 or other major events affecting livelihoods, make things worse because of the uncertainty they create, which further raises RRRS.

4.3 *Game Theory, NPVs Animal Spirits and Workouts*

In financing transactions, workouts, and operational turnarounds, the strategy that should be chosen by a party can be reflected either through the largest NPV of the deal or no deal at all for each party.[20] By calculating the NPV of the available strategies and alternatives, a party can make the best, most rational

19 George A. Akerlof and Robert J. Shiller, *Animal Spirits: How Human Psychology Drivers the Economy, and Why It Matters for Global Capitalism* (New Jersey: Princeton University Press, 2010).

20 Han T. J. Smit and Lenos Trigeorgis, "Strategic NPV: Real Options and Strategic Games under Different Information Structures," *Strategic Management Journal* 38, no. 13 (April 2017).

decision based upon the available data, and would be able to choose the best strategy. While there are other tools and indicators with which to measure, what is important is that all parties are on the same page on which valuation method will be used. NPVs are well understood and what is typically chosen as the best strategy based upon all the collected data regarding a player's strategic moves and countermoves. Relying upon NPVs is an educated decision, but it does not mean it will be correct.

NPV, while in name sounds financial-like, is deeply affected by the human behavior of animal spirits. "The NPV model does not aim at solving decision problems as decision makers have actually defined them, but at solving decision problems as decision makers should have 'rationally' defined them."[21]

This is a very large obstacle in refinancing and workout negotiations. A gross divergence in the value of the hotel greatly increases the chances of not reaching an agreement. If parties do not agree on an approximate value of the hotel, who will calculate it, or how it will be calculated, there is very little possibility of a cooperative agreement.

4.4 *Cooperation v. Litigation*

Navigating workout scenarios is a form of art. They require soft skills and understanding of the other party's position, but also hard and aggressive negotiation skills. There are three likely different scenarios:

(i) The three parties (lender, owner–borrower, and operator) will cooperate when the NPV of its share of the NPV of the business is higher through cooperation than litigation. If, John, Roe Inc., and Star Bank all obtain a larger return, then they have an incentive to cooperate. If the dominated strategy for all three players is litigation, then they should cooperate.

They "should" cooperate, because it is possible that a player will not understand or will not seek professional advice that indicates to the party that litigation results in the worst outcome, brinkmanship aside, which means that litigation is a dominated strategy for the party if a higher NPV can be obtained through cooperation. A higher NPV will consider a litigation scenario. It is not unusual if one or more players value the hotel, the project, and its sunk costs (costs already incurred and that cannot be recovered) and not the NPV.

---

21 Carlo Alberto Magni, "Reasoning the 'Net-Present-Value' Way: Some Biases and How to Use Psychology for Falsifying Decision Models," September 7, 2010, 43, http://dx.doi.org/10.2139/ssrn.1673371.

(ii) Two parties will also cooperate when the NPV of its share of the NPV of the hotel is higher than not cooperating, even if one party does not cooperate. That is, two parties will collaborate if their dominate strategies are to collaborate, even if the remaining party's best strategy is to not cooperate.
For instance, if John and Roe Inc. have a larger NPV cooperating, even if Star Bank's dominate strategy is litigating, John Ltd and Roe Inc. will collaborate without Star Bank. Hence, two parties can collaborate to obtain a larger NPV even with a party not willing to cooperate.

(iii) There will be no cooperation at all when the NPV is higher for two of the three parties to not cooperate rather than to cooperate. The dominated strategy for the three players is cooperation.

As mentioned before, animal spirits, personal perceptions, and feelings may distort the view regarding the NPV of the hotel. On top of that, the COVID-19 pandemic distorted valuations and because the future is still uncertain, the divergence on valuations has increased.

A party will accept a strategy when it obtains its best possible NPV. However, cooperation also includes competition.

4.5 *Dividing the "Pie": Cooperation Is in Fact Cooperation + Competition*

It is not correct to completely differentiate cooperation and competition. Cooperation is an overall win-win, but splitting the value is still a zero-sum game, which is why there is "coopetition."[22]

A zero–sum game is "when the gains made by winners in an economic transaction equal the losses suffered by the losers."[23]

Simply put, the worst "coopeting" strategy must be at the very least marginally better than the best competing/litigating alternative. It must be better in absolute terms. If that is the case, then parties should be willing to cooperate, and within that framework of cooperation players will compete. There is no rational basis to split any additional gain from cooperation. Existing values that each party bring into the barganing should not fix the outcome. Once there is willingness to cooperate, the game turns into a zero-sum game where the parties will compete to split the marginal increase in the value of cooperation amongst themselves. This is "coopetition".

---

22 Adam Brandenburger and Barry Nalebuff, "The Rules of Co-opetition," Harvard Business Review (January-February 2021), accessed April 14, 2022, https://hbr.org/2021/01/the-rules-of-co-opetition.

23 "Economics A-Z terms beginning with Z," The Economist, accessed April 24, 2022, https://www.economist.com/economics-a-to-z/z#node-21529327.

Parties involved should strive to obtain the best NPV possible for themselves, which always will be in detriment of the NPV of the other parties. The NPV of the investment, such as the hotel, is finite. Parties may find solutions that increase the value of the hotel (cooperation) and increase the NPV for all parties, but the value will still be finite and will have to be divided in a zero–sum negotiation (competition). That is, the win–win negotiation mantra is partially true, because each party will try to maximize its position relative to the other party. Even if all players win, some will win more than others. Thus, it is more like WIN-WIN–win. The NPV of the business in absolute terms and/or in relative terms for some or all the parties will be reduced. The "coopeting" NPV of the lender shall be at the very least marginally better than the NPV of the lender when litigating to enforce the loan, considering the "value grabbing" by the owner and operator and the time to repossess. Likewise, the NPV of the owner-borrower and operator must also be marginally better than the NPV in a "value grabbing" process.

Remember that the lender must raise the capital that it lends. On top of that, banking regulations may add additional layers of cost, and if it is an alternative lender, the cost of capital requires additional returns that offset the risk of investing in non-regulated alternative lenders. In a full legal scenario, repossession might be years away, there is a tax impact on the acquisition, and potentially high litigation costs.

The equity stakeholders of the owner-borrower may see all their equity gone if the lender repossesses, and thus a negative return on its investment. The owner-borrower would obtain very low or most likely negative RRR and no return on the investment going forward. The owner-borrower is aware that while they can delay a mortgage enforcement, in the end, it will lose the hotel and all its investment in the equity.

The operator also may see its contract terminated or not renewed and any capital expenditure invested in the hotel lost. The nature of the business in which the operator conducts itself necessitates that its economic interests will gravitate towards the bank if repossession becomes probable.

Thus, the players involved should have an expected NPV that considers both the value of the business, in this case a hotel, and what strategies the other parties may follow regarding its NPV.

This zero-sum game means that it is not necessary to split the gains, or the value-taking based on what contributions/reductions each player brings to the table. That is, it does not matter that the lender brings the largest contribution or the owner-borrower the smaller one. What really matters is that each "coopeting" strategy is marginally better than a litigating alternative, because in absolute terms, that player will be in a better position. But in a zero-sum game, previous contributions should not be the basis for splitting the gains in a "coopetition" agreement. All players can increase/reduce the NPV independently from their previous contributions.[24] Hence, whatever they previously contributed, and how it was valued, does not have to set the split of the additional value. What is important is the willingness to "coopete" and generate value. The player that may bring/destroy more value should be the player that, in the zero-sum game, gains the most in relative terms.

5 The Art of Brinkmanship and the Prisoner's Dilemma

The prisoner's dilemma has a twist in a secured lending scenario. In the worst outcome for Star Bank, it will recover at least part of its investment with the repossession and subsequent sale of the hotel,[25] while the owner-borrower may get nothing for their equity aside from the return through "value grabbing." The owner will only get equity after the lender has collected the outstanding balance of the financing.

Still, while the bank may prevail after repossession in absolute terms, from an NPV perspective, the owner and operator must calculate their NPVs to decide whether to cooperate or not. For instance, it is likely that John Ltd will lose the hotel to Star Bank. However, if during the enforcement process, through value grabbing John Ltd reaches a better NPV than through cooperating, then it does not matter what Star Bank does. Rationally, John Ltd does not have to cooperate.

From those positions, the lender is in a better position to practice both brinkmanship and the chicken game generally (its loans will be senior to the other debt holders and equity), but this still usually is tested on a case-by-case basis.

A common way to reach a "coopeting" agreement is to express an obvious willingness to use irresistible or overwhelming force (contractual and legal remedies).[26] Mere words may not suffice, and real action should be taken, for instance, taking legal action not only through mortgage enforcement but also demanding the bankruptcy of a lender. A party only using words might be seen

24 Bary Nalebuff and Adam Brandenburger, "Rethinking Negotiation," Harvard Business Review (November-December 2021), accessed April 9, 2022, https://hbr.org/2021/11/rethinking-negotiation.

25 Assume that the secured lending has some sort of collateral of value that, while it may be reduced, it may not be fully destroyed.

26 Bruce D. Henderson, "Brinkmanship in Business," Harvard Business Review (March 1967), accessed April 24, 2022, https://hbr.org/1967/03/brinkmanship-in-business.

as bluffing, and if read, the downside is very high. Additionally, even if wrongly read by other players as bluffing, Star Bank may then be compelled to take action that it otherwise would not because it put itself in a position it did not need to be in by not acting, resulting in a chicken game with undesired consequences for all players. However, acting itself simultaneously reduces the risk of being read incorrectly and has the additional benefit of putting up a barrier to the loss. For instance, if the three parties' negotiations are fruitless and the position of the owner-borrower cannot be accepted by the lender-bank, then initiating a mortgage enforcement, demanding some personal guarantees, or even demanding the bankruptcy of the owner-borrower signals the maximum loss the lender is willing to accept. The bank, thus, tries to protect its investment by accelerating the time to repossess. On the other hand, the owner-borrower may request some ad-hoc or legal injunction that would stop enforcement for a period of time or carry out some form of corporate restructuring that would delay enforcement.

6 Value Grabbing

Another important aspect to be considered is "value grabbing." Value grabbing encompasses the tactics or moves to increase the NPV of one player through the reduction of the NPV of the other parties. While those tactics will reduce the NPV of the other players, the increase in the NPV of the actor is not guaranteed. Value grabbing could result in a lose-lose game. Potentially, those tactics may not be within the law (even could be a criminal offense), and it is common that those tactics will be on the edge of legality but may be taken with the ultimate purpose to generate a better NPV for the actor.

For instance, if the lender is enforcing in a low loan to value scenario ("LTV," or the share of the loan with respect to the value of the collateral), a rational owner-borrower should file as many oppositions, motions, and appeals as possible to delay repossession while "value grabbing," which will affect the future distribution of cash flow and/or time, reducing the NPV of the loan and potentially also of the hotel. Another example may be the lender accelerating the loan in the low LTV to generate default interest and value grab the equity in the collateral, while the owner-borrower intended to negotiate a workout. A final example may be that the owner-borrower of the hotel does not comply with some municipality order that forces the hotel to close, with a great cost to be reopened once repossessed.

Assuming a fixed value of the hotel, if one player increases its cash flow or reduces the NPV of the hotel in prejudice of another player, the NPV of the second player will decrease and that player may be incentivized to share its expected gains.

The exact extent of "value grabbing" may be extremely difficult to calculate in advance. Ethical and behavioral considerations must be taken into account on a case-by-case basis; thus, animal spirits again have an impact on the NPV forecasts.

It is likely that the owner-borrower and the operator will see their NPVs cut short upon the repossession of the hotel in an enforcement scenario, because the lender-bank is senior in the payment waterfall and they will try to maximize its return, grabbing any value possible.

"Value grabbing" can also happen in a "coopeting" scenario and will form part of the resulting settlement. However, if they are known and not accepted by the suffering player, there is a high probability of preventing a "coopeting" outcome. The value grabbing in this scenario, and thus the value added to the NPV of the owner-borrower, should be in smaller absolute terms than in a litigation scenario. If the value grabbing was larger, then the NPV of the lender-bank (the most likely affected player) would be lower in a "coopeting" scenario than in a litigation scenario. Therefore, the lender should choose to litigate.

This means that the lender-bank must calculate its NPV post "value grabbing," at the very least with those facts that can be realistically predicted, to properly understand its different strategies with the owner-borrower and the operator. For example, if the repossession process will take 2 years and the owner-borrower informs the lender that the kitchen of the hotel it is in a part of the building that was not mortgaged, then the lender must calculate in its NPV whatever additional costs the lender will have to incur to make sure the hotel has a kitchen and can therefore operate as a hotel.

In that scenario, if the NPV post "value grabbing" is still better than the NPV through "coopetition", the lender-bank, will enforce the loan, litigate, and then repossess the hotel or sell it to a third party. This tends to happen if the collateral, such as the hotel, has a high LTV and/or high default interest rate that value grabs. Then the bank is more incentivized to accelerate the loan, enforce it and litigate. In that case, the owner-borrower and the operator must consider whether the NPV they may get after the enforcement, which is the leftover equity, is higher than value grabbing. At that point, the owner-borrower and the operator would have four different strategies:

(i) Oppose and value grab;
(ii) Oppose and not value grab;
(iii) Not oppose and value grab; or
(iv) Not oppose and not value grab.

From those four, they will have to choose the strategy that gives a higher NPV. This is much easier said than done.

The lender's decision to "coopete" or litigate also depends on what the owner-borrower and the operator may do. Independent of the "coopetition" or litigation, if the lender has a dominant strategy on the position of the owner-borrower and the operator, then the lender will likely choose this one. The same must be said about owner-borrower and the operator. However, the reality is that in a hotel workout scenario, the lender is better positioned than the owner-borrower and the operator, but still needs "coopetition" to reach its best NPV.

7 PARTS and Strategy

Game theory has five basic elements: (i) players; (ii) added values; (iii) rules; (iv) tactics; and (v) scope.[27] Given the impact the COVID-19 pandemic has had on the hotel industry, previous commercial relationships have been severely altered. Outside of COVID-19, any event out of the ordinary has a potentially exponential impact on the value of the hotel, from a terrorist attack in a nearby location to a world financial crisis.

Because of COVID-19, part of the NPV of each player has been destroyed, and no one can predict when or what will be recovered. In the meantime, a higher RRR and a longer-term contract may be required to fulfill new risk appetites. This means that the agreements pre-COVID-19 may no longer be valid from a commercial point of view because the temporary shutdown of the hotel means that the previous agreements cannot be honored with their existing terms and conditions. There was little to no cash flow to honor the agreements, and those agreements will likely be terminated or amended to reflect the impact that COVID-19 has had on them.

COVID-19 now requires that parties need to consider the PARTS elements to find their best NPV, while the PARTS elements themselves may need to be altered in the wake of the pandemic.

7.1 *Players*

Players are those parties involved in the possible agreements or mortgage enforcement actions. The parties are not fixed, and some parties may find it useful to change some or all of them, add new players, or forge coalitions among current players or new players, and then analyze the resulting NPV.

---

27 Adam M. Brandenburger and Barry J. Nalebuff, *Co-opetition* (Profile Books, 1997), 9.

The different possibilities must be considered on a case-by-case basis, considering the unique circumstances of each situation.

7.2 *Added (or Destructed) Value*

Added value is what players add to the game (financing, ownership, operation), the sum of which is the total added value. With hotels, this is the total value of the hotel as an ongoing concern, including what the players may detract through value grabbing. A party should know not only what it can do to generate value, but also what value it can take or destroy from others. For example, investing in capital expenditures (CAPEX) or destroying value by losing the hotel operating license.

A player will want to bring more value or subtract more value, thus making its position more valuable vis-à-vis the others. The party that changes the NPV value of the hotel the most, whether bringing or destroying value, will have a better position in the "coopeting" game. For example, while John Ltd, the owner-borrower may bring an additional value of 1, Star Bank may destroy a value of 2, putting Star Bank in a better position in the "coopeting" game because it has more leverage under brinkmanship. But if John Ltd brings an additional value of 3, then John Ltd would be in a better position. This does not mean that the additional contribution or destruction must be valued equally; it means it has more power in the zero-sum game.

In a "coopeting" game, the player who can bring/destroy more value is also the player that is better positioned to obtain more value under any "coopeting" alternatives.

7.3 *Rules*

Rules include legal, contractual, and customary or trade practice rules. In the hotel industry, contractual terms will be amended (workout solutions), terminated (enforcement of the loan), or insolvency of the borrower will be filed. But during a major event such as COVID-19, these rules are not necessarily fully applicable. In that case, a player will depart from a *pacta sunt servanda*[28] to a *clausula rebus sic stantibus*[29] perspective and try to reach a new outcome, either through "coopetition" or litigation, which suits their interests better in NPV terms.

The change in circumstances means there is a need to change the rules, and the larger the change in circumstances, the larger the need to change the

---

28 *Pacta sunt servanda* means "agreements shall be kept."

29 *Clausula rebus sic stantibus* means that an agreement becomes inapplicable because of a fundamental change of circumstances.

applicable rules. While the law cannot be changed by the players, the players can agree to change the contractual terms. Because trade practice rules are common rules of trade and considering that events such as the COVID-19 pandemic are not common, trade practice rules are likely not applicable.

7.4 *Tactics*

Tactics are actions, or a lack of action, taken by the players. Because parties cannot predict the future and a NPV is just a valuation method of the future, there is a high degree of uncertainty. Tactics influence how players perceive this uncertainty and how they act in response to their perception, for instance, brinkmanship in the chicken game or bluffing and the Hobbesian trap. Note that animal spirits have a direct impact on the tactics used and they will mold their strategy accordingly.

7.5 *Scope*

Scope is the relationship between the players, not only in the hotel investment but beyond as well, such as personal and business relationships that may not be intrinsically related to the hotel but still essential in a broader context among some of the players.

8 Why Do Agreements Fail?

There are several circumstances that may derail a "coopeting" agreement. A PARTS analysis may help to find different strategies that increases the NPV of a "coopeting" agreement, making a consensual solution more likely.

Patterns of similar sovereign financings and defaults in the same period have had very different rescheduling outcomes (or no rescheduling, with negative consequences for all parties).[30] That means that when faced with a similar problem, with similar alternatives, there have been very important deviations in the strategies that were followed and the resulting outcomes. While there have been several reasons for those different outcomes based on a PARTS analysis, animal spirits have been a main reason for that deviation. This can be especially true due to the impact of COVID-19 in valuations (or any other major event), where parties may have a vastly different idea of the NPV after COVID-19 than they would have prior to the pandemic.

30 Vinod K. Aggarwal, *Debt Games: Strategic Interaction in International Debt Rescheduling* (Cambridge University Press, 1996), 41.

9 Practical Example

Here is a practical example combining all these concepts.

9.1 *Background*

John Ltd, the owner-borrower, opened his five-star hotel Marbella, Málaga, Spain, with 300 rooms, swimming pools, a spa, a beach club, golf courses, and a two-star Michelin restaurant. It is operated through a lease agreement by an independent third party, Roe Inc., the operator. The loan is secured by a first ranking mortgage for 30.000.000,00€. The pre-COVID-19 NPV of the hotel was 50.000.000,00€, meaning that the loan to value of the hotel pre-COVID-19 was 60%; therefore, John Ltd had 40% equity in the hotel.

The lease agreement stipulated quarterly payments of 600.000,00€, equal to 80% of the revenues, which was 750.000,00€. Now, however, Roe Inc., the operator, has not obtained the expected revenue. As a result, there was no variable rent, only fixed rent, and because there was no variable rent, the owner, John Ltd, decided not to invest in the required CAPEX. Roe Inc. invested in some FF&E, but the quality was not as expected for the class of hotel. The hotel lease agreement stipulated a renegotiation of the rents after seven years, which would have given John Ltd the opportunity to receive a higher rent at the current market levels, or to take control over the hotel exploitation. However, John Ltd did not do anything, as Roe Inc. was paying the owner under the table and away from the eyes of the trade and financial creditors.

Revenue per available room ("RevPAR") fell in a vicious cycle; the clients and guests were not happy with the hotel, and their opinions were that the hotel was subpar. Roe Inc. missed and/or delayed payments to John Ltd, alleging that the lack of investment in CAPEX had obliged him to close several rooms. John Ltd was forced to refinance with the bank when he became at risk of defaulting on his monthly instalments. In exchange, the bank increased its security package with a pledge over the bank accounts and the credit rights of the lease agreement and increased the default interest to Euro Interbank Offered Rate ("Euribor") by 10%. The bank expected that there would be a default and positioned itself to be able to dilute the equity in case it had to enforce the loan and repossess. The REVpar subsequently nosedived.

When COVID-19 hit Spain, hotels were obliged to close by mid-March 2020. John Ltd was advised wrongly by Hagen, the consigliere, who was more versed in other types of businesses rather than hotels and did not take advantage of COVID-19 laws. John Ltd was slow to react, and the loan was subsequently accelerated by the bank. Roe Inc. stopped paying rent to John Ltd, alleging

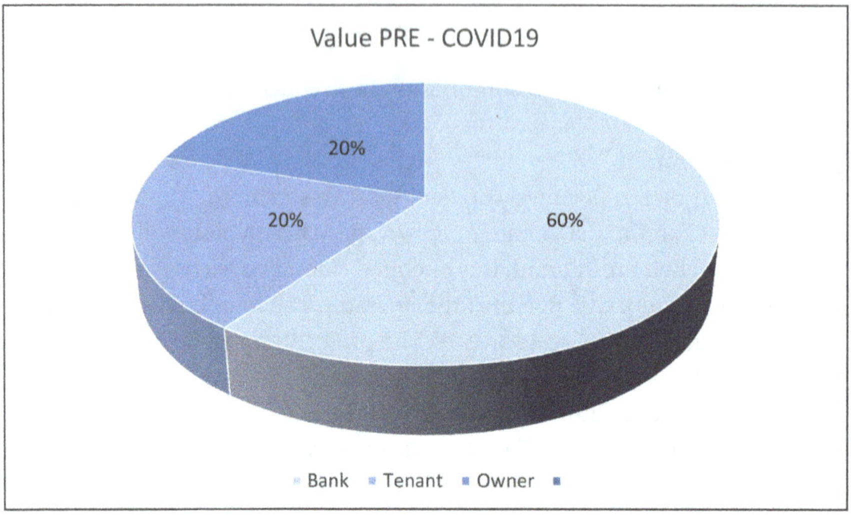

FIGURE 2.3 Value pre-COVID-19

clausula rebus sic stantibus,[31] believing that there was a fundamental change in the circumstances and that he was not obliged to pay the rent. Roe Inc. forgot that the rent had not been adjusted to market for several years.

Note that the hotel belongs to a special purpose vehicle (a company created to hold the hotel and isolate the liabilities), John Ltd, and that Star Bank has no recourse to John's other assets.

The NPV of the hotel after COVID-19 was drastically reduced to slightly above 30.000.000,00€ and the LTV was 89%. Roe Inc. has seen his equity in the value of the hotel destroyed by half, and John Ltd has seen his equity reduced to 1% of the value pre-COVID-19.

In the post-COVID-19 scenario, the NPVs of the three players are no longer aligned and therefore action must be taken.

Star Bank, John Ltd, and Roe Inc can either "coopete" or litigate. Each player must decide what strategy to follow, and they will investigate its best strategy to maximize its return from the hotel.

9.2 *The Size of the Pie, the Value and Each Player's Slice*

Each player will then try to understand its situation post-COVID-19:

31 The *clausula rebus sic stantibus* doctrine only applies when the substantial change in circumstances reduces the expected NPV. However, it is not applicable when the change benefits the tenant, but not the owner or both.

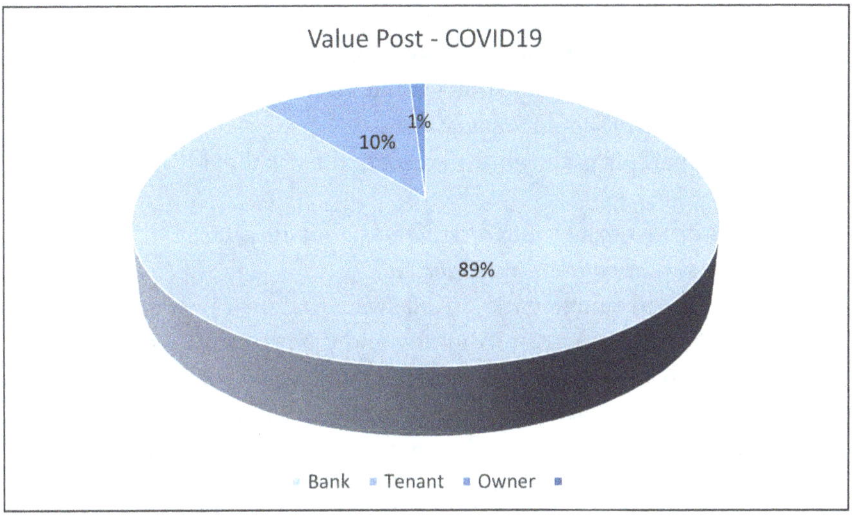

FIGURE 2.4 Value post-COVID-19

(i) The value of the hotel based on future cash flows; and
   a. How much value and when it will be obtained, and
   b. How much is left over to divide between the three players.

(ii) The RRR of their respective investors and its creditors.

That is, the NPV of the business and the NPV for each player, or how much the hotel is worth and how much each player will receive from it.

9.3 *Pre- vs. Post-COVID-19 slices (NPVs)*

Each player will then compare its own post-COVID-19 NPV to its pre-COVID-19 NPV before analyzing and deciding on a strategy.

(i) If the post-COVID-19 NPV is smaller than the pre-COVID-19 NPV, then the player should try to increase it.

(ii) If the post-COVID-19 NPV is at least the same as the pre-COVID-19 NPV, then the player has no incentive to increase it without considering the other players' strategies.
However, because there is only one hotel, and its NPV must be split among Star Bank, John Ltd, and Roe Inc., if one or more players are in category (i), then the player or players in category (ii) will see their NPV negatively affected. Thus, a recalculation of a NPV will be required to add value grabbing, which will result in the post-COVID-19 NPV plus value grabbing.

(iii) If the post-COVID-19 NPV plus value grabbing is at least the same as the pre-COVID-19 NPV, then the player has no incentive to increase it. That player has a dominant strategy, and no matter what the other parties do, that party should follow its NPV.

Beware of animal spirits and always consider the risk that involves.

9.4 *Post-COVID-19 NPV and after Value Grabbing after PARTS: "Coopetition" v. Litigation*

Star Bank, John Ltd, and Roe Inc. are all aware that their post-COVID-19 NPVs are smaller than their pre-COVID-19 NPV and the previously agreed commercial terms are no longer valid. All parties are aware that each player is capable of value grabbing and each player should compare its post-COVID-19 NPV plus the value after value grabbing, and then determine if they should "coopete" or litigate:

(i) If the post-COVID-19 NPV and after value grabbing means that "coopeting" is better for all players as opposed to litigating, then Star Bank, John Ltd, and Roe Inc. will "coopete". They will look for a WIN-WIN-win.

(ii) If the post-COVID-19 NPV and after value grabbing means "coopeting" is better for two of the three parties, then two parties will "coopete" and litigate against the other player.
For instance, John Ltd and Roe Inc will "coopete" and litigate against Star Bank.

(iii) If the post-COVID-19 NPV and after value grabbing means litigating is better for two or more players rather than "coopeting", then the parties will litigate.

In each of these scenarios, a party should consider PARTS before going forward and executing an action plan. Players should consider changing their plan to maximize the value of their NPV for each of them individually and/or as a group. Star Bank, John Ltd, and Roe Inc. can apply PARTS to each of their plans to maximize its post-COVID-19 NPV, including value grabbing, and then decide which is their best strategy.

Practical matters that Star Bank, John Ltd, and Roe Inc. could consider, and when appropriate share with other players, include:

(i) Players:
   a. Star Bank, the lender, can trade the loan at a discount. Star Bank should then compare the NPV of selling the loan versus being involved in a "coopeting" scenario or a litigation scenario. Star Bank could contact any personal guarantors to help Star Bank reach a "coopting" solution on better terms.
   b. John, the owner-borrower, can either sell the shares of the owner company, John Ltd, or sell the collateral. John should then

compare the NPV of selling the shares and/or selling the collateral versus being involved in a "coopeting" scenario or a litigious scenario.

c. Roe Inc., the hotel operator, can terminate or sell the contract.

d. John Ltd and Roe Inc. can join forces against Star Bank.

(ii) Added Values:

a. Star Bank may be willing to invest in CAPEX.

b. John Ltd may be willing to renegotiate a write-off with trade creditors.

c. John may be willing to dissolve John Ltd if it is impossible to obtain a new hotel license.

d. Roe Inc. may be willing to invest in FF&E.

(iii) Changing the rules:

a. Star Bank may be willing to enforce the mortgage.

b. John Ltd may be willing to sell the hotel and repay the loan.

c. John Ltd may be willing to file for bankruptcy protection and force a write–off, an automatic stay[32] of Star Bank, or renegotiate new lease terms with Roe Inc.

d. Roe Inc. may be willing to change from a lease to management agreement.

(iv) Tactics:

a. Brinkmanship: Star Bank may initiate enforcement.

b. Value grabbing: John Ltd may stop paying some taxes, or Roe Inc. may stop paying rents.

c. Hobbesian trap: Each player may wish to have a friendly working relationship and avoid having any party take an action that may make a consensual solution impossible.

(v) Scope:

a. Star Bank may have other business with Roe Inc.

b. John may be a large shareholder of Star Bank.

Even when the players agree to agree, a second, additional game is also played. Agreeing to agree may be a result of acts taken when the players are aware that a consensual-"coopeting" scenario should deliver a better NPV than a litigation scenario. Players, through their respective actions, agreed that they can maximize the pie, and within that, a second zero-sum game may be played. The parties will then compete in that second level of game. There is no rule on

32 An automatic stay is a legal provision that temporarily prevents creditors from collecting their loans or seizing assets of the insolvent company. The automatic stay reduces the NPV of a loan.

whether that second game will be played together or separately, as it depends on the PARTS of each player and can be part of the negotiation process.

A two-step process is recommended, where all players believe that they will first win, and then WIN–WIN–win. In NPV terms, "coopeting" is usually better than litigating. Only in cases where litigating is undoubtedly the dominant strategy should this strategy be followed.

CHAPTER 3

The Importance and Impact of Risk Allocation Clauses for Payment Obligations in Hospitality Contracts as Demonstrated by COVID-19 Litigation

John D. Wilburn, Richard D. Holzheimer, Jr. and Kang He

1 Introduction

The World Health Organization declared COVID-19 a pandemic on March 11, 2020,[1] and a global shutdown ensued. Many countries responded to COVID-19 with some form of a lockdown which, collectively, limited the movement and activities of billions of people.[2] Some nations, like the United States, enacted strict quarantine procedures, closing non-essential businesses, barring non-essential travel, and requiring social distancing. International travel for leisure or business was out of the question.

With its heavy dependence on travel and gatherings, the hospitality industry was hit particularly hard by COVID-19. Pre-pandemic, the industry was growing faster than the world's economy.[3] But in the United States alone, the lockdown that was imposed to battle the virus led to an unprecedented 42% annual decline in travel spending.[4] For U.S. hotels, occupancy was down 42.3%, and revenue per available room fell 51.9% in March 2020 compared to March 2019.[5] Restaurant sales similarly dropped, with $659 billion in sales in

1 "WHO Director-General's Opening Remarks at the Media Briefing on COVID-19," World Health Organization, March 11, 2020, https://www.who.int/director-general/speeches/detail/who-director-general-s-opening-remarks-at-the-media-briefing-on-covid-19---11-march-2020.

2 Daniel Dunford et al., "Coronavirus: The World in Lockdown in Maps and Charts," BBC News, April 7, 2020, https://www.bbc.com/news/world-52103747.

3 "2020: A Year in Review," World Tourism Organization, accessed March 31, 2022, https://www.unwto.org/covid-19-and-tourism-2020.

4 "Weekly Coronavirus Impact on Travel Expenditures in the U.S.: January 22, 2021 Update," U.S. Travel Association, January 22, 2021, https://www.ustravel.org/sites/default/files/media_root/document/TE_Coronavirus_WeeklyImpacts_01.22.21.pdf.

5 HNN Newswire, "STR: US Hotel Performance for March 2020," CoStar, April 21, 2020, https://www.costar.com/article/64781317.

 | DOI:10.1163/9789004514874_005

2020 compared to the $863 billion in sales in 2019.[6] Internationally, COVID-19 caused a 74% decline in global tourism in 2020, as shown in the image below from the World Tourism Organization.[7]

The pandemic led many hotels and restaurants to shut their doors, either permanently or temporarily.[8] When governments began allowing parts of the hospitality industry to reopen under limited conditions, the general fear created by the pandemic led some consumers to still remain at home. In August 2020, occupancy of U.S. hotels was only 48.6%, representing the worst occupancy level on record for an August.[9] According to a survey by the American Hotel & Lodging Association, as of November 2020, hotels were still struggling because they were "unable to rehire all their staff, let alone make mortgage payments, due to the historic drop in travel demand."[10] Over half of the hotels surveyed claimed they were in danger of foreclosure.[11]

Fast forward to 2021, the data shows that the hospitality industry is recovering.[12] In April 2021, travel spending in the United States tallied $73.9 billion, reflecting a drop of only 24% below April 2019 levels.[13] In June 2021, the U.S. hotel industry recorded its highest monthly occupancy since October 2019, with occupancy rates down only 9.8% compared to June 2019.[14] In 2022, more than 80% of American travelers "are excited to travel … the highest

6 Alicia Kelso, "U.S. Restaurant Industry Finished the Year $240 Billion Below Pre-Pandemic Sales Estimates," Forbes, January 26, 2021, https://www.forbes.com/sites/aliciakelso/2021/01/26/the-us-restaurant-industry-finished-the-year-240-billion-below-pre-pandemic-sales-estimates/?sh=759cc2dc4ebf.

7 World Tourism Organization, *supra* note 3.

8 HNN editorial staff, "Following COVID-19 Developments, Industry's Response," CoStar, November 25, 2020, https://www.costar.com/article/806551678.

9 HNN Newswire, "STR: US Hotel Performance for August 2020," CoStar, September 18, 2020, https://www.costar.com/article/1433099331.

10 "AHLA Front Desk Feedback: Survey of Hotels on Financial Crisis," American Hotel & Lodging Association, accessed March 31, 2022, https://www.ahla.com/covid-19s-impact-hotel-industry.

11 *Id.*

12 As of April 2021, intra-country tourism was on the rise, but international tourism remained bleak. "April 2021 Travel Data Report," U.S. Travel Association, accessed May 5, 2021, https://www.ustravel.org/research/monthly-travel-recovery-data-report. The World Tourism Organization expected that international tourism would not return to pre-pandemic levels until 2023 at the earliest. See World Tourism Organization, *supra* note 3.

13 "April 2021 Travel Data Report," U.S. Travel Association, accessed May 5, 2021, https://www.ustravel.org/research/monthly-travel-recovery-data-report.

14 "U.S. Hotel Performance for June 2021," STR, July 21, 2021, https://str.com/press-release/str-us-hotel-performance-june-2021.

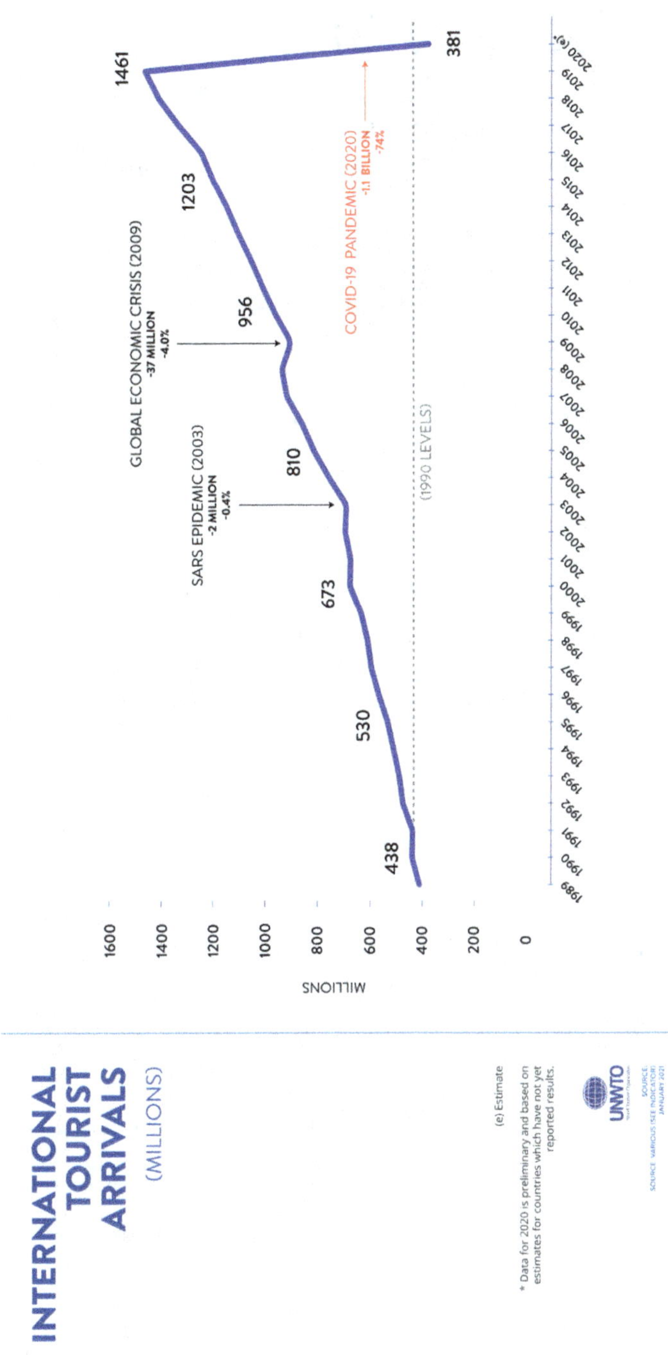

FIGURE 3.1 International tourist arrivals from 1989 to 2020

ID.

level since the start of the pandemic."[15] According to the American Hotel & Lodging Association, however, "full recovery is still several years away."[16]

The road to recovery is rife with obstacles. The industry must contend with increased health and safety spending for the safety of guests and employees.[17] Indeed, the American Hotel & Lodging Association dubbed 2022 as the "year of the 'new' traveler," who places "a premium on safe and sanitary environments, flexible and no-penalty booking policies, convenient customer service, sustainable products, and a positive social impact."[18] Despite governmental restrictions being lifted, some hotels and restaurants could or did not operate at full capacity or provide pre-COVID level of services because of labor shortages or financial issues, among other reasons,[19] and the rise of COVID-19 variants could impact the hospitality industry's recovery. The way the world dines and travels has evolved, and businesses and consumers will experience new obstacles as they attempt to broker a balance between the economic consequences of COVID-19 and customer satisfaction.

Industry players litigated over unpaid franchise or royalty fees that accrued during the pandemic. Many businesses have filed lawsuits in the United States (and worldwide) to litigate the impact of COVID-19 on contractual payment obligations. The decisions from these cases demonstrate the importance of carefully drafted risk allocation clauses and the need for cooperation, creativity, and flexibility to achieve practical, growth-oriented resolutions moving forward.

2 Background about Risk Allocation Clauses

Risk allocation is a key component to commercial bargaining. Beyond price negotiations, contract negotiators try to anticipate what happens if something goes wrong or the unexpected occurs. The results of that concern are risk allocation provisions that represent the parties' agreement as to which side bears

15 "March 2022 Travel Data Report," U.S. Travel Association, accessed March 31, 2022, https://www.ustravel.org/research/monthly-travel-recovery-data-report.

16 "The Year of the 'New' Traveler," American Hotel and Lodging Association, January 24, 2022, 2, https://www.ahla.com/sites/default/files/AHLA%20SOTI%20Report%202022%201.24.22.pdf.

17 *Id.* at 6, 11.

18 *Id.* at 11.

19 Alison Kosik, "America's Worker Shortage is Real and Getting Worse By the Day, US Chamber CEO Says," CNN, June 1, 2021, https://www.cnn.com/2021/06/01/economy/worker-shortage-us-chamber-of-commerce/index.html.

the consequences of a future event. Commercial contracts are generally filled with risk allocation clauses, such as warranty, indemnification, liquidated damages, fee-shifting, and *force majeure* provisions. Like an insurance policy, the goal is to avoid having to invoke risk allocation clauses but having them just in case the unexpected happens.

From a COVID-19 perspective, the importance of negotiating risk allocation clauses is highlighted in *NetOne, Inc. v. Panache Destination Management*, which involves a dispute between a travel service company, Panache, and one of its corporate clients, NetOne.[20] In December 2019, NetOne and Panache entered a contract for the latter to provide transportation, guided tours, and recreational activities for a NetOne-sponsored event scheduled to take place in March 2020.[21] The contract contained a general *force majeure* provision that covered a pandemic.[22] After NetOne cancelled the event due to COVID-19 restrictions, Panache failed to return NetOne's deposits, so NetOne sued.[23] Importantly, the *force majeure* provision gave NetOne a right to cancel the event without penalty. Equally important, but missing, however, was a clause about returning the deposits.[24] Finding that the contract did not require the deposits to be returned in the event of a *force majeure* cancellation, the court held that Panache would be able to keep portions of the deposit for work performed in preparation for the event.[25] Because the contract was silent on whether the deposits would be repaid in the event of a *force majeure* cancellation, the court refused to allocate all the risk to Panache.

As demonstrated in the *NetOne* case, when unforeseen disasters occur, the *force majeure* clause steals the litigation spotlight. French for "superior force," *force majeure* relieves or suspends a party's duty under a contract in the event of extraordinary, unforeseeable circumstances that prevent a party from fulfilling its obligation. Typical *force majeure* events include natural disasters like hurricanes, floods, earthquakes, acts of God, fire, war or terrorism, riots, labor strikes, and governmental actions beyond the party's reasonable control. More broadly, *force majeure* covers unforeseen and extraordinary events that are beyond the control of the parties.[26]

---

20 *NetOne, Inc. v. Panache Destination Mgmt.*, No. 20-cv-00150-DKW-WRP, 2020 U.S. Dist. LEXIS 201129, 1 (D. Haw. Oct. 28, 2020).

21 *Id.* at 4.

22 *Id.* at 6.

23 *Id* at 7.

24 *Id* at 8–9.

25 *Id.*

26 Some jurisdictions, however, do not require that the event be unforeseeable unless the contract expressly requires lack of foreseeability. See, *e.g.*, *TEC Olmos LLC v. ConocoPhillips*

The concept of *force majeure* is not new to American or global jurisprudence—it has been around for centuries.[27] Historically, quarantines, epidemics, and pandemics have qualified as *force majeure* events under common law. For instance, in 1850s Maine, a millworker named Peter Lakeman agreed to work the year's sawing season.[28] Mr. Lakeman worked for parts of the season, but then quit due to a cholera breakout. Because Mr. Lakeman left his post before the end of the season, his employer refused to pay him for the time worked. Mr. Lakeman sued for wages. In awarding payment to Mr. Lakeman, the court found that his duty to work the remainder of the season "became impossible by the act of God."[29] The court explained:

> [Mr. Lakeman] was under no obligation to imperil his life by remaining at work in the vicinity of a prevailing epidemic so dangerous in its character that a man of ordinary care and prudence, in the exercise of those qualities, would have been justified in leaving by reason of it, nor does it make any difference that the men who remained there at work after the plaintiff left were healthy, and continued to be so. He could not then have had any certain knowledge of the extent of his danger. He might have been in imminent peril, or he might have been influenced by unreasonable apprehensions. He must, necessarily, have acted at his peril, under the guidance of his judgment.[30]

Then, in the early 1900s, a vessel called the *Santona* sailed to transport cargo between the United States and Panama.[31] On its way back from Panama, the vessel was required to quarantine in Texas, which caused a 10-day delay.[32] The company who hired the *Santona* refused to pay the agreed-upon sum because of the delay, and so the *Santona*'s owner sued.[33] Finding that the quarantine qualified as *force majeure*, the court forgave the delay and required payment.[34]

Co., 555 S.W.3d 176, 183 (Tex. App. 2018) ("[W]hen parties specify certain *force majeure* events, there is no need to show that the occurrence of such an event was unforeseeable.").

27 Not every jurisdiction calls the doctrine *force majeure*. Some call it a "material adverse change," and others rely on the common law doctrine of impossibility. Either way, the gist of these concepts is the same—an unforeseeable event not attributable to the parties that made it impractical or impossible for one party to perform its contractual duty.

28 *Lakeman v. Pollard*, 43 Me. 463 (1857).

29 *Id.* at 467.

30 *Id.*

31 *Clyde Commercial S. S. Co. v. W. India S. S. Co.*, 169 F. 275 (2d. Cir. 1909).

32 *Id.* at 278.

33 *Id.*

34 *Id.* at 279.

Today, many commercial contracts contain *force majeure* provisions.[35] But "[n]ot that long ago, the force majeure clause risked being dismissed as a laundry list of potential catastrophes, each unlikely to happen, embedded in the boilerplate at the back end of a commercial contract."[36] With COVID-19, *force majeure* clauses have captured the attention of courts and businesses around the world.

3 Judicial Treatment of Risk Allocation Clauses for Missed Payments during COVID-19

Successfully invoking *force majeure* to excuse payment obligations generally involves three things. First, the party seeking to be excused must prove that the event at issue falls within the contract's definition of *force majeure*.[37] Second, the party must show that the event caused an inability to perform the contractual duty at issue. Third, the parties must not have already agreed to allocate the risks of nonpayment on the payor.

For contracts executed before COVID-19, proving that the pandemic qualified as a *force majeure* event seemed to be the easy part. But many businesses struggled to show that the pandemic caused an inability to pay. Under the legal standard for causation, the pandemic must have made it objectively impossible to pay, as opposed to just making it harder, impractical, or even subjectively impossible.[38] Even if causation was shown, however, a well-crafted provision

35 If a contract does not have a *force majeure* provision, the defense could still be invoked under the common law defenses of impossibility, frustration of purpose, or impracticability. Although this paper does not address the common law defenses, many of the principles and guidance on *force majeure* overlap with such defenses.

36 Paula M. Bagger, "The Importance of Force Majeure Clauses in the COVID-19 Era," American Bar Association, March 25, 2021, https://www.americanbar.org/groups/litigation/committees/commercial-business/boilerplate-contracts/force-majeure-clauses-contracts-covid-19/.

37 In drafting a *force majeure* clause, parties should consider whether a *no contra proferentem* clause would be appropriate to avoid having any ambiguities construed against the drafter. Another rule to keep in mind is *ejusdem generis*, which means that when a broad catch-all phrase, such as "or other events beyond the parties' control," follows a list of more specific events, the catch-all phrase will be confined to events similar to the specific events listed.

38 Timothy Murray, *Corbin on Contracts: Force Majeure and Impossibility of Performance Resulting From COVID-19* (Matthew Bender & Company, Inc., 2020), § 1.03, Section 2.F (collecting cases).

allocating the risks of nonpayment on the payor would defeat any chance of the payment being excused.

3.1 *Whether the COVID-19 Pandemic Qualified as* Force Majeure

In the modern era, commercial entities define the scope of *force majeure* within the contract. So, to determine if COVID-19 qualifies as *force majeure*, courts looked to the contract's definition. Not every *force majeure* clause, however, expressly identifies a quarantine, epidemic, or pandemic. Ordinarily, an event will qualify as *force majeure* only if the clause identifies it, whether specifically or through an applicable catch-all.[39] The maxim behind listing each qualifying event is *expressio unius est exclusio alterius*, meaning the explicit mention of one thing excludes all others not listed. Thus, in some instances, a party seeking to excuse its failure to perform due to COVID-19 could be out of luck if the *force majeure* clause did not contain the phrase "quarantine," "epidemic," "pandemic," or something else to that effect.[40]

With COVID-19, the growing trend of the U.S. judiciary was to couch the pandemic under catch-all or broader phrases, such as "circumstances beyond our reasonable control,"[41] "act of God,"[42] "act of nature,"[43] "calamities,"[44] or "natural disaster."[45] For example, in *JN Contemporary Art LLC v. Phillips Auctioneers LLC*, the contract called for an art auction to occur in May 2020.[46] The auction house postponed the event due to government-imposed restrictions due to COVID-19.[47] The custodian of the artwork sued the auction house for breach of contract, and the court had to interpret the scope of the *force majeure* clause, which covered "circumstances beyond our or your reasonable control, including, without limitation, as a result of natural disaster, fire, flood, general strike,

39 Richard A. Lord, *Williston on Contracts*, 4th. ed. (Thomson West, 2003), § 77:31 ("What types of events constitute *force majeure* depend on the specific language included in the clause itself.").

40 To realize how contracts may treat the phrase "pandemic" differently, see the studies mentioned in *AB Stable VIII LLC v. Maps Hotels & Resorts One LLC*, No. 2020-0310-JTL, 2020 Del. Ch. LEXIS 353, 164–66 (Nov. 30, 2020).

41 *JN Contemporary Art LLC v. Phillips Auctioneers LLC*, 507 F. Supp. 3d 490, 496 (S.D.N.Y. 2020).

42 *See La Simple Co. v. SLP Enters., LLC*, No. 21-10058-LTS, 2021 U.S. Dist. LEXIS 81209, 17 (D. Mass. Apr. 27, 2021).

43 *Free Minn. Small Bus. Coalition v. Walz*, No. 62-cv-20-3507, 2020 Minn. Dist. LEXIS 256, 50 (Ramsey Cty. Sept. 1, 2020).

44 *AB Stable VIII LLC*, 2020 Del. Ch. LEXIS 353, at 149.

45 *JN Contemporary Art LLC*, 507 F. Supp. 3d at 501.

46 *Id.* at 495.

47 *Id.* at 497.

war, armed conflict, terrorist attack or nuclear or chemical contamination."[48] Although the clause did not specifically identify quarantine, pandemic, or epidemic, the court classified the COVID-19 pandemic and the resulting quarantine restrictions as "circumstances beyond the parties' reasonable control" and a "natural disaster."[49] As the court noted, "[i]t cannot be seriously disputed that the COVID-19 pandemic is a natural disaster."[50]

One court in Delaware has expressly rejected the argument that COVID-19 was caused by humans, as opposed to nature. "Some individuals, concerned about conspiracies, have suggested that humans created COVID-19 as a bioweapon. If true, that could undermine its status as a *natural* disaster. The record in this case does not support a finding that the virus was anything other than a natural product of germ evolution."[51] In Texas, one court observed: "[w]hile humans can take precautions to slow the spread of COVID-19 or engage in behavior that fosters contagion, the possibility of slowing the virus spread does not suggest that humans caused the pandemic."[52]

The judiciary's treatment of a pandemic as an "act of God" or "natural disaster" is not novel. In 1891, the U.S. Supreme Court said that "sudden deaths and illnesses" have been held to be "acts of God."[53] In 1906, the highest court in the state of Washington deemed the tuberculosis outbreak an "act of God."[54] Also, in 1920, an English court in *Lebeaupin v. Crispin* classified epidemics as an "act of God."[55] In line with these historic cases, the growing trend amongst the judiciary is to find some way to include COVID-19 within the ambit of a *force majeure* provision.

3.2 *Whether the COVID-19 Pandemic or the Resulting Economic Downturn Caused an Inability to Pay*

While the judiciary has expressed sympathy for the devastation and business interruption caused by COVID-19, courts remain strict on the scope of contractual duties that may be excused by way of *force majeure*, particularly payment obligations. Although the majority trend is to qualify the COVID-19 pandemic as a *force majeure* event, that qualification does not necessarily mean that

48 *Id.* at 496.
49 *Id.* at 501.
50 *Id.*
51 *AB Stable VIII LLC*, 2020 Del. Ch. LEXIS 353, at 132 n.214.
52 *Easom v. US Well Servs.*, No. H-20-2995, 2021 U.S. Dist. LEXIS 52941, 21 (S.D. Tex. Mar. 19, 2021).
53 *Gleeson v. Va. M. R. Co.*, 140 U.S. 435, 439 (1891).
54 *Grover v. Zook*, 87 P. 638, 640 (Wash. 1906).
55 *Lebeaupin v. Richard Crispin & Co* [1920] 2 K.B. 714 (UK).

courts will excuse payment obligations. That is because the next step to invoke *force majeure* requires a party to prove that the pandemic caused an objective inability to pay.

"Causation" can be analogized simply by reference to the popular dilemma about "which came first: the chicken or the egg?" In litigation, however, proving causation can be as complex and vexing as the different answers to that dilemma. When deciding whether to apply *force majeure,* courts ask whether the event at issue prevented performance.[56] As simple as that question may seem, the legal standard for causation has an intricate foundation that does not favor payors.

To understand why causation does not favor payors, it is important to first understand that financial difficulty or economic hardship will rarely excuse a party's contractual obligation.[57] As one federal court put it, "[t]he state of the market is one of the things on which the parties are gambling when the contract ... is made."[58] Thus, in the aftermath of the 2008 financial crisis,[59] *force majeure* clauses offered no protection to companies who failed to satisfy their payment obligations. In the commercial lease case of *Route 6 Outparcels, LLC v. Ruby Tuesday, Inc.*, a New York court classified the "[2008] worldwide economic meltdown" as an event beyond Ruby Tuesday's control.[60] Citing to causation, however, the court explained that "the critical inquiry" was whether the crisis prevented Ruby Tuesday from constructing a restaurant on the property and paying rent.[61] Finding that Ruby Tuesday's failure to construct a restaurant and to thus pay rent was due to the company's decision to apply its limited financial resources towards other obligations, the court's answer was no.[62] The

56 See, *e.g.*, *Route 6 Outparcels, LLC v. Ruby Tuesday, Inc.*, 910 N.Y.S.2d 408 (N.Y. Sup. Ct. 2010), *aff'd*, 931 N.Y.S.2d 436 (N.Y. App. Div. 2011).

57 *In re: Millers Cove Energy Co., Inc.*, 62 F.3d 155, 158 (6th Cir. 1995) (stating that "[c]ourts and commentators generally refuse to excuse lack of compliance with contractual provisions due to economic hardship, unless such a ground is specifically outlined in the contract"); see also *Svanaco, Inc. v. Brand*, No. 15-cv-11639, 2021 U.S. Dist. LEXIS 115059, 16 (N.D. Ill. June 21, 2021) ("[T]he financial difficulty in performing an obligation pursuant to a contract cannot by itself operate to extinguish that obligation.").

58 *Seaboard Lumber Co. v. United States*, 41 Fed. Cl. 401, 417 (1998).

59 Eric Rauchway, "The 2008 Crash: What Happened to All That Money?," History, September 14, 2018, last modified January 20, 2021, https://www.history.com/news/2008-financial-crisis-causes.

60 *Route 6 Outparcels, LLC*, 910 N.Y.S.2d at 408.

61 *Id.*

62 *Id.*

adverse change in economic conditions simply made it more burdensome and difficult to perform, but not objectively impossible.[63]

COVID-19 adds an extra layer to the causation argument. For the 2008 financial crisis, businesses looking to excuse their contractual obligations relied on a financial crisis caused by market destabilization. With COVID-19, however, businesses cite to a financial crisis caused by a global pandemic. Despite the differences between a market crash and a global pandemic, when it came to payment obligations during COVID-19, most courts stood fast on their reluctancy to accept economic hardship as a defense.

The question being asked by the courts is whether the pandemic made it objectively impossible for a party to pay, as opposed to just making it harder, impractical, or subjectively impossible.[64] To illustrate, in *Palm Springs Mile Assocs. v. Kirkland's Stores, Inc.*, Kirkland stopped paying rent under a commercial lease.[65] Citing to a *force majeure* provision that excused delays in performance due to government-imposed restrictions, Kirkland argued that the government-mandated quarantine suspended its obligation to pay rent.[66] The federal court in Florida rejected Kirkland's arguments, finding that the quarantine did not "actually prevent[] Kirkland from making rent payments."[67]

Likewise, in *Dominion Energy Cove Point LNG v. Mattawoman Energy, LLC*, a federal court rejected the defendant's *force majeure* defense because the COVID-19 restrictions did not legally preclude access to capital financing to pay the monthly fees.[68] The court duly noted that "from a practical perspective, judicial recognition of COVID-19 as [a valid defense to payment obligations] would wreak havoc on settled economic expectations and destabilize the economy by rendering most of [2020's] bargained-for exchanges voidable."[69] If the failure to pay started before the pandemic, or if the business itself was

63 *Id.*

64 Corbin, *supra* note 38, at Section 2.F ("An inability to pay the rent generally is deemed subjective, as opposed to objective, impossibility, and it does not excuse performance. When the hardship is unique to the party seeking to be excused from performing, a court might call that 'subjective,' as opposed to objective, impossibility.").

65 *Palm Springs Mile Assocs. v. Kirkland's Stores, Inc.*, No. 20-21724-Civ, 2020 U.S. Dist. LEXIS 163880, 2 (S.D. Fla. Sept. 8, 2020).

66 *Id.* at 5.

67 *Id.* at 6–7.

68 *Dominion Energy Cove Point LNG, L.P. v. Energy*, No. 1:20-cv-611, 2020 U.S. Dist. LEXIS 253335, 22–23 (E.D. Va. Oct. 20, 2020).

69 *Id.* at 23.

permitted to operate during the months in question, virtually no court sympathized with the defaulting party.[70]

Two bankruptcy courts have felt differently about the causation issue. In *In re Hitz Restaurant Group*, the restaurant claimed that the government mandate barring on-premise consumption of food and beverages suspended its rent obligations.[71] The *force majeure* clause excused the parties "in the event, but only so long as the performance of any of its obligations are prevented or delayed, retarded or hindered by ... orders of government[,] [except that] [l]ack of money shall not be grounds for Force Majeure."[72] Avoiding the lack-of-money clause, the bankruptcy court in Illinois found that the shutdown order "was unquestionably the proximate cause of [the restaurant's] inability to pay rent, *at least in part*, because it prevented [the restaurant] from operating normally and restricted its business to take-out, curbside pick-up, and delivery."[73] Thus, the restaurant's obligation to pay rent was partially excused.[74]

Similarly, in *In re Cinemex USA Real Estate Holdings, Inc.*, a bankruptcy court in Florida excused a movie theater from paying rent during the months when the government did not allow the operation of theaters.[75] The court noted, however, that once it was legal for the movie theater to reopen, the rental obligation resumed in full regardless of capacity.[76]

Defaulting parties, however, should not latch onto the minority decisions from *In re Hitz Restaurant Group* and *In re Cinemex USA* as reasons to avoid their payment obligations. The circumstances will differ from case to case,[77] and the language will differ from contract to contract. Neither *In re Hitz Restaurant*

70 *Id.*; see also *Gap Inc. v. Ponte Gadea N.Y. LLC*, 524 F. Supp. 3d 224, 237–38 (S.D.N.Y. 2021) ("[T]he undisputed evidence shows that Gap in fact operated a retail business at the stores at issue in this case by way of curbside pick-up, and operated other retail locations on an in-person basis, during the pandemic. The fact that its continued performance may be burdensome, 'even to the extent of insolvency or bankruptcy,' does not render Gap's performance objectively impossible under New York law.") (internal citation omitted).

71 *In re Hitz Rest. Group*, 616 B.R. 374 (Bankr. N.D. Ill. 2020).

72 *Id.* at 377.

73 *Id.* at 377–78 (emphasis added).

74 As the restaurant could still operate take-out services and used 25% of the building's square footage, the restaurant had to pay 25% of the rent. *Id.* at 379. The court also noted that as restrictions on dining would be lifted, the rental payments would likely increase. *Id.*

75 *In re Cinemex USA Real Estate Holdings, Inc.*, 627 B.R. 693 (Bankr. S.D. Fla. 2021).

76 *Id.* at 701–02.

77 *See id.* at 702 n.19 ("The circumstances regarding full closure and reopening may differ from lease to lease and certainly from state to state. Therefore, the Court wants to make clear that parties should not assume that the findings and the holdings of this particular dispute will necessarily translate to litigation involving other leases.").

Group nor *In re Cinemex USA* establishes precedent that courts from other jurisdictions must follow. Both cases involved parties in bankruptcy, and parties outside of a bankruptcy proceeding may not receive the same treatment. What is more, these cases will likely not apply to excuse payment obligations for a business that was legally allowed to re-open but did not do so.

Ultimately, courts will rarely excuse payment obligations under a commercial contract, even considering the devastation caused by COVID-19. The root cause of a party's inability to pay must be the *force majeure* event itself, as opposed to a resulting economic hardship.[78] In cases where a party is subjectively unable to pay due to lack of funds, courts find the cause to be economic hardship. As a result, payors seeking forgiveness for past due payments that accumulated during the pandemic rarely succeed in court.

3.3 *Whether the Payor Assumed the Risk*

Another hurdle to the *force majeure* defense is whether the payor agreed to assume the risk. If the parties allocate the risk to one side, the courts are generally bound to enforce that allocation, regardless of the equities. For example, in *Victoria's Secret Stores v. Herald Square Owner LLC*, Victoria's Secret sought to avoid paying rent, citing the forced closure of the store under state law as the basis for its inability to perform.[79] The lease, however, contained a provision that exempted Victoria's Secret's inability to pay due to unforeseen circumstances as a valid defense.[80] Relying on the parties' agreement, the court summarily dismissed the lawsuit in favor of the landlord, noting that Victoria's Secret's claim "is premised on the mistaken theory that the parties did not allocate the risk of the tenant not being able to operate its business and that the tenant is therefore somehow forgiven from its performance by virtue of a state law."[81]

The effects of risk allocation rippled on a nationwide scale for Chuck E. Cheese venues throughout the United States.[82] In the leases, the commercial landlords bargained for the tenant's inability to pay rent to be excluded from

78 *E.g., In re: Millers Cove Energy Co., Inc.*, 62 F.3d 155, 158 (6th Cir. 1995) ("Courts and commentators generally refuse to excuse lack of compliance with contractual provisions due to economic hardship, unless such a ground is specifically outlined in the contract").

79 *Victoria's Secret Stores v. Herald Square Owner LLC*, No. 651833/2020, 2021 N.Y. Misc. LEXIS 3827 (N.Y. Sup. Ct. Jan. 7, 2021).

80 *Id.*

81 *Id.*

82 *In re CEC Entm't, Inc.*, 625 B.R. 344 (Bankr. S.D. Tex. 2020).

the protections of the *force majeure* clause.[83] The court respected the bargain and denied the tenant's request to reduce the rent balance.[84]

Not every risk allocation clause is as clear as it may seem. *In re Hitz Restaurant Group* is an exceptional case, where the court shifted some risk of nonpayment to the landlord, despite the parties' agreement that "[l]ack of money shall not be grounds for *Force Majeure*."[85] In searching for flexibility to partially excuse the rent payments, the court explained that the "lack of money" clause conflicted with the "governmental action" clause, the latter of which was a valid basis to invoke *force majeure*.[86] Because government regulations forced the restaurant to shut down in-person dining, the court found the "governmental action" clause more specific to the circumstances and thus controlling.[87] Although *In re Hitz Restaurant Group* is an outlier, the case highlights the importance of drafting risk allocation clauses carefully and perhaps with greater detail.

Even with COVID-19 and the droves of opinions calling for flexible interpretation of *force majeure* clauses, most courts continue to enforce risk allocation clauses.[88] That respect demonstrates the transactional importance of discussing risk allocation during contract negotiations and identifying how much risk is allocated to each side.[89]

4 Allocating Risk of Nonpayment Moving Forward

Needless to say, *force majeure* is a hard defense to invoke to excuse payment obligations. The maxim of *pacta sunt servanda* mandates that contracts are to

83 *Id.* at 353–57.

84 *Id.* at 364.

85 *In re Hitz Rest. Group*, *supra* note 71, at 377–79.

86 *Id.* at 378.

87 *Id.*

88 Risk allocation clauses are not automatically enforceable. A party could still launch certain defenses to the enforceability of such clauses, such as duress, undue influence, or unconscionability. While it is unlikely a court would apply one of these defenses to a contract negotiated between two sophisticated commercial entities, the opportunity to raise such defenses creates more litigation over what may seem to be a clear-cut issue.

89 Another risk to allocate in future contracts is the cost of increased cleaning protocols and other safety/health related measures. In some places, those measures may be required by the government. But even where it is not required, the hospitality industry has been voluntarily implementing these measures for its consumers. Unless the contract expressly allocates such costs, franchisees may carry that burden by default.

be kept as written.[90] "Generally, once a party to a contract has made a promise, that party must perform or respond in damages for its failure, even when unforeseen circumstances make performance burdensome."[91] The concept of *pacta sunt servanda* is alive and well in American jurisprudence.[92] Thus, parties should negotiate for a risk allocation clause that spells out what happens to payment obligations during an economic downturn caused by a *force majeure* event. In doing so, contract negotiators should consider (i) whether to shift all the risk to one side or share in the risk, (ii) the use of general and specific terms, and (iii) that semantics matter. Although neither this chapter nor the courts can change how prior contracts were originally drafted, this section provides guidance on how litigants can settle current litigation or modify those contracts moving forward.

4.1 *To Share or Not to Share?*

Risk allocation can be one-sided or shared. "Hell or high water" is a common term used to describe a one-sided clause that binds a party to continue making payments no matter what happens. Under a "hell or high water" scenario, the payment obligation is regarded as absolute and unconditional.[93] Courts generally enforce "hell or high water" provisions.[94] As one court noted, "[t]o deny their effect as a matter of law would seriously chill business."[95]

The following is an example of a "hell or high water" provision: "[Entity]'s obligations to pay all amounts due [under this agreement] are absolute and unconditional and shall not be subject to any abatement, reduction, set off, defense, counterclaim, interruption, deferment or recoupment for any reason whatsoever."[96] When it comes to risk allocation clauses, redundant clauses may help if litigation arises. Thus, to build on the foregoing "hell or high water" provision (or to expressly limit the extent of a *force majeure* clause), a party may consider adding something to this effect: "Neither general economic downturn or conditions nor [Entity]'s financial inability to perform the terms

---

90 See Corbin, *supra* note 38, at Section 2.A; *Pinero v. Zapata*, 306 So. 3d 1117 (Fla. Dist. Ct. App. 2020) (finding that the trial court erred by rewriting the parties' agreement to provide one party with additional time to make payments due to COVID-19 difficulties).

91 See Corbin, *supra* note 38, at Section 2.A.

92 *Id.*

93 *In re O.P.M. Leasing Servs., Inc.*, 21 B.R. 993, 1005–07 (Bankr. S.D.N.Y. 1982).

94 *Id.* at 1006–07 ("More specifically, courts have uniformly given full force and effect to 'hell and high water' clauses in the face of various kinds of defaults by the party seeking to enforce them.").

95 *Id.* at 1007.

96 *Hitachi Data Sys. Credit Corp. v. Precision Discovery, Inc.*, No. 17-cv-6851-SHS, 2019 U.S. Dist. LEXIS 136555, 2 (S.D.N.Y. Aug. 13, 2019).

of this agreement will be a defense to breach, even if the downturn, condition, or inability is caused by a *force majeure* event."

A risk allocation clause can also be one sided in favor of excusing payment. The bankruptcy case of *In re Old Carco,* LLC dealt with an automobile plant that closed before the agreed date.[97] The plant shut down because of economic hardship caused by the 2008 financial crisis.[98] Because the *force majeure* clause specifically included "change to economic conditions," the closing of the plant did not arise to a breach of the contract.[99]

In contrast to one-sided allocation clauses, parties may instead agree to share the risk. If a *force majeure* event causes an economic fallout, the payment obligation could be reduced by a certain percentage, either a set number or based on variables, like revenue, occupancy, or use of the premises. In the outlier case of *In re Hitz Restaurant Group*, the court allocated the risk based on the percentage-use of the building.[100] As the restaurant could still operate takeout services and used 25% of the building's square footage, the court still made the restaurant pay 25% of the rent.[101] The court also noted that, as restrictions on dining would be lifted, the rent would likely increase.[102] For hotel leases, the same concept could be applied to occupancy levels. Between franchisors and franchisees, royalty fees may already be based on a fixed amount, plus a variable amount determined by revenue or occupancy. But during an economic fallout caused by a *force majeure* event, the parties could agree to reduce or eliminate the fixed amount or change the base figure used to calculate the variable amount. The parties should carefully define what constitutes an "economic fallout" sufficient to trigger a payment-related shared allocation of risk.

Whether the parties should agree to one-sided or shared allocation depends on several factors, like the purpose of the relationship, the length of the contract, the history and rapport between the parties, other dealings between the parties, the financial assets of each side, the current or projected economic climate, and other business-related concerns. Even if a franchisor or landlord has the upper hand in choosing the terms of the contract, a franchisee or tenant should not downplay their ability to negotiate. The success and profitability of a franchise enterprise depends on the quality and quantity of franchisees. Every lost franchise is a lost source of revenue for the franchisor. Commercial

---

97 *In re Old Carco* LLC, 452 B.R. 100 (Bankr. S.D.N.Y. 2011).

98 *Id.* at 112.

99 *Id.* at 118–26.

100 *In re Hitz Rest. Grp., supra* note 71, at 379.

101 *Id.*

102 *Id.*

landlords may not want to lose a reliable, longstanding tenant, and there may not be other suitable tenants for quite some time. Moreover, litigants can always find some way to challenge the enforceability and interpretation of a one-sided risk allocation clause and make the other side endure a lawsuit and incur attorneys' fees.[103] A well-crafted risk allocation clause may contribute to faster resolution of the case, such as on a motion to dismiss or a motion for summary judgment.[104] But resolution of the case is separate from collection, which can be even trickier and take even longer. Some companies, like single-purpose entities, may be judgment-proof.

In the end, even if the contract contains an airtight, one-sided risk allocation clause, enforcing it, while a viable legal option, may not be the best, or even a practical solution. The global and devastating impact of the pandemic should prompt commercial parties to consider whether to amend existing risk allocation clauses. Litigants may want to consider settling on mixed allocation terms. Each scenario is different, and the best path forward depends on an individualized inquiry of the past, present, and future circumstances.

4.2 *Specific or General Terms? Why Not Both?*

An effective risk allocation clause should be both specific and general—specific enough to leave no wiggle room that a certain event or condition is covered, but general enough to cover everything in-between. Being general is important given the doctrine of *expressio unius est exclusio alterius*, which means the express mention of certain items excludes those items that were omitted. To illustrate, if an agreement specifically defines *force majeure* as extreme weather, war, or fire, then a pandemic may not be covered. That is why some contracts may contain the phrase "act of God," "unforeseen events beyond human control," or "other events like those previously listed." Still, parties should not rely solely on general clauses, which may be viewed as ambiguous. For instance, some litigants have argued (without success) that the pandemic is not an act of God or beyond human control.[105] In the same way, parties will fight about what qualifies as an "economic fallout." If the parties have a specific event or

103 One way to recoup the expenses of litigation is a fee-shifting clause that makes the losing party pay the prevailing party's attorneys' fees and costs. A fee-shifting provision, however, has its own risks. Thus, having a fee-shifting provision in the contract may not fully alleviate the original concern that it was designed to address.

104 Cf. *Hiatt v. Brigham Young Univ.*, No. 1:20-CV-00100-TS, 2021 U.S. Dist. LEXIS 3269 (D. Utah Jan. 7, 2021) (in a tuition refund case, denying the college's motion to dismiss for lack of a clear risk allocation clause).

105 See *supra* notes 52, 53 and accompanying text.

definition in mind, identify it. Contract drafters should consider including both specific and general terms in their risk allocation clause.

Parties can also argue whether a phrase is specific or general. Take the term "war," for example, which is commonly listed in *force majeure* clauses. According to the U.S. Constitution, an armed conflict is not considered "war" unless declared by Congress.[106] Under that definition, the United States has not been involved in a "war" since World War II.[107] That means the "Vietnam War" and the "Gulf War" technically do not count if "war" is regarded as a specific term defined by the U.S. Constitution. On the other hand, "war" could be interpreted broadly to include acts of war, armed conflicts, terrorism, use of military force, or cyberwarfare. If the parties only want the constitutional definition of "war" to count, then the phrase "Congressionally-declared war" would be a better term. If parties want to be more general, then they could broaden the phrase to "acts of war, armed conflicts, terrorism, cyberwarfare, and other like conflicts." Disputes like this may be avoided with deliberate drafting and proactive scrutiny.

4.3 *Semantics Matter!*

Semantics matter. Take the case of *Gibson v. Lynn University*, for example, where a college student sued for a partial tuition refund after the University, in response to COVID-19, switched to remote learning.[108] The contract had allocated the risk to the students, stating "[t]here will be no refund of tuition ... *in the event the operation of the University is suspended* at any time as a result of [a *force majeure* event]."[109] The University moved for summary dismissal of the claim, arguing that the plain language of the risk allocation clause barred any refund.[110] But the student pointed out that the school did not "suspend" its operations.[111] Rather, the school moved operations to an online platform.[112] The court expressed concern over the student's interpretation, explaining that the school may have been entitled to keep all tuition had it just shut down entirely.[113] Yet the dispute over the semantics of one word caused enough doubt to keep the claim alive.[114]

106 U.S. Const. art. I, § 8, cl. 11.

107 See United States House of Representatives, "Power to Declare War," accessed March 31, 2022, https://history.house.gov/Institution/Origins-Development/War-Powers/.

108 *Gibson v. Lynn Univ., Inc.*, 504 F. Supp. 3d 1335 (S.D. Fla. 2020).

109 *Id.* at 1338 (emphasis added).

110 *Id.*

111 *Id.* at 1340.

112 *Id.*

113 *Id.*

114 *Id.* at 1342.

Further, in the case of *In re Cinemex USA*, all it took was a romanette for a movie theater tenant to avoid paying rent, despite a risk allocation clause that seemed to favor the landlord.[115] There, the lease said:

> If either party to this Lease, as the result of any (…) (iv) acts of God, governmental action (…), or (v) other conditions similar to those enumerated in this Section beyond the reasonable control of the party obligated to perform (*other than failure to timely pay monies required to be paid under this Lease*), fails punctually to perform any obligation on its part to be performed under this Lease, then such failure shall be excused and not be a breach of this Lease by the party in question, but only to the extent occasioned by such event.[116]

The court noted that the phrase "other than failure to timely pay monies required to be paid under this Lease" was part of romanette (v)—the "other conditions" phrase—and not part of romanette (iv), which covered acts of God or government action.[117] Because the court classified COVID-19 as part of romanette (iv), the risk allocation clause under romanette (v) did not apply.[118] Thus, the tenant was excused from paying rent during the months when movie theaters closed by state regulations.[119]

Gibson and *In re Cinemex USA* emphasize the importance of drafting risk allocation clauses carefully, with deliberation over the choice of words and even punctuation. The purpose of a risk allocation clause is to create certainty in the event of the unforeseen. That purpose is ill-served if the clause is poorly drafted or ambiguous.

5 Conclusion

COVID-19 challenged the hospitality industry. But the industry stood strong and is on the road to recovery. As consumers start to travel and dine in restaurants more, they desire pre-COVID levels of service (or better), despite the

115 *In re Cinemex USA*, *supra* note 75.

116 *Id.* at 699 (emphasis added).

117 *Id.* at 700.

118 *Id.*

119 One could argue that, had the provision at issue used semicolons instead of commas to separate the categories of *force majeure* events, the court may have applied the risk allocation clause to every listed event.

labor and financial challenges the industry still faces. One hurdle to satisfying this expectation is the uncertainty from litigation over reoccurring expenses, like rent and royalty fees, that went unpaid during the pandemic. The COVID-19 lawsuits about these issues emphasize the importance of carefully drafting risk allocation clauses for payment obligations. One-sided clauses may not be the best solution in every situation, even if the clause is airtight. Shared allocation and flexibility may be better, either during the drafting phase or in settlement negotiations, to achieve a practical, growth-oriented resolution. In the end, COVID-19 negatively impacted every player in the hospitality industry. The industry banded together, however, and collectively survived. The same collective mentality should govern the resolution of these disputes. When discussing overdue payment obligations, whether for this pandemic or a future catastrophe, it would be remiss to consider them without evaluating the business relationship, financial circumstances, future growth and revenue, and consumer demands. When the industry players fail to work together, they risk losing again, but this time, in the eyes of their consumers.

CHAPTER 4

Disputes under Hotel Management Agreements: before, during, and after COVID-19

Thomas R. Snider and Greig Taylor

1 Introduction[1]

This chapter addresses key features of hotel management agreements ("HMAs") and assesses the current and future implications of COVID-19 and disputes that arise in relation to them.[2] When the business is healthy, clauses in HMAs are rarely considered, yet disputes under HMAs arise for many reasons even in "normal" times. However, in times of extreme disruption, *e.g.*, during the COVID-19 era, existing issues may be exacerbated, and entirely new considerations and disputes may arise because of prolonged, significant decreases in occupancy and revenues, especially in the context of *force majeure* claims and frustration of purpose, resulting in potential defaults and/or termination of HMAs.

This chapter commences with a discussion of the purpose and nature of HMAs. It then addresses *force majeure* and frustration claims in the context of HMA disputes, followed by a consideration of disputes arising from the owner-operator relationship, the calculation of management fees, and performance test considerations in relation to owner termination rights. This chapter then considers the future of disputes under HMAs before concluding.

1 Thomas R. Snider is a Partner and the Head of International Arbitration at Charles Russell Speechlys LLP in Dubai. Greig Taylor is a Managing Director at AlixPartners in New York.

2 HMAs are common in the Middle East and Asia. They comprise a different contractual regime from franchise agreements, which are common in regions such as the United States and Africa and are becoming increasingly more popular in the Middle East region. Franchise agreements can be attractive to operators, as there is less risk than a management role, and are attractive to owners as they have more control over the hotel. Franchise agreements (and other contractual arrangements such as the so-called "manchise," which may initially function like an HMA, but contains an option to move to a franchise after a period of time) are not addressed specifically in this chapter.

 | DOI:10.1163/9789004514874_006

2 HMAs: Context and Background

HMAs are typically used to record the relationship between the owner and operator of a hotel and broadly regulate the risk allocation between them on a long-term basis. Under these management contracts, investors, who make significant investments in building, maintaining, and upgrading properties, often have limited hotel-management experience, and so contract out the management of their property to independent operators. The operator is responsible for the day-to-day running of the hotel, driving occupancy and revenues, managing operational costs, and often has almost exclusive control in this regard. In addition to the general management of the hotel, an operator can also provide the owner the opportunity to reap the benefits of a well-known brand. In return for the right to trade under that brand, a hotel owner surrenders much of the control and decision-making process related to the property to the operator. The level of control that may be exerted over the hotel operations by an owner varies from owner to owner depending upon their approach. However, generally, the hotel owner ultimately takes the commercial risk that the hotel will not be successful with obligations, typically limited to requiring the owner to provide any required working capital for the venture and financing the operation of the hotel (this includes the funds for the furniture, fittings, and equipment reserve and the capital expenditure).[3]

Hotel operators will often invest substantial time, effort, and resources into the training for and implementation of "brand standards" and procedures into the management of a new hotel. Consequently, standard-form HMAs for branded operators tend to be long-term and require owners to enter multi-year contracts (often 15 or more years). As these brand operators are generally reputable and well-established, hotel owners are often willing to make these long-term commitments.

An HMA will typically contain detailed provisions to give parties certainty as to their respective rights and obligations under the agreement. HMAs will typically reserve the owner's right to approve the annual budget of the hotel. However, this right is usually caveated so that the owner may not object to expenditure that is required to maintain the hotel in compliance with the operator's "brand standards," fire, life, and safety requirements, or applicable law. In addition, owners will often require approval rights over certain important operational matters, such as payments out of the hotel accounts above a

3 Dalal Al Houti, "5 Tips on How to Avoid Hotel Management Disputes,"' Al Tamimi & Co., accessed January 21, 2022, https://www.tamimi.com/law-update-articles/5-tips-on-how-to-avoid-hotel-management-disputes/.

certain monetary threshold, the appointment of key staff (such as the General Manager and Director of Finance), significant contracts (including third-party food-and-beverage and retail leases), and high-value litigation.

Owners will usually also have the right to terminate the agreement for specified acts of default or if agreed upon performance targets are not met by the operator. The performance test provisions in an HMA also commonly reserve the right for the operator to make cure payments (which are often limited to a maximum number) to compensate the owner for the failure of the performance and avoid termination. They also typically include carve-outs, where the operator can avoid failing the performance test, if such failure is caused by external factors that are beyond its control.

At the same time, the owner retains most of the risk from the operation of the business and provides the working capital required for the hotel to continue running (if there is insufficient working capital generated from hotel revenues). An operator will typically seek to limit its liability to gross negligence or wilful default. Operators may, in addition to their management fees, also charge additional fees to cover the costs for providing centralized services.

Accordingly, the relationship between owner and operator is inevitably complex and susceptible to fluctuations in the market during the normal course of business. This already complex relationship was tested further in the face of extreme disruptions, such as those posed by COVID-19. Indeed, the hospitality industry saw considerable uncertainty and upheaval because of the COVID-19 pandemic. With occupancy numbers plummeting and hotels undergoing periods of closure, there were inevitable impacts on hotels' financial performances, bringing into focus the arrangements pertaining to the management of hotels. As discussed further below, such significant reductions in hotel revenue can often lead to greater tension between the hotel owner, who may have existing debt obligations relating to the hotel that still need to be serviced, and the operator, whose operational performance may be placed under greater scrutiny by the owner as a result. In view of the impact of the COVID-19 pandemic, HMAs in the future may well see more detailed negotiations regarding the parties' obligations, with both owners and operators trying to limit their exposure to liability and financial hardship.

3 Foreseeable Disputes under COVID-19: *Force Majeure* and Frustration

Disputes involving the legal concepts of *force majeure* and frustration raise several questions, including when, how, and who determines whether the relevant "event" has occurred. These clauses may be subject to more intense negotiations in the future, and parties to HMAs will need to understand the differences between the various bodies of law that typically govern HMAs in this regard.

Parties often negotiate HMAs bearing in mind their need for certainty under a long-term agreement. Common law jurisdictions will generally uphold the sanctity of the contract, even when the allocation of risk shifts during the contract. Consequently, parties to common law HMAs must perform their contractual obligations unless a common law doctrine such as frustration (discussed in more detail below) can be invoked[4] to discharge parties of their obligations. Conversely, civil law jurisdictions may allow parties to rely on principles of good faith, judicial intervention, or the doctrine of unforeseeability, where unforeseen circumstances operate to impose an excessive contractual burden on the parties.[5]

Accordingly, in the context of COVID-19, HMAs may be significantly impacted by the governing law of the agreement. In the hospitality industry, many branded HMAs are governed by English law, which, as expected from its common law approach, broadly gives primacy to the terms of the written agreement and seeks to preserve the sanctity of the original contract. Under English law, *force majeure* is a creature of contract and, therefore, a matter of contractual construction – where the agreement provides for an appropriately drafted *force majeure* clause, parties may be relieved of their obligations by relying on such a clause. Accordingly, hotel owners and operators looking to rely on *force majeure* clauses in their agreements should ensure that the clause is bespoke to the parties' relationship and clearly defines what constitutes a *force majeure* event.[6] Although some HMAs do refer to "events beyond the reasonable control" of the parties or provide for "epidemics, quarantine or any other public health restrictions or public health advisories," the construction of such clauses may be too general and, therefore, unenforceable. In addition, *force majeure* clauses may not capture the unique circumstances presented by COVID-19, which is a more prolonged and global event unlike the more one-off

4 *Taylor v Caldwell* [1863] 3 B&S 826.

5 Christopher Brunner, "Chapter 3: The Concept of Non-performance, Section 6: The Concept of Non-performance Under General Contract Principles," in *Force Majeure and Hardship under General Contract Principles: Exemption for Non-performance in International Arbitration* (Alphen aan den Rijn: Kluwer Law International, 2008), 57–74.

6 Mohamed S. Abdel Wahab, "Chapter 1: Dispute Prevention, Management and Resolution in Times of Crisis Between Tradition and Innovation: The COVID-19 Catalytic Crisis," in *International Arbitration and the COVID-19 Revolution*, eds. Maxi Scherer, Niuscha Bassiri, and Mohamed S. Abdel Wahab (Kluwer Law International, 2020), 1–26.

and localized events often considered in the context of *force majeure* (*e.g.*, floods and other natural disasters).

Nonetheless, even common law jurisdictions may differ in their interpretation of an HMA, and, consequently, the rights and remedies available to parties. US case law, for example, demonstrates that owners may terminate HMAs at will even in non-default situations, based on agency principles. For instance, in *Hotel TOC v. Trump International*,[7] the HMA contained a clause reserving the right of the owner to terminate the agreement under the agency law of New York. This right, however, does not extend to protect the owner from resulting damages. Conversely, in English law, an HMA is unlikely to give parties any implied rights (in relation to termination, for instance), and rights and obligations are construed as a matter of construction.

Meanwhile, the concepts of *force majeure* and material adverse change may have the force of law and be defined and recognized by certain civil codes. For instance, the French Civil Code defines *force majeure* under Article 1218 and allows parties to suspend their obligations (temporarily or permanently depending on the duration of the relevant event).[8] Although construction of the clause and its operation in the contract is considered, *force majeure* in civil law jurisdictions tends to be wider than it is under English law. As a result, civil law courts may be willing to go beyond the express provisions of the contract in their interpretation of a *force majeure* clause.[9]

At the same time, however, the standard that must be met in civil law jurisdictions to establish a *force majeure* event can be high. In the United Arab Emirates, for example, the concept of *force majeure* is interpreted narrowly; the party claiming *force majeure* will have to establish that performance was impossible (not merely difficult).[10] In the context of a long-term contract such as an HMA, such a showing may be particularly challenging to make.

Going forward, more HMAs may see the specific inclusion of pandemics as *force majeure* events. Indeed, HMAs are being much more prescriptive,

7 *Hotel TOC, Inc. v. 1. Trump Panama Hotel Management LLC, 2. Trump International Hotels Management, LLC*, ICC Case No. 23149/MK, Final Award, 20 March 2020, para. 128.

8 Alfons H. Puelinckx, "Frustration, Hardship, Force Majeure, Imprévision, Wegfall der Geschäftsgrundlage, Unmöglichkeit, Changed Circumstances: A Comparative study in English, French, German and Japanese Law," *Journal of International Arbitration* 3, no. 2 (June 1986): 47–66.

9 Christoph Brunner, "Chapter 3: Rules on Force Majeure as Illustrated in Recent Case Law," in *Hardship and Force Majeure in International Commercial Contracts: Dealing with Unforeseen Events in a Changing World*, eds. Fabio Bortolotti and Dorothy Ufot (Paris: ICC Services Publications Department, 2018), 82–112.

10 UAE Civil Code, Federal Law No. 5 of 1985, as amended, Art. 273.

including defining events such as travel bans and even "general disinclination to travel" as *force majeure* events. Where language to that effect is not provided, parties should consider whether it is caught by a different concept, such as "an Act of God," "action by the government," or a catch-all provision, but these less prescriptive terms often do not capture relevant events as tightly. In an arbitration for the termination of an HMA for a hotel in North Africa, for example, the tribunal concluded that, under the terms of the contract at issue, an event amounted to *force majeure* only when it materially affected the tourism in the country where the hotel was situated and if the effects persisted for six months.[11] The tribunal took the view that *force majeure* was invoked on the basis of a review of hotel occupancy statistics over a period of five years, which demonstrated a material effect on tourism.[12] Post-COVID-19 HMAs may similarly include performance indicators as a basis for invoking *force majeure* clauses.

Force majeure clauses may be an effective mechanism to avoid reliance on the legal doctrine of frustration. Frustration may not offer the same kind of certainty provided under a contract and generally requires a much higher threshold to be met[13] – parties must demonstrate that the obligations impacted by the event or circumstances are fundamental to the contract and commercially impossible to perform. Additionally, the requisite times for the prevention of performance may differ under *force majeure* and frustration. While contractual clauses may categorically define what constitutes a significant period for the purposes of non-performance (a long-stop date or specified timeframe for extension),[14] courts may take the view that an HMA subsisting over 20 years is not incapable of being performed, even if the hotel were to be closed for a period of time.[15]

11 Romain Dupeyré, "ICC Arbitration in the Hospitality Industry," *ICC Dispute Resolution Bulletin* 26, no. 2 (2016).

12 *Id.*

13 Bevis Mak, "Physical Impossibility and Frustration," *Arbitration: The International Journal of Arbitration, Mediation and Dispute Management* 64, no. 2 (May 1998): 137–148.

14 Tara Marlow and Ian Arnott, "Coronavirus: hotel management agreements and force majeure," Al Tamini & Co, accessed 13 January 2023, https://www.tamimi.com/law-update-articles/coronavirus-hotel-management-agreements-and-force-majeure/.

15 *National Carriers Ltd v Panalpina (Northern) Ltd* [1981] AC 675. In *National Carriers Ltd*, the 20-month interruption of the contract was not considered sufficient grounds to terminate a lease subsisting 10-years.

4 Potential HMA-Specific Disputes Relating to COVID-19

Many disputes arising under HMAs relate to operational matters, and certain categories of disputes often recur under HMAs. This is no less true in the COVID-19 era. These disputes often relate to the owner-operator relationship, in particular the calculation of management fees, and performance test considerations in relation to owner termination rights. These categories of disputes are discussed in more detail below.

4.1 *Owner-Operator Relationship*

In the aftermath of COVID-19 restrictions and closures, it is likely that both owners and operators will be looking to maximize revenues and profits. However, owners and operators will have different stakeholders, *e.g.*, operators' stakeholders include shareholders interested in the enterprise value of the company and brand as a whole, whereas owners are focused on debt coverage and lender requirements, which may cause tension in the owner-operator relationship. As noted above, under an HMA, an owner effectively takes on the commercial risk that the hotel will not be successful, while surrendering most of the operational control of the property to the operator. On the other hand, the operator remains dependent on the owner for the capital required for growth and development and is constrained in respect to certain key decisions. As such, in times of extreme disruption, there is likely to be considerable divergence in the parties' interests.

As discussed above, a typical HMA (especially with reputable international brands) gives a high degree of control to the operator for the day-to-day management of the hotel. While the agreement normally provides for certain core responsibilities and obligations, the operator generally has the freedom to exercise its discretion in the running of the hotel, including wide powers to direct and manage employees, even though the owner employs the staff of the hotel. As a result, the owner is unlikely to be able to require operators to act in specific ways in relation to the management of the business. This extends to the post-COVID-19 response. While hotel owners may primarily be concerned with maximizing revenue and profits, an operator, particularly a branded one, is likely to be alert to the wider public relations issues associated with reopening post-pandemic. Hotel closures and suspensions are not always addressed in an HMA – the general position is that closure and re-opening is within the ambit of the operator, with an obligation to consult with the owner (although this can sometimes be subject to mutual agreement between the parties). However, where an operator is mindful of protecting the brand's reputation and conscious of safety regulations relating to management of the property, it will want to retain control of the decision-making in this regard. Consequently, an owner with a low degree of control is unlikely to be able to require operators to respond to the pandemic in a certain way; for instance, how to price rooms when capacity or occupancy is low, or how to re-open in line with government restrictions.

4.2 *Calculation of Management Fees*

Broadly speaking, a balancing of risks and rewards exists over the long-term duration of an HMA. On one hand, owners do very well when the economy is strong, but in more challenging economic times, they are required to continue providing working capital and funding while also covering their debt service and other commitments. On the other hand, operators' remuneration is generally relatively constant, as they earn their fees for managing the property primarily from the revenues, and any upsides are limited to incentive fees.

In this regard, management fees payable to operators are typically calculated on a percentage of gross revenue (a base management fee), plus an incentive management fee based on operating profits, or a combination of both. Lower financial performance, brought on by COVID-19-related restrictions, may negatively impact management fees given lower revenue and likely failure to meet the requisite profit thresholds for any incentive management fees. However, some HMAs provide protection for operators with the inclusion of a minimum management fee irrespective of actual performance.

In times of such financial distress, the operator may be willing to offer short-term relief by way of a temporary deferral of base management fees or a lower base management fee percentage. In the near-to medium-term, this may then be ramped back up to the contractually specified amount.

Throughout this entire period, there are likely no incentive management fees as the hotel looks to recover to pre-pandemic profitability levels. As a result, longer-term, operators may seek to focus more on receiving a minimum management fee which is not based on any performance metric to ensure that they are able to cover their overhead and general operating expenses in the event of any future catastrophic events.

A further consideration should also be given to the impact of insurance proceeds, *e.g.*, any business interruption proceeds, if the owner is required to carry business interruption insurance per the HMA. Depending upon the recoverability of such amounts, which is a hotly contested issue globally between the hospitality industry and insurance carriers because of COVID-19, it is important to understand who is entitled to receive such amounts, and how they are recorded in the books and records of the hotel. For example, if the insurance proceeds are designed to replace the lost revenues of the hotel and recorded under gross revenues per the Uniform System of Accounts in the Lodging Industry ("USALI") or otherwise, then management fees will likely be calculated on such insurance proceeds.

4.3 *Owner Termination Rights*

As discussed above, most HMAs contain owner terminations rights if the operator fails an agreed performance test over a specified period unless there is the ability to cure, and the operator does in fact cure. These performance tests can take several forms. One form is by reference to the hotel's profits against a pre-determined threshold, which typically increases each year over the life of the initial term of the HMA, and which may be reset for any extension periods. To the extent the actual performance in the test period (typically two consecutive years) falls below such applicable thresholds, this constitutes a failure of the performance test, which can result in termination of the HMA by the owner unless the operator pays the shortfall, which resets the performance test period. The idea behind this test is to ensure the operator works toward increasing the profits of the hotel each year and to guarantee the owner a minimum return on its investment and cover of its debts.

Alternatively, a two-pronged performance test may include both a profit test based on the hotel's performance against its budget and a revenue test based on the comparative performance of an agreed upon peer group (a "Competitive Set"). The profit test, typically based on gross operating profit ("GOP"), compares the actual GOP achieved by the hotel in a test year against the budgeted GOP for that year. If the actual GOP is less than a specified percentage of the budgeted GOP, then the operator fails the profit test for that period. The revenue test, typically Revenue Per Available Room ("RevPAR"), compares revenue at the hotel against the competitive set. This is possible due to the availability of industry data from benchmarking services such as STR. If the hotel's RevPAR in the test period is less than a specified percentage of the Competitive Set's average RevPAR, then the operator will fail the RevPAR Test for that test period.

The single-prong profit performance test becomes more difficult to pass in the latter years of the initial term of a HMA given the annual threshold increases and may be severely impacted by an event such as COVID-19. However, events such as COVID-19 may constitute a *force majeure* event for purposes of this performance test and performance is excused for however long it is determined the qualifying event exists, which may include any period required for the hotel to recover to pre-pandemic levels of profitability, which are currently forecast to be anywhere between one and four years depending upon the hotel.

The two-prong profit and revenue performance test require the operator to fail both tests to fail the performance test. Because of COVID-19, most hotels suffered a precipitous decline in occupancy, revenues, and profits, and so for the first year of the pandemic at least, it is likely that they failed the profit test, *i.e.*, in 2020. This is because the 2020 budgeted GOP would have been set at the end of 2019 which did not consider the impact of COVID-19. Given that the revenue test is based upon a Competitive Set of hotels, typically in a similar location and of a similar standard, COVID-19 is likely to have impacted all such hotels in a similar manner, and therefore the hotel may still have passed the revenue test in 2020. Therefore, the operator is likely not to have failed the performance test in 2020 because of COVID-19.

Furthermore, regardless of which performance test is contained within the HMA, most performance tests can only be triggered if the operator fails for two consecutive testing years. For the single-prong test, this determination rests upon the ability of the operator to continue to declare a *force majeure* event, if available. For the two-prong test, operators will be carefully preparing budgets to consider the eventuality of continuing financial impacts due to COVID-19 and so will likely not fail the profit test. For the revenue test, the hotel will need to ensure its performance at least matches that of its Competitive Set as they ramp back up to pre-COVID-19 performance levels. Ultimately, however, the operator could choose to cure any shortfall or failure of the performance test to avoid termination and pay such required amounts to the owner to preserve the HMA.

Performance-related disputes under HMAs previously saw arbitral tribunals recognizing the owner's right of termination for subpar managerial performance. In times of extreme disruption and economic downturn, while the standard will typically be contained in the contract, disputes under HMAs may see the triers of fact reconsidering what "commercially reasonable efforts" or similar clauses entail. This may, for instance, be determined by reference to industry-wide performance at a given time. For instance, in *Jnah v Marriott*, an obligation on the operator to maintain the hotel as a "full service, first class international hotel"[16] was interpreted by the arbitral tribunal as an obligation to manage the hotel to a standard that was broadly comparable to the top tier hotels in that market over the life of the HMA.

Owners may also have the ability or right to unilaterally terminate an HMA coupled with the express provision to pay damages to the operator. Such damages may be premised upon the payment of liquidated damages based upon a historical period of actual management fees paid to the operator, multiplied

16 *Jnah Development S.A.L. v Marriott International Hotels Inc. (II)*, ICC Case No. 13894/EBS/VRO.

by an amount designed to reflect the remaining term of the HMA at the date of termination. Liquidated damages are intended to reflect the parties best estimate of damages as contemplated at the time of drafting the HMA. However, because of events such as COVID-19, the end result may be very different to what was anticipated. In *SC SJ Holding LLC, et al.* the HMA was terminated by the debtors, who then asserted that damages were to be calculated under the liquidated damages provision, which was based on an aggregate trailing 12-month period of actual management fees paid to the operator, and a multiplier.[17] The impact of COVID-19 on the financial performance of the hotel and the significant reduction in management fees for 2020 and 2021, coupled with a termination date of early 2021, resulted in a calculation of liquidated damages by the debtors at a fraction of what it would have been absent the impact of COVID-19. Amongst other issues, the operator contested the debtor's application of liquidated damages, arguing that the (alleged manipulated) timing of the termination under-compensated the operator vis-à-vis the remaining term of the HMA.

5 The Future: HMA Disputes after the Pandemic

As a result of the pandemic, the hospitality sector has suffered considerable financial tumult and uncertainty, and future HMAs are likely to be subject to considerable negotiation in the aftermath of the pandemic. On one hand, prominent branded operators may be perceived as safer than independent, "white-label" operators, leading to an expansion of established brands. In turn, this may give hotel owners less flexibility and control in negotiating the terms of the HMA, particularly since the degree of control usually afforded to them is already minimal. Conversely, in a tight revenue environment, owners may seek to reduce the cost of the business by negotiating fee structures differently and reducing franchise royalty fees to operators.[18] Ultimately, post-pandemic, risk allocation will be a key concern for owners and operators alike, with each party seeking to shift the liability onto the other.

While dispute resolution mechanisms for HMAs will depend entirely on the circumstances and relationship between parties, it is likely that international arbitration will continue to hold prominence as a mechanism for resolving

---

17 *SC SJ Holding LLC, et al.* (*Debtors*), Case No. 21–10549 (JTD) (Bankr. D. Del. 2021).

18 "Hotel Management Agreements Post-COVID-19: A New World?," Womble Bond Dickinson, June 1, 2020, https://www.womblebonddickinson.com/uk/insights/articles-and-briefings/hotel-management-agreements-post-covid-19-new-world.

conflicts between parties.[19] The 2021 White & Case and Queen Mary University International Arbitration Survey found that international arbitration is the "preferred method of resolving cross-border disputes for 90% of respondents," with 59% of respondents to the survey stating international arbitration together with alternative dispute resolution as their preferred method of resolving cross-border disputes post-COVID-19. The very nature of HMA disputes – generally involving fact-and industry-specific issues at the operational level – makes them likely to fall within this preferred method of dispute resolution, as parties will have the ability to select decision-makers with the requisite familiarity with the hospitality industry and these sorts of disputes.

Moreover, the involvement of international hotel operators in such disputes demands flexibility, while also ensuring robust enforcement measures are in place across the world. Parties to an international HMA will wish to ensure the outcomes of their disputes are binding and enforceable globally. In the context of worldwide disruption to the hospitality industry, international arbitration is likely to remain an attractive dispute resolution mechanism, keeping in mind the (perceived) greater neutrality of a tribunal over a party's national court, the increased confidentiality, and the ability to select arbitrators to the tribunal.

6 Conclusion

The hospitality industry, having faced considerable economic downturn and change, is likely to see an increase in the number of disputes arising from non-performance of contractual obligations in HMAs. The effects of COVID-19 – restrictions on travel and an increased focus on safety regulations – will continue to impact occupancy and revenues, exacerbating existing issues or giving rise to entirely new ones, especially in relation to termination and default. As HMAs attract further scrutiny, greater tensions between owners and operators will result in increased disputes regarding the long-term allocation of risk and liability. Most of these disputes, favoring current trends in the industry, will be subject to arbitration, with parties seeking neutrality, flexibility, and enforceability from their chosen form of dispute resolution.

19 White & Case LLP, "2021 International Arbitration Survey: Adapting Arbitration to a Changing World," Queen Mary University of London, May 6, 2021, https://arbitration.qmul.ac.uk/media/arbitration/docs/LON0320037-QMUL-International-Arbitration-Survey-2021_19_WEB.pdf .

Acknowledgements

The authors would like to thank Patricia D. Cruz Trabanino for her insightful input on this article and leading a discussion of the article at the conference on Construction and Hospitality Disputes Post-COVID held on 15 October 2021 in Geneva. The authors would also like to thank Ian Arnott, Humayun Ahmad, Jeanne Visser, and Priyanjoli Bose for their valuable input and research assistance for this chapter. Any errors or omissions are the sole responsibility of the authors.

CHAPTER 5

Government Measures and Investment Treaty-Based Claims

Eckhard Hellbeck

1 Introduction

In response to the rise of the COVID-19 pandemic, on January 30, 2020, the Director-General of the World Health Organization ("WHO") declared a Public Health Emergency of International Concern, defined as an "extraordinary event [that] is determined ... to constitute a public health risk to other States through the international spread of disease and to potentially require a coordinated international response."[1] On March 11, 2020, the WHO declared a pandemic.[2] Reacting to the pandemic, many States took various measures that both directly and indirectly impacted almost all economic sectors, especially the hospitality and construction sectors. Many foreign investors considered arbitration claims against these governments under contracts and/or investment treaties on the basis that these measures violated the States' obligations under investment protection treaties.

These arbitration claims are likely to confront arbitrators with the difficult task of weighing legally protected private investments against the sovereign authority of the State to take emergency measures to protect the health of the general population. In some cases, this may involve determining whether certain government measures were justified by the pandemic or whether the government merely used the pandemic as a pretext for its own, different agenda.[3]

1 WHO, *International Health Regulations*, 3rd edition (France: World Health Organization, 2005), Art. 1(1) ("IHR"); see also "Statement on the Second Meeting of the International Health Regulations (2005) Emergency Committee Regarding the Outbreak of Novel coronavirus (2019-nCoV)," WHO, January 30, 2020, https://www.who.int/news/item/30-01-2020-statement-on-the-second-meeting-of-the-international-health-regulations-(2005)-emergency-committee-regarding-the-outbreak-of-novel-coronavirus-(2019-ncov).

2 "WHO Director-General's Opening Remarks at the Media Briefing on COVID-19 – 11 March 2020," WHO, March 11, 2020, https://www.who.int/director-general/speeches/detail/who-director-general-s-opening-remarks-at-the-media-briefing-on-covid-19---11-march-2020.

3 See, *e.g.*, Cosmo Sanderson, "Mexico Faces Potential Claims over Pandemic Response," Global Arbitration Review, May 22, 2020, https://globalarbitrationreview.com/article/1227136/mexico-faces-potential-claims-over-pandemic-response (reporting that foreign investors in

 | DOI:10.1163/9789004514874_007

The ultimate issue confronting arbitrators will likely be the question of whom should bear the cost of losses resulting from legitimate government measures taken to combat the pandemic.

The hospitality and construction sectors were among the most affected sectors of the economy. The pandemic's impact on the hospitality industry was immediate when government restrictions stopped almost all travel in early 2020 due to serious concerns that travel and congregation in indoor spaces would further spread infection.[4] The International Labour Organization ("ILO") estimated that "[t]he pandemic and global efforts to contain it could cause the international tourism economy to contract by between 45 and 70 percent."[5] The construction sector also was severely impacted by the pandemic, including by the lockdowns and other health and safety measures imposed by governments.[6] In some countries, certain construction activities, however, were deemed essential and thus were exempted from lockdowns.[7] Given its sensitivity to economic cycles, the construction industry nonetheless also suffered greatly from the general economic downturn triggered by the pandemic.[8]

To the extent international businesses in the hospitality and construction sector have entered contracts with the relevant State, they may be able to pursue claims under those contracts to seek compensation for losses suffered because of the States' pandemic-related measures. Such claims will be governed by

---

Mexico's renewable energy sector are considering investment treaty claims concerning certain measures that Mexico enacted in April 2020, which gave preferential grid access to non-renewable electricity generation facilities and restricted such access for renewable energy generators. While Mexican authorities reportedly sought to justify the measures referring to a decreasing demand for electricity because of the COVID-19 pandemic, foreign investors apparently believe this is a mere pretext to strengthen domestic, State-owned electricity generation from non-renewable sources).

4 See, *e.g.*, "AHLA's State of the Hotel Industry 2021," American Hotel & Lodging Association, January 21, 2021, 3, https://www.ahla.com/sites/default/files/2021_state_of_the_industry_0.pdf ("The hotel industry experienced the most devastating year on record in 2020, resulting in historically low occupancy, massive job loss, and hotel closures across the country. Hotels were one of the first industries affected by the pandemic after travel was forced to a virtual halt in early 2020, and it will be one of the last to recover. The impact of COVID-19 on the travel industry so far has been nine times that of 9/11").

5 "ILO Sectoral Brief: The Impact of COVID-19 on the Tourism Sector," International Labour Organization, May 2020, 2, https://www.ilo.org/wcmsp5/groups/public/---ed_dialogue/---sector/documents/briefingnote/wcms_741468.pdf.

6 "ILO Sectoral Brief: Impact of COVID-19 on the Construction Sector," International Labour Organization, January 2021, 2, https://www.ilo.org/wcmsp5/groups/public/---ed_dialogue/---sector/documents/briefingnote/wcms_767303.pdf.

7 *Id.*

8 *Id.* at 1.

national law, which will differ from one country to another. Separately, international businesses may be able to pursue treaty claims against States, governed primarily by international law. This chapter focuses on the latter.

After providing a brief overview of government measures affecting the hospitality and construction sectors, this chapter addresses substantive treaty rights that may protect foreign investments against such measures, in particular protections against uncompensated expropriation and violation of the State's obligations to accord foreign investors and their investments fair and equitable treatment. The chapter then discusses exceptions from treaty protections for measures taken to protect public health and in times of emergency. It goes on to discuss a rule of treaty interpretation that could be used to limit treaty protections in favor of public health or the measures taken to protect public health. This chapter also addresses the defense of *force majeure* under international law.

2 Government Measures

This section provides examples of pandemic-related government measures that may lead to treaty claims. As each government has enacted its own measures based on its own legal system, there is no uniformity among such measures, and any attempt to prepare a comparative analysis of measures enacted around the world inevitably would go beyond the scope of this chapter.

2.1 *Measures Affecting the Hospitality Industry*

In response to the pandemic, most countries enacted travel restrictions and even total entry prohibitions.[9] These direct travel restrictions inevitably caused significant damage to the hospitality sector, which relies heavily upon tourism and the free travel of individuals for income. Additional, indirect damage was inflicted on the hospitality industry by government-imposed lockdowns in most "non-essential" economic sectors, curfews, and stay-at-home orders, all of which caused a general economic downturn, which also affected supply chains supporting the hospitality industry.

As an example, on March 17, 2020, the Italian government issued a decree authorizing the requisitioning of hotels to quarantine people. While the decree provided for compensation by reference to the asset's current market value, it

9 See "COVID-19 Travel Regulations Map," International Air Transport Association Travel Centre, accessed April 27, 2022, https://www.iatatravelcentre.com/world.php.

did not specify the method of calculating the market value nor the form of payment of compensation.[10] By a separate decree, the Italian government imposed a lockdown confining all persons to their homes and suspending all industrial and commercial activities, except for those activities that were expressly designated as "strategic."[11]

2.2 *Measures Affecting the Construction Industry*

As mentioned above, some countries declared certain construction activities to be of strategic or essential importance, and for this reason exempted them from lockdowns and other restrictions.[12] In addition to indirect impacts from the slowdown of economic activity, the construction sector also suffered severe, direct impacts from a variety of government measures that ostensibly were designed to protect the public from the economic impact of the pandemic as well as against infection. The following examples involve arbitration claims considered or initiated against States by foreign investors and concessions to build and operate toll roads and airport terminals.

In May 2020, Peru's legislature passed a law suspending the collection of tolls by concessionaires of toll roads.[13] The stated purpose of the suspension was to facilitate the transport of essential goods and workers during the pandemic, which had caused many Peruvians to lose their income.[14] As the law did not offer any compensation to the concessionaires, foreign investors in six concessionaires reportedly considered filing investment arbitration claims against Peru.[15] Soon after the legislation was passed, the government initiated a proceeding before Peru's Constitutional Court challenging it

10 See Massimo Benedettteli, Caterina Coroneo, and Nicolò Minella, "Could COVID-19 Emergency Measures Give Rise to Investment Claims? First Reflections from Italy," Global Arbitration Review, March 26, 2020, https://globalarbitrationreview.com/coronavirus/could-covid-19-emergency-measures-give-rise-investment-claims-first-reflections-italy.

11 See *id*; see also "Italy: COVID-19 – Urgent Measures to Limit the Spread of Coronavirus: Tax & Legal Alert," KPMG, March 24, 2020, https://assets.kpmg/content/dam/kpmg/us/pdf/2020/03/tnf-italy-march24-2020.pdf (summarizing the Italian Government Decree of 22 March 2020).

12 *Id.*

13 Cosmo Sanderson, "Peru Threatened Over Coronavirus Emergency Measure," Global Arbitration Review, June 5, 2020, https://globalarbitrationreview.com/coronavirus/peru-threatened-over-coronavirus-emergency-measure.

14 *Id.*

15 *Id.*

constitutionality.[16] In August 2020, the Constitutional Court issued its decision, finding that the legislation violated the principle of freedom of contract under Article 2 of the Constitution.[17] The Court also found that the legislation failed to explain sufficiently how forcing the concessionaires to stop collecting tolls was to assist in mitigating the pandemic.[18] In light of this failure, the Court found that the true goal of the legislation was rather to "grant an economic benefit to transportation activities."[19] Because the Court invalidated the legislation, none of the foreign investors initiated arbitration against Peru.

More recently, in August 2021, two French airport operators filed claims against Chile at the International Centre for Settlement of Investment Disputes ("ICSID") related to a concession to build and operate a new airport terminal.[20] They claimed compensation for losses suffered because of government measures taken in response to the COVID-19 pandemic, including the closure of flight routes and requiring additional sanitary measures.[21] Reportedly, the claimants argued that these measures, combined with the government's refusal to renegotiate the terms of the concession, violated the Chile-France bilateral investment treaty, as the measures leave investors with no income to offset expenses due to government intervention.[22]

16 Lisa Bohmer, "Peru Round-Up: An Update on Arbitration Threats and Pending Cases Against the State," IAReporter, September 15, 2020, https://www.iareporter.com/articles/peru-round-up-an-update-on-arbitration-threats-and-pending-cases-against-the-state/.

17 *Id.*

18 *Id.*

19 *Id.*

20 Toby Fisher, "Chile Hit with Claim Over Airport Pandemic Disruption," Global Arbitration Review, August 16, 2021, https://globalarbitrationreview.com/chile-hit-claim-over-airport-pandemic-disruption.

21 *Id.*; see also *ADP International S.A. and Vinci Airports S.A.S. v. Republic of Chile*, ICSID Case No. ARB/21/40 (registered on August 13, 2021), https://icsid.worldbank.org/cases/case-database/case-detail?CaseNo=ARB/21/40.

22 "Three Are In Place to Hear Claims Under the Chile-France BIT," IAReporter, March 29, 2022, https://www.iareporter.com/articles/three-are-in-place-to-hear-claims-under-the-chile-france-bit/; Lisa Bohmer, "French Airport Investors Make Good on Earlier Threat to Bring Treaty-Based Claims Against Chile in Relation to Reduced Air Traffic During the COVID Pandemic," IAReporter, August 13, 2021, https://www.iareporter.com/articles/french-airport-investors-make-good-on-earlier-threat-to-bring-treaty-based-claims-against-chile-in-relation-to-reduced-air-traffic-during-the-covid-pandemic/.

3 Substantive Treaty Rights

While foreign investors will first look to the provisions of any contract they might have with the State to investigate potential claims, these investors also may have the right to bring concurrent claims under international law. International investment protection treaties, for example, allow a foreign investor to bring separate claims against the State separate from the contract claims, which are not mutually exclusive with one another.

As a first step, a foreign investor must determine whether (i) a contractual relationship exists with the State, and (ii) whether any investment treaties may apply to the investor and the investment. Second, the investor must identify any dispute resolution clauses contained in any applicable contract and/or treaty and determine their scope. For example, some investment treaties provide for broad consent to international arbitration of "all disputes" or "any dispute" related to the investment, which arguably allows an arbitral tribunal to consider both contractual claims and treaty claims.[23] Other treaties more narrowly provide for consent to arbitrate only disputes concerning alleged treaty violations.[24] The scope of the respective dispute resolution clauses will determine whether the investor may submit both contractual and treaty-based claims to the same arbitral tribunal.

When assessing whether a State acted appropriately with its COVID-19 response measures to determine if a claim exists under international treaty law, a foreign investor should consider both substantive treaty rights, such as the State's obligations of expropriation and fair and equitable treatment, as well as the relevant exceptions that exist to these treaties, such as public health exceptions or emergencies. If an exception applies, this may legitimize the government measure that would otherwise violate an investor's rights under the treaty.

---

23 See, *e.g.*, *Salini Costruttori S.P.A. and Italstrade S.P.A. v. Kingdom of Morocco*, ICSID Case No. ARB/00/4, Decision on Jurisdiction, 23 July 2001, 42 I.L.M. 609, 623–624, paras. 59–61 (finding that Article 8 of the applicable bilateral investment treaty, which provided that the arbitral tribunal had jurisdiction to decide "[a]ll disputes or differences … concerning an investment," covered both treaty claims and claims arising out of a contract to which the State is a party).

24 See, *e.g.*, *Ioannis Kardassopoulos v. Georgia*, ICSID Case No. ARB/05/18, Decision on Jurisdiction, 6 July 2007, para. 249 (noting that, under Article 26(1) of the Energy Charter Treaty, an arbitral tribunal has jurisdiction over a dispute only if it "concern[s] an alleged breach of an obligation of the [host State] under Part III" of that Treaty).

3.1 *Expropriation*

Under well-established customary international law, expropriation generally refers to the power of a State to take private property from an individual, organization, group, or investor in exchange for prompt, adequate and effective compensation. Additionally, the measure of expropriation must serve a public purpose, must not be arbitrary or discriminatory, and must follow principles of due process. Investment treaties typically reflect this standard.[25] Thus, if the host State takes a foreign investment without compensation, it may be liable to pay compensation under such a treaty as well as independently under customary international law, regardless of the specific treaty provision.

While an expropriation may be direct (State takes legal title to, or physical possession of, an asset), the COVID-19 related measures mostly resulted in indirect expropriation. An indirect, or *de facto*, taking occurs when the State's measure substantially deprives the investment of its value, but does not result in a change of title or physical possession, as the ICSID tribunal in *Tecmed v. Mexico* explained:

> [I]t is understood that the measures adopted by a State, whether regulatory or not, are an indirect *de facto* expropriation if they are irreversible and permanent and if the assets or rights subject to such measure have been affected in such a way that 'any form of exploitation thereof' has disappeared; *i.e.*, the economic value of the use, enjoyment or disposition of the assets or rights affected by the administrative action or decision have been neutralized or destroyed. Under international law, the owner is also deprived of property where the use or enjoyment of benefits related thereto is exacted or interfered with to a similar extent, even where legal ownership over the assets in question is not affected, and so long as the deprivation is not temporary. The government's intention is less important than the effects of the measures on the owner of the assets or on the benefits arising from such assets affected by the measures; and the form of the deprivation measure is less important than its actual effects. To determine whether such an expropriation has taken place, the Arbitral Tribunal should not 'restrict itself to evaluating whether a formal dispossession or expropriation took place, but should look beyond mere

25 See Rudolf Dolzer and Christoph Schreuer, *Principles of International Investment Law*, 2nd edition (Oxford University Press, 2012), 99–100.

appearances and establish the real situation behind the situation that was denounced.'[26]

In this respect, COVID-related measures could constitute indirect expropriation if the government action substantially deprived the investor of the economic value of the use, enjoyment, or disposition of the assets or rights affected by the measure. A temporary deprivation, however, does not qualify as expropriation. To the extent the use and enjoyment of the asset is restored after the measures are lifted, it is not possible to claim compensation for expropriation in the interim period.

Thus, there are several key difficulties in claiming compensation for an unlawful indirect expropriation in connection with government measures targeting the COVID-19 pandemic. These difficulties exist when an investor wishes to establish (i) a substantial deprivation, (ii) that is permanent rather than temporal, and (iii) that the police powers doctrine does not apply.

Even if a claimant establishes that an indirect taking has occurred under (i) and (ii), there is a further implicit element of expropriation that must be considered. Under customary international law, the police powers doctrine provides that the valid exercise of a State's police powers does not constitute an expropriation.[27] In *Philip Morris v. Uruguay*, a case concerning cigarette packaging requirements, the arbitral tribunal stated that "[p]rotecting public health has long since been recognized as an essential manifestation of the State's police power" under customary international law.[28] The *Philip Morris* tribunal further explained that treaty obligations must be interpreted in light of any relevant rules of international law that are applicable between the parties to the treaty, in accordance with Article 31(3)(c) of the Vienna Convention on the Law of Treaties.[29] This includes rules of customary international law. Accordingly, there has been "a consistent trend [in investment treaty decisions] in favor of differentiating the exercise of police powers from indirect expropriation."[30]

---

26 *Tecnicas Medioambientales Tecmed S.A. v. The United Mexican States*, ICSID Case No. ARB(AF)/00/2, Award, 29 May 2003, para. 116 (internal references omitted); see also *Bayindir Insaat Turizm Ticaret Ve Sanayi A.S. v. Islamic Republic of Pakistan*, ICSID Case No. ARB/03/29, Award, 27 August 2009, para. 443 (same).

27 See *Philip Morris Brands SÀRL et al. v. Oriental Republic of Uruguay*, ICSID Case No. ARB/10/7, Award, 8 July 2016, paras. 287–290.

28 *Id.* at para. 291.

29 *Id.* at para. 290.

30 *Id.* at para. 295; see also *Tecnicas Medioambientales Tecmed S.A.*, *supra* note 26, at para. 119 ("The principle that the State's exercise of its sovereign power within the framework of its

The arbitral tribunal in *Saluka v. Czech Republic* explained the scope, conditions, and effects of the police powers doctrine as follows: "It is now established in international law that States are not liable to pay compensation to a foreign investor when, in the normal exercise of their regulatory powers, they adopt in a non-discriminatory manner *bona fide* regulations that are aimed to the general welfare."[31]

Referencing various cases, the *Philip Morris* tribunal found that "[t]he powers doctrine has been applied in several cases to reject claims challenging regulatory measures designed specifically to protect public health."[32] Indeed, more than a century ago, the Germany-Venezuela Mixed Claims Commission dismissed a claim for compensation for a German national's carriage, where during a smallpox epidemic, the Venezuelan police detained the carriage because it supposedly transported two people afflicted with the disease and the carriage was damaged during its detention.[33] The Claims Commission observed that "[i]t seems to be well settled by the authorities that in the case of an original wrongful taking of personal property the owner is not bound to receive the property in an injured condition."[34] Ultimately, however, it held that "[c]ertainly during an epidemic of an infectious disease there can be no liability for the reasonable exercise of police powers."[35]

Methanex v. United States involved a claim for compensation after measures adopted by California prohibited the fuel additive MTBE on the ground that it was harmful to public health.[36] The tribunal rejected the investor's expropriation claim, finding that "as a matter of general international law, a non-discriminatory regulation for a public purpose, which is enacted in accordance with due process and, which affects, *inter alios*, a foreign investor or investment is not deemed expropriatory."[37]

---

police power may cause economic damage to those subject to its powers as administrator without entitling them to any compensation whatsoever is undisputable").

31 *Saluka Investments BV v. The Czech Republic*, UNCITRAL, Partial Award, 17 March 2006, para. 255.

32 *Philip Morris Brands SÀRL et al.*, *supra* note 27, at para. 298.

33 *Bischoff Case*, Germany-Venezuela Mixed Claims Commission, Award, 1903, 10 RIAA 420, 420–421.

34 *Id.* at 420.

35 *Id.*

36 *Methanex Corporation v. United States of America*, UNCITRAL, Final Award on Jurisdiction and Merits, 3 August 2005, Pt. II, Ch. D, paras. 2, 14–19.

37 *Id.* at Pt. IV, Ch. D, para. 7.

In *Chemtura v. Canada*, where Canada had prohibited the sale of lindane, an agricultural insecticide, as harmful to human health and the environment, the tribunal similarly rejected the expropriation claim, stating:

> Irrespective of the existence of a contractual deprivation, the Tribunal considers in any event that the measures challenged by the Claimant constituted a valid exercise of the Respondent's police powers. ... [T]he [Pest Management Regulatory Agency of Canada] took measures within its mandate, in a non-discriminatory manner, motivated by the increasing awareness of the dangers presented by lindane for human health and the environment. A measure adopted under such circumstances is a valid exercise of the State's police powers and, as a result, does not constitute an expropriation.[38]

The *Philip Morris* tribunal ultimately found that the cigarette packaging regulations imposed by Uruguay "were taken ... with a view to protect public health in fulfilment of its national and international obligations[,] ... were non-discriminatory[,] and were not 'arbitrary and unnecessary' but rather were potentially 'effective means to protecting public health.'"[39] The tribunal concluded that the measures "were a valid exercise by Uruguay of its police powers for the protection of public health [and could not] constitute an expropriation of the Claimants' investment."[40]

3.2 *Fair and Equitable Treatment*

Investment treaties generally obligate the host State to treat foreign investors and their investments fairly and equitably. The Fair and Equitable Treatment ("FET") obligation is broad and undefined, and therefore it may apply in different circumstances.[41] Tribunals have held the FET obligation to be breached when State conduct was "arbitrary, grossly unfair, unjust or idiosyncratic, [or] discriminatory."[42] Tribunals have not, however, defined these terms clearly and, as a result, their use often overlaps.

38 *Chemtura Corporation v. Government of Canada*, UNCITRAL, Award, 1 August 2010, para. 266.

39 *Philip Morris Brands SÀRL et al.*, *supra* note 27, at para. 306.

40 *Id.* at para. 307.

41 *Id.* at paras. 319–320.

42 *Waste Management, Inc. v. United Mexican States*, ICSID Case No. ARB/(AF)/00/3, Award, 30 April 2004, para. 98; see also *Biwater Gauff (Tanzania) Ltd. v. United Republic of Tanzania*, ICSID Case No. ARB/05/22, Award, 24 July 2008, para. 597 (same); *Hochtief AG*

The International Court of Justice ("ICJ") has defined "arbitrary" or "arbitrariness" under international law as "a willful disregard of due process of law, an act which shocks, or at least surprises, a sense of juridical propriety."[43]

Partially overlapping with the element of arbitrariness, the term "grossly unfair" generally refers to the concepts of procedural fairness and due process, which are considered core elements of the FET obligation.[44]

The terms "unjust or idiosyncratic" overlap with the elements of arbitrariness and due process but can be understood to refer more precisely to substantive due process, in other words, to the State's obligation to base its measures on "established sources of law."[45] They also refer to the State's obligation to apply its laws and regulations consistently.[46]

A measure also can violate the FET obligation if it is unreasonable. This requires determining "the existence of a rational policy; and the reasonableness of the act of the state in relation to the policy."[47] This calls for a determination of whether there is "an appropriate correlation between the state's public policy objective and the measure adopted to achieve it. This has to do with the nature of the measure and the way it is implemented."[48]

A tribunal also may consider whether a measure is disproportionate.[49] For a measure to be proportionate, it must be "suitable and necessary to achieve the legislative intent."[50] Suitability "does not … requir[e] more than a relationship

---

v. Argentine Republic, ICSID Case No. ARB/07/31, Decision on Liability, 29 December 2014, para. 219 (same); *Philip Morris Brands SÀRL et al., supra* note 27, at paras. 323–324 (same).

43 *Elettronica Sicula S.p.A. (ELSI) (United States of America v. Italy)*, Judgment, 20 July 1989, 1989 I.C.J. Rep. 15, 76 para. 128; *Philip Morris Brands SÀRL et al., supra* note 27, at 390 (same).

44 See August Reinisch and Christoph Schreuer, *International Protection of Investments – The substantive standards* (Cambridge University Press, 2020), 376–427, paras. 618–876.

45 *Mondev International Ltd. v. United States of America*, ICSID Case No. ARB(AF)/99/2, Award, 11 October 2002, para. 119; *Ioan Micula et al. v. Romania*, ICSID Case No. ARB/05/20, Award, 11 December 2013, para. 507.

46 *Cargill, Inc. v. United Mexican States*, ICSID Case No. ARB(AF)/05/2, Award, 18 September 2009, para. 296.

47 *AES Summit Generation Limited and AES-Tisza Erömü Kft v. The Republic of Hungary*, ICSID Case No. ARB/07/22, Award, 23 September 2010, paras. 10.3.7–10.3.9; see also *RWE Innogy GmbH and RWE Innogy Aersa S.A.U. v. Kingdom of Spain*, ICSID Case No. ARB/14/34, Decision on Jurisdiction, Liability, and Certain Issues of Quantum, 30 December 2019, para. 644 (same).

48 *AES Summit Generation Limited and AES-Tisza Erömü Kft, supra* note 47; *Electrabel S.A. v. Hungary*, ICSID Case No. ARB/07/19, Award, 25 November 2015, para. 179 (same); see also *RWE Innogy GmbH and RWE Innogy Aersa S.A.U., supra* note 47.

49 *RWE Innogy GmbH and RWE Innogy Aersa S.A.U., supra* note 47, at 648–649; *Electrabel S.A., supra* note 48, at para. 179.

50 *RWE Innogy GmbH and RWE Innogy Aersa S.A.U., supra* note 47, at 551.

of suitability between the measure and the objective to be achieved."[51] On the other hand,

> the question of whether a measure is necessary will typically involve some analysis as to whether there were any less restrictive means reasonably available to the State for meeting the given objective. If it is established that – even according a margin of appreciation to the State – less restrictive means were reasonably available, it is difficult to see how the given measure can be considered necessary.[52]

Arguments may be made in favor of either position on whether a government measure was "necessary" or more extreme than necessary to achieve the intended goal.

A measure that is discriminatory also may violate the FET obligation. A government's decision to label certain businesses as "strategic" or "essential," allowing them to continue operating while other businesses cannot, may create claims of arbitrary discrimination by investors whose businesses were forced to shut down or reduce operations if the government's decision was not based on clear and rational criteria.

4 Treaty Exceptions

While these international investment treaties allow foreign investors to have claims against States for their actions, some investment treaties contain explicit exceptions for public health measures or emergency situations.

4.1 *Public Health Exceptions*

Some investment treaties contain general exceptions or incorporate the general exceptions set out in the General Agreement on Tariffs and Trade ("GATT")[53]

51 *Id.* at 554.

52 *Id.*

53 See "General Agreement on Tariffs and Trade 1994," Marrakesh Agreement Establishing the World Trade Organization, April 15, 1994, Annex 1A, 1867 U.N.T.S. 187, 33 I.L.M. 1153 (1994), Art. XX(b), https://www.wto.org/english/docs_e/legal_e/legal_e.htm ("Subject to the requirement that such measures are not applied in a manner which would constitute a means of arbitrary or unjustifiable discrimination between countries where the same conditions prevail, or a disguised restriction on international trade, nothing in this Agreement shall be construed to prevent the adoption or enforcement by any contracting party of measures: ... necessary to protect human, animal or plant life or health.").

and the General Agreement on Trade in Services ("GATS").[54] These agreements allow a party to adopt or enforce measures to protect human life or health, provided that the measures are not arbitrary or discriminatory. For example, the Japan-Peru bilateral investment treaty ("Japan-Peru BIT") provides:

> Subject to the requirement that such measures are not applied in a manner which would constitute a means of arbitrary or unjustifiable discrimination against the other Contracting Party, or a disguised restriction on investments of investors of the other Contracting Party in the Area of a Contracting Party, nothing in this Agreement other than Article 14 shall be construed to prevent a Contracting Party from adopting or enforcing measures … necessary to protect human, animal or plant life or health.[55]

Several recent investment treaties reflect a slightly different approach. Rather than providing a general exception for health protection measures, they contain provisions specifically exempting such measures only from the scope of indirect expropriation. For example, the Comprehensive Economic and Trade Agreement between Canada and the European Union ("CETA") provides that "non-discriminatory measures of a Party that are designed and applied to protect legitimate public welfare objectives, such as health, safety and the environment, do not constitute indirect expropriations," except "in the rare circumstances when the impact of a measure or series of measures is so severe in light of its purpose that it appears manifestly excessive."[56] The United States introduced a similar provision in its 2004 Model Bilateral Investment Treaty,[57]

54 See "General Agreement on Trade in Services," Marrakesh Agreement Establishing the World Trade Organization, Annex 1B, 1869 U.N.T.S. 183, 33 I.L.M. 1167 (1994), Art. XIV(b), https://www.wto.org/english/docs_e/legal_e/26-gats_01_e.htm ("Subject to the requirement that such measures are not applied in a manner which would constitute a means of arbitrary or unjustifiable discrimination between countries where like conditions prevail, or a disguised restriction on trade in services, nothing in this Agreement shall be construed to prevent the adoption or enforcement by any Member of measures: … necessary to protect human, animal or plant life or health").

55 Agreement Between Japan and the Republic of Peru for the Promotion, Protection and Liberalisation of Investment ("Japan-Peru BIT"), signed November 21, 2008, Art. 19(1)(a), https://investmentpolicy.unctad.org/international-investment-agreements/treaty-files/1733/download.

56 Comprehensive Economic and Trade Agreement between Canada and the European Union (and its Member States) ("CETA"), signed October 30, 2016, Annex 8-A sec. 3, https://investmentpolicy.unctad.org/international-investment-agreements/treaty-files/5380/download.

57 See 2004 U.S. Model BIT, Annex B, para. 4(b), https://investmentpolicy.unctad.org/international-investment-agreements/treaty-files/2872/download ("Except in rare

which has been adopted in bilateral investment treaties and investment chapters of free trade agreements concluded by the United States since that time.[58]

As most COVID-19-related measures were designed to protect public health, they generally would appear to fall within the scope of such exceptions, unless an investor could demonstrate that they weforre arbitrary, disproportionate, or discriminatory. For example, the above-mentioned Peruvian legislation suspending toll collections might be considered disproportionate because it had the effect of shifting an economic burden on investors without meeting its ostensible goal of protecting public health.

4.2 *Emergency Provisions*

Several investment treaties also contain emergency provisions, including so-called "war clauses" and "essential security" provisions, which exempt States from certain treaty obligations or restrict those obligations in certain circumstances.

A war clause typically provides for national and most-favored nation treatment in the event of war, a national state of emergency, or similar events. For example, Article IV(3) of the United States-Argentina bilateral investment treaty ("US-Argentina BIT") provides:

> Nationals or companies of either Party whose investments suffer losses in the territory of the other Party owing to war or other armed conflict,

circumstances, non-discriminatory regulatory actions by a Party that are designed and applied to protect legitimate public welfare objectives, such as public health, safety, and the environment, do not constitute indirect expropriations."); see also 2012 U.S. Model BIT, Annex B, para. 4(b), https://investmentpolicy.unctad.org/international-investment-agreements/treaty-files/2870/download (same).

58 See, *e.g.*, Treaty Between the United States of America and the Oriental Republic of Uruguay Concerning the Encouragement and Reciprocal Protection of Investment, signed November 4, 2005, Annex B, para. 4(b), https://investmentpolicy.unctad.org/international-investment-agreements/treaty-files/2380/download ("Except in rare circumstances, non-discriminatory regulatory actions by a Party that are designed and applied to protect legitimate public welfare objectives, such as public health, safety, and the environment, do not constitute indirect expropriations"); Colombia-United States Trade Promotion Agreement, signed November 22, 2006, Annex 10-B, para. 3(b), https://investmentpolicy.unctad.org/international-investment-agreements/treaty-files/2737/download (same); United States-Mexico-Canada Agreement ("USMCA"), signed November 30, 2018, Annex 14-B, para. 3(b), https://investmentpolicy.unctad.org/international-investment-agreements/treaty-files/6008/download ("Non-discriminatory regulatory actions by a Party that are designed and applied to protect legitimate public welfare objectives, such as health, safety and the environment, do not constitute indirect expropriations, except in rare circumstances").

> revolution, state of national emergency, insurrection, civil disturbance or other similar events shall be accorded treatment by such other Party no less favorable than that accorded to its own nationals or companies or to nationals or companies of any third country, whichever is the more favorable treatment, as regards any measures it adopts in relation to such losses.[59]

The effect of such a clause is to make provisions such as those concerning expropriation or FET inapplicable in the event certain conditions occur. Instead, the State is obligated only to refrain from discriminating as against its own nationals or nationals of third States.

Essential security provisions are typically found in investment treaties of the United States. For example, Article XI of the US-Argentina BIT provides:

> This treaty shall not preclude the application by either party of measures necessary for the maintenance of public order, the fulfilment of its obligations with respect to the maintenance or restoration of international peace or security, or the protection of its own essential security interests.[60]

Under these investment treaty clauses, a State could make the argument that the COVID-19 pandemic amounts to a "state of national emergency" or a "similar event," or presents a threat to its essential security interests, and claim that it is exempted from liability for its measures taken to combat the pandemic.[61] It is important to note, however, that such exemptions from liability are limited to the duration of the emergency.[62] Once the emergency situation passes, the treaty obligations resume.[63]

---

59 Treaty between United States of America and the Argentine Republic Concerning the Reciprocal Encouragement and Protection of Investment ("US-Argentina BIT"), signed November 14, 1991, Art. IV(3), https://investmentpolicy.unctad.org/international-investment-agreements/treaty-files/127/download.

60 *Id.* at Art. XI.

61 See *LG&E Energy Corp., LG&E Capital Corp. and LG&E International Inc. v. Argentine Republic*, ICSID Case No. ARB/02/1, Decision on Liability, 3 October 2006, para. 261.

62 *Id.*

63 *Id.*

5 Interpreting Investment Treaties under the World Health Organization's International Health Regulations

Absent any specific treaty provisions addressing public health or emergencies, Article 31(3)(c) of the Vienna Convention on the Law of Treaties ("VCLT") directs that "any relevant rules of international law applicable in the relations between the parties" must still be considered when interpreting a treaty.

Such rules of international law can be found in the WHO's 2005 International Health Regulations ("IHR"), a set of rules which is legally binding on all WHO Member States.[64] In particular, the IHR limits the sovereign right of States to adopt "additional health measures," including entry regulations, in response to a disease outbreak. Thus, Article 43(2) of the IHR requires States to "base their determinations [on whether to implement health measures] upon: (a) scientific principles; (b) available scientific evidence of a risk to human health ...; and (c) any available specific guidance or advice from WHO." In addition to having a legitimate basis, under Article 43(1) of the IHR, the health measures must be the least restrictive means to achieve the appropriate level of health protection. Further, under Article 43(3) of the IHR, a State implementing health measures "which significantly interfere with international traffic shall provide to WHO the public health rationale and relevant scientific information for it." The provision defines "significant interference" as "refusal of entry or departure of international travellers, baggage, cargo, containers, conveyances, goods, and the like, or their delay, for more than 24 hours."[65]

The WHO noted in February 2020 that the economic and social effects of travel restrictions can be severe:

> In general, evidence shows that restricting the movement of people during public health emergencies is ineffective in most situations and may divert resources from other interventions. Furthermore, restrictions may interrupt needed aid and technical support, may disrupt businesses, and may have negative social and economic effects on the affected countries.[66]

---

64 See generally IHR, *supra* note 1. The IHR were adopted by the World Health Assembly under Article 21 of the WHO Constitution. Article 22 provides in relevant part that "[r]egulations adopted pursuant to Article 21 shall come into force for all Members." WHO Constitution, entered into force April 7, 1948, Arts. 21, 22, https://apps.who.int/gb/bd/pdf_files/BD_49th-en.pdf#page=6.

65 IHR, *supra* note 1, at Art. 43(3).

66 "Updated WHO Recommendations for International Traffic in Relation to COVID-19 Outbreak," WHO, February 29, 2020, https://www.who.int/news-room/articles-detail/updated-who-recommendations-for-international-traffic-in-relation-to-covid-19-outbreak.

But in April 2020, the WHO endorsed "appropriate and proportionate restrictions on non-essential domestic and international travel."[67]

Depending on the circumstances of a specific case, the IHR may influence the interpretation and application of treaty obligations concerning expropriation and FET. For example, an immigration restriction based solely on a traveler's nationality, rather than on their country or region of origin, may be found to be disproportionate because there is no rational connection between a traveler's nationality and the likelihood of infection. Conversely, differential treatment based on country or region of origin may be justified by statistics showing differing levels of infection by country or region. Uncertainty also may arise as to what travel qualifies as "essential" or "non-essential." Absent adoption of a uniform set of criteria, each country will apply its own definitions. In the event of a dispute, a tribunal likely would be able to review such definitions, applying standards of reasonableness and proportionality.

6 The *Force Majeure* Defense under International Law

Respondent States may invoke the defense of *force majeure* under customary international law against any treaty claims. The elements of *force majeure* under international law may differ from those under the national law of any given jurisdiction. The International Law Commission of the United Nations ("ILC") has codified the *force majeure* defense under customary international law as follows:

1. The wrongfulness of an act of a State not in conformity with an international obligation of that State is precluded if the act is due to *force majeure*, that is the occurrence of an irresistible force or of an unforeseen event, beyond the control of the State, making it materially impossible in the circumstances to perform the obligation.
2. Paragraph 1 does not apply if:
   (a) the situation of *force majeure* is due, either alone or in combination with other factors, to the conduct of the State invoking it; or
   (b) the State has assumed the risk of that situation occurring.[68]

67 "COVID-19 Strategy Update – 14 April 2020," WHO, April 14, 2020, 5, https://www.who.int/publications/i/item/covid-19-strategy-update---14-april-2020.

68 Articles on Responsibility of States for Internationally Wrongful Acts, Art. 23, annexed to UNGA Res. 56/83 (12 December 2001).

As the ILC's commentaries to this provision explain, the following three elements must be met: "(a) the act in question must be brought about by an irresistible force or an unforeseen event; (b) which is beyond the control of the State concerned; and (c) which makes it materially impossible in the circumstances to perform the obligation."[69] The arbitral tribunal in *Rainbow Warrior* held that *force majeure* applied only to cases of absolute and material impossibility, but not to circumstances merely rendering performance more difficult or burdensome.[70] Given this high threshold, it is not surprising that, while often invoked, the plea of *force majeure* rarely succeeds. Moreover, although the frequent inclusion of *force majeure* clauses in transnational commercial contracts has led to several decisions by arbitral tribunals involving *force majeure*, these decisions generally focus on the standard formulated in those contracts and under the chosen national law, and thus have no bearing on the standard under public international law.[71]

Additionally, when considering *force majeure* under international law, it is important to keep in mind that, even where the plea succeeds, it has the effect of precluding the wrongfulness of the government measure at issue only for the period during which the impossibility of performance persists. Once performance is no longer impossible, the underlying obligation "regains full force and effect."[72] This means that the existence of *force majeure* does not extinguish, but merely delays, the underlying obligation to perform. It does, however, exonerate the State from liability to compensate for a situation to which it did not contribute and over which it had no control.[73]

---

69 International Law Commission, "Report of the International Law Commission on the Work of its Fifty-Third Session," *Yearbook of the International Law Commission* 2, no. 2 (August 2001): 76 (Art. 23, cmt. 2).

70 *Rainbow Warrior* (*New Zealand v. France*), Award, 30 April 1990, 20 RIAA 215, at 252–253, para. 77.

71 See International Law Commission, *supra* note 69, at 78 (Art. 23, cmt. 8); James Crawford, *State Responsibility: The General Part* (United Kingdom: Cambridge University Press, 2013), 295.

72 International Law Commission, *supra* note 69, at 86 (Art. 27, cmt. 1).

73 See Articles on Responsibility of States for Internationally Wrongful Acts, *supra* note 68, at Art. 27 ("The invocation of a circumstance precluding wrongfulness in accordance with this chapter is without prejudice to: (a) compliance with the obligation in question, if and to the extent that the circumstance precluding wrongfulness no longer exists; (b) the question of compensation for any material loss caused by the act in question."); James Crawford, *supra* note 71, at 319 ("[I]t is doubtful that force majeure (arguably ... an excuse in that it does not clearly render conduct lawful; it just compels it) can give rise to an obligation to compensate. By definition, a state relying on force majeure has not contributed to the situation and so ... is no more responsible for any material loss than the state suffering it").

7 Conclusion

Undoubtedly, it will be a difficult task for tribunals to adjudicate investment treaty claims brought by foreign investors in response to emergency measures enacted by States to combat the COVID-19 pandemic. Investment treaty tribunals in the past have held that States have a margin of appreciation in exercising their sovereign powers, especially in emergency situations, but they also have reviewed such measures under the principles of reasonableness and proportionality. As such, they may scrutinize government measures to combat the COVID-19 pandemic, but they may also grant deference to States' measures given the unprecedented scale of the pandemic and the associated risks posed to public health, especially considering the limited and continuously evolving nature of scientific knowledge on how to effectively fight the pandemic.

It is important for international businesses in the construction and hospitality sectors to understand that they may have the ability to pursue international treaty claims against States for their COVID-19 responses in addition to any potential claims under their contracts. These international treaty claims provide standards under which States must act and provide methods of compensation for foreign investors who have been wronged by State actions. Foreign investors should consider their substantive treaty rights and whether State actions violated treaty obligations regarding expropriation and the fair and equitable treatment of the investors and their investments. While considering these claims, investors should be sure to investigate exceptions a State may have to these treaty obligations, such as public health or emergency exceptions, and whether these substantive rights and exceptions apply in their specific circumstances.

CHAPTER 6

The Private and Public International Law Dimension of Arbitrations Arising out of the Hospitality Industry as a Result of the COVID-19 Pandemic

Bernhard Maier and Olivia Flasch

1 Introduction

Since the beginning of the COVID-19 pandemic in early 2020,[1] disputes lawyers have been preparing for an increase in litigation and arbitration,[2] following the unprecedented scale and scope of emergency measures taken by governments worldwide in response to the virus.

These measures included far-reaching travel restrictions,[3] forced closures of businesses, and even hotel room capacity being requisitioned for other

1 "WHO Director-General's opening remarks at the media briefing on COVID-19 – 11 March 2020," World Health Organization, accessed July 16, 2021, https://www.who.int/director-general/speeches/detail/who-director-general-s-opening-remarks-at-the-media-briefing-on-covid-19---11-march-2020.

2 See "Cashing in on the pandemic: how lawyers are preparing to sue states over COVID-19 response measures," Corporate Europe Observatory, accessed July 16, 2021, https://corporateeurope.org/en/2020/05/cashing-pandemic-how-lawyers-are-preparing-sue-states-over-covid-19-response-measures; see also "Call to give companies 'breathing space' on coronavirus litigation," Financial Times, accessed July 16, 2021, https://www.ft.com/content/61bca6a9-1a12-4068-9b5d-1baa1b9dc063. In May 2020, the International Institute of Sustainable Development, a think tank, even tabled the idea of a bilateral or multilateral suspension of investment treaty arbitration in response to COVID-19 related measures. See "Consultations on a Concerted Response to COVID-19 Related ISDS Risks," International Institute of Sustainable Development, last modified June 2020, https://www.iisd.org/events/consultations-concerted-response-covid-19-related-isds-risks-0.

3 Interestingly, as of August 23, 2021, travellers from the US were able to enter the EU and the UK but not *vice versa*, leading to questions as to the motivation behind travel bans and their manifest negative (and potentially one-sided) impact on transatlantic trade in goods and services. See Elena Sánchez Nicolás, "EU and UK frustrated at US travel ban extension," EU Observer, July 29, 2021, https://euobserver.com/coronavirus/152557.

 | DOI:10.1163/9789004514874_008

purposes.[4] As a result of some of these measures, valuable assets such as cruise-ships and aircrafts have had to be mothballed, often at great expense to their owners and operators.[5]

Due to its high dependence on the physical movement of individuals – both domestically and internationally – the hospitality sector[6] has suffered disproportionately from wide-ranging and restrictive government measures in response to the pandemic.[7] While a number of governments put in place interim support packages,[8] questions will arise as to whether these support measures were applied fairly, evenly and for a sufficient duration. The appropriate balancing of national public health imperatives with economic considerations will be one of the key questions occupying politicians and lawyers alike.

In Britain, travel companies and industry associations criticized the government's constantly changing[9] "traffic light" system for travel destinations as

4 See Mark Townsend, "UK hotels to become homeless shelters under coronavirus plan," The Guardian, March 21, 2020, https://www.theguardian.com/world/2020/mar/21/uk-hotels-homeless-shelters-coronavirus.

5 See "Coronavirus: Airlines all over the world park planes as pandemic plays out," USA Today, accessed July 16, 2021, https://eu.usatoday.com/picture-gallery/travel/airline-news/2020/04/09/coronavirus-airlines-all-over-world-park-planes-amid-pandemic/5122560002/; Richard Luscombe, "End of the cruise? Industry struggles through rough waters of coronavirus crisis," The Guardian, March 16, 2020, https://www.theguardian.com/travel/2020/mar/16/end-of-the-cruise-industry-struggles-through-rough-waters-of-coronavirus-crisis; Will Feuer and Seema Mody, "CDC bans U.S. cruises through September, citing 'ongoing' coronavirus outbreaks on ships," CNBC, July 16, 2020, https://www.cnbc.com/2020/07/16/cdc-bans-us-cruises-through-september-citing-expanding-coronavirus-outbreaks.html; see also "Spain maintains ban on cruise ships even as tourism sector reopens," CGTN, June 28, 2020, https://news.cgtn.com/news/2020-06-28/Spain-maintains-ban-on-cruise-ships-even-as-tourism-sector-reopens-RGRvQWMfss/index.html.

6 Strictly speaking, the hospitality industry comprises businesses such as hotels, bars, and restaurants that offer people food, drink, or a place to sleep. However, and because there is a significant interrelationship between the hospitality industry and the travel industry, this paper will also address potential disputes involving the latter.

7 See "BA warns Gatwick staff it may not resume flights there," Financial Times, accessed July 16, 2021, https://www.ft.com/content/5e9f183f-2866-471a-b60b-3b1471686272; see also "British Airways owner IAG slashes flight schedules as losses hit €1.3bn," Financial Times, accessed July 16, 2021, https://www.ft.com/content/b48b036c-5e34-45ea-a059-71d2cafe6792.

8 See Larry Elliott, "Rishi Sunak unveils £4.6bn relief package for UK retail and hospitality sectors," The Guardian, January 5, 2021, https://www.theguardian.com/politics/2021/jan/05/rishi-sunak-unveils-46bn-relief-package-for-uk-retail-and-hospitality-sectors.

9 Gwyn Topham, "COVID traffic light system could cost UK airports £2.6bn this summer," The Guardian, June 10, 2021, https://www.theguardian.com/business/2021/jun/10/covid-traffic-light-system-uk-airports-summer-airline.

arbitrary and devoid of any scientific basis.[10] The uncertain, unpredictable and ever-changing nature of some restrictions made meaningful commercial planning nearly impossible for the hospitality sector.

What legal recourse, if any, is available to actors in the hospitality industry who were and continue to be impacted by the emergency measures? Under what circumstances and to what extent can hospitality companies seek compensation? What defences, if any, are available to governments where allegations of breaches of national and international law are levied against them? What level of hindsight, if any, will courts and tribunals apply in deciding legal disputes?

In attempting to answer these questions, this chapter will frame the legal debate around potential areas of dispute between private actors in the hospitality sector on the one hand and States and State entities on the other. Rather than focusing on specific jurisdictions, this paper will aim to provide a snapshot of the international dimension of these disputes, with reference to relevant national legislation and international legal instruments, where appropriate.

At the heart of this debate is the tension between a State's sovereign right to regulate its internal affairs in the face of a crisis and compliance with its international obligations, whether under bilateral or multilateral treaties or otherwise. This is of course also relevant to global emergency scenarios beyond the pandemic.

2 What International Obligations Do Governments Owe Actors in the Hospitality Sector and What Would Amount to a Breach of These Obligations?

Host state obligations *vis-à-vis* qualifying investors are enshrined in international law instruments such as bilateral or multilateral investment agreements or private law contracts such as concession agreements or public private partnership frameworks. In the aftermath of the pandemic, bilateral investment treaties ("BITS") are likely to be useful tools in the toolkit of foreign investors in the hospitality sector. The substantive protection standard clauses of BITS may offer qualifying foreign investors the ability, in certain narrowly defined circumstances, to seek compensation from the host State for the adverse economic effects of actions taken by, or otherwise attributable to, the State.

10 Julia Buckley, "How the UK's travel regulations fell behind the rest of Europe," CNN, June 21, 2021, https://edition.cnn.com/travel/article/uk-travel-regulations-industry-future/index.html.

By way of example, the fair and equitable treatment clause allows investors in certain circumstances to hold host States to written or verbal assurances made in relation to specific projects. The foreign investor seeking to rely on this substantive protection standard will need to demonstrate that these assurances were sufficient to establish actionable expectations.

In this regard, a foreign investor – such as a large hotel or restaurant group, travel agency or airport operator – might argue that a temporary reduction in certain taxes to protect struggling hospitality businesses from insolvency[11] gives rise to an expectation that these taxes will not be levied retroactively at a later date. Tax authorities may be tempted to do so in specific circumstances, for example if it turns out that revenues for certain businesses were higher during the pandemic than originally anticipated. These expectations will of course need to be balanced with a government's right to take appropriate measures to safeguard public health. Governments will likely be afforded significant latitude, especially to account for that fact that certain decisions may appear arbitrary, discriminatory or unfair with the benefit of hindsight. As such, the judicial interpretation of a host State's inherent "right to regulate" as well as the "police powers doctrine" will take center stage.

Another standard BIT provision that hospitality businesses may seek to rely on is the so-called "umbrella clause." Depending on the precise wording, this provision can elevate the breach of an investment agreement (ordinarily a private law contract) to a breach of the relevant treaty (and thus cause it to be governed by principles of public international law). What is more, even obligations assumed through unilateral declarations, such as legislative acts or executive decrees, may be protected by an umbrella clause. In the hospitality context, this could translate into claims pursued against a host State following emergency changes to a licensing or taxation regime. The provision may also be invoked in circumstances where, as a result of the pandemic, a host State considers itself relieved from certain contractual obligations entered into with a foreign investor in the hospitality sector.

Foreign investors may also rely on the most-favored-nation clause in raising a claim against a host State. Governments worldwide have put in place significant rescue packages for companies adversely impacted by the pandemic.[12]

---

11 See "UKHospitality Budget Submission January 2021," UKHospitality, accessed July 16, 2021, https://view.publitas.com/ukh/ukh-budget-submission-january-2021/page/1.

12 For example, financial and fiscal aid for small and medium-sized enterprises include measures such as guaranteed recovery of delayed payments, indirect financing to suppliers through their buyers, tax credits and other fiscal benefits to firms and co-financing of development programmes. See "Investment Policy Monitor – Investment Policy Responses

Where this financial support is deployed unequally and in a discriminatory fashion – preferring certain hospitality companies over others – there may be scope for seeking compensation under applicable treaties. Specific questions of state aid and EU competition law may also arise but are outside the scope of this paper.

A BIT may also give a qualifying foreign investor the ability to seek direct recourse against a host State before an international tribunal, rather than having to seek recourse before the local courts of the host State. This means that in certain circumstances a foreign investor may have better prospects of obtaining appropriate compensation than a comparable hospitality enterprise incorporated in and owned by nationals of the host State. As such, domestic investors may be "protected less than foreign investors covered by investor-state arbitration treaties because there is no domestic recovery for public interest or non-public interest regulation."[13]

As at early 2022, the authors are aware of only one action initiated by a foreign investor against a host State for alleged violations of the substantive protection provisions of a BIT (or any other international investment agreement) for alleged losses suffered as a result of measures implemented in response to the pandemic. *ADP v Chile*[14] was initiated on 13 August 2021 and arises out of Chile's reported refusal to renegotiate the terms of an airport concession despite the investor incurring significant losses as a result of the pandemic. In the authors' view, future claims of this nature are highly likely.

3 What Legal Defences Are Available to States?

Having identified some of the potential legal causes of action against a host State, it is also essential to address potential host State defences. This section will discuss individual rights in the human rights sphere as well as potentially compensable rights in the investment treaty context.

---

to the COVID-19 Pandemic," United Nations Conference on Trade and Development, May 2020 https://unctad.org/system/files/official-document/diaepcbinf2020d3_en.pdf.

13 Alison Giest, "Interpreting Public Interest Provisions in International Investment Treaties," *Chicago Journal of International Law* 18, no. 1 (2017): 321, 334.

14 *ADP International S.A. and Vinci Airports S.A.S. v Republic of Chile*, ICSID Case No. ARB/21/40.

3.1 *The State of Emergency in the Context of Human Rights*

By early 2020, all 50 US states as well as the federal government had declared a state of emergency under US law.[15] The US was not alone. 108 countries worldwide had, in 2021, officially declared a national emergency pursuant to their respective national legislation.[16] These declarations granted the relevant national and state governments the power to pass emergency legislation in order to maintain public safety, regardless of whether these measures restricted fundamental rights. In most cases, this legislation was notoriously difficult, if not impossible, to challenge before local courts.[17] In the context of the COVID-19 pandemic, this included issuing far-reaching stay-at-home orders, bans on gatherings and the closure of certain businesses.[18]

States of emergencies had also been declared in the human rights context.[19] By 2021, nine member states[20] of the Council of Europe had notified the Council of their intention to invoke Article 15 of the European Convention

15 On 13 March 2020, then-US President Donald Trump issued Proclamation 9994, declaring that the COVID-19 outbreak constitutes a national emergency. See U.S. President, Proclamation, "Declaring a National Emergency Concerning the Novel Coronavirus Disease (COVID–19) Outbreak," *Federal Register* 85, no. 53 (18 March 2021): 15337, https://www.federalregister.gov/documents/2020/03/18/2020-05794/declaring-a-national-emergency-concerning-the-novel-coronavirus-disease-covid-19-outbreak.

16 "COVID-19 Civic Freedom Tracker," ICNL, accessed July 16, 2021, https://www.icnl.org/covid19tracker/?location=&issue=5&date=&type=.

17 "Briefing – States of emergency in response to the coronavirus crisis: Situation in certain Member States IV," European Parliamentary Research Service, July 2020, https://www.europarl.europa.eu/RegData/etudes/BRIE/2020/652002/EPRS_BRI(2020)652002_EN.pdf.

18 *E.g.*, measures ordered in: 1) South Africa: Disaster Management Act 2002: Amendment of Regulations Issued in Terms of Section 27(2), GN R. 398 of GG 43148 (March 25, 2020); 2) France: "Coronavirus: Spain and France announce sweeping restrictions," BBC, March 15, 2020, https://www.bbc.co.uk/news/world-europe-51892477; 3) Italy: "Italy suspends all China flights as coronavirus cases confirmed in Rome," The Local, January 31, 2020, https://www.thelocal.it/20200131/italy-suspends-all-china-flights-after-coronavirus-cases-confirmed-in-rome/; 4) UK: "Coronavirus: UK brings in strict curbs on life to fight virus," BBC, March 24, 2020, https://www.bbc.co.uk/news/uk-52014472.

19 Audrey Lebret, "COVID-19 pandemic and derogation to human rights," *Journal of Law and the Biosciences* 7, no. 1 (2020): 1–15.

20 Albania, Armenia, Estonia, Georgia, Latvia, North Macedonia, Republic of Moldova, Romania, San Marino, Serbia – see full list at "Reservations and Declarations for Treaty No. 005 – Convention for the Protection of Human Rights and Fundamental Freedoms," Council of Europe, accessed July 16, 2021, https://www.coe.int/en/web/conventions/full-list/-/conventions/treaty/005/declarations?module=declarations-by-treaty&numSte=005&codeNature=0.

on Human Rights ("ECHR") as a response to the COVID-19 pandemic.[21] Article 15 "affords to Contracting States, in exceptional circumstances, the possibility of derogating, in a limited and supervised manner, from their obligations to secure certain rights and freedoms under the Convention."[22] This is a significant step beyond the margin of appreciation afforded to Member States in non-emergency situations pursuant to Article 1 to the Protocol to the ECHR. Article 1 to the Protocol emphasizes a Member State's right "to enforce such laws as it deems necessary to control the use of property in accordance with the general interest."[23]

Not all the Contracting States who invoked Article 15 of the ECHR specified which precise rights they intended to derogate from. Of those States which did specify particular rights, there is a notable emphasis on derogations from Article 5 (right to liberty and security), Article 6 (right to a fair trial), Article 8 (right to respect for private and family life) and Article 11 (freedom of assembly and association) of the ECHR, Article 2 of the Additional Protocol (right to education) and Article 2 of Protocol No. 4 (freedom of movement).[24]

Similarly, ten Latin American States derogated from the American Convention on Human Rights, using its equivalent provision, Article 27.[25]

21 Some of these notifications were made in early 2020 and have now been withdrawn, whereas others are still in force and/or were made in 2021. "Reservations and Declarations for Treaty No.005 – Convention for the Protection of Human Rights and Fundamental Freedoms," Council of Europe, accessed July 16, 2021, https://www.coe.int/en/web/conventions/full-list/-/conventions/treaty/005/declarations?module=declarations-by-treaty&numSte=005&codeNature=0.

22 European Convention for the Protection of Human Rights and Fundamental Freedoms, entered into force September 3, 1953, 213 U.N.T.S. 222, Article 15(1), which states: "*In time of war or other public emergency threatening the life of the nation any High Contracting Party may take measures derogating from its obligations under [the] Convention to the extent strictly required by the exigencies of the situation, provided that such measures are not inconsistent with its other obligations under international law.*"

23 Article 1 of the Protocol to the Convention for the Protection of Human Rights and Fundamental Freedoms, Treaty No.009, which entered into force on 18 May 1954, https://rm.coe.int/168006377c.

24 Council of Europe, *supra* note 21.

25 American Convention on Human Rights "Pact of San Jose, Costa Rica," entered into force July 18, 1978, 1144 U.N.T.S. 123, Article 27, which states: "*In time of war, public danger, or other emergency that threatens the independence or security of a State Party, it may take measures derogating from its obligations under the present Convention to the extent and for the period of time strictly required by the exigencies of the situation, provided that such measures are not inconsistent with its other obligations under international law and do not involve discrimination on the ground of race, color, sex, language, religion, or social origin.*" Kushtrim Istrefi and Isabel Humburg, "To Notify or Not To Notify," Opinio Juris, April 18, 2020,

Additionally, at least 14 countries notified the UN Secretary-General of their intention to derogate from the International Covenant on Civil and Political Rights as a result of the pandemic.[26]

Through these notifications, countries made use of their express legal right to be relieved from certain of their international legal obligations for the duration of the pandemic. State measures prohibiting people from attending certain public venues and forcing such venues to remain closed struck at the core of fundamental freedoms such as the freedom of movement and the freedom of assembly. As a consequence of these and other derogations, industries such as the hospitality and travel industries were negatively impacted.

Importantly, if States can attain their public policy objectives without invoking measures which limit human rights, they are under an obligation to do so.[27] However, during the pandemic, States faced the nearly impossible task of balancing public health policy with the fundamental rights of individuals on the basis of imperfect information. As a result of the wide discretion afforded to States during the pandemic under existing human rights legislation and the uncertainty surrounding COVID-19, any *ex post facto* procedural and substantive review of States' exercise of their emergency power is likely to be limited.

3.2 *The Right to Regulate and Emergency Clauses in Investment Treaties*

In addition to declaring an internal state of emergency in order to suspend national and international legal obligations in the human rights context, States also have a customary international law right to regulate and to exercise their police powers in the public interest. This includes measures to protect public health. The manner in which this right is exercised and its interplay with international law obligations is subject to significant discussion in international investment law. This right is supplemented by express treaty provisions emphasizing a State's right – not only in times of crisis – to take certain measures that would otherwise be contrary to their international law obligations.[28]

---

https://opiniojuris.org/2020/04/18/to-notify-or-not-to-notify-derogations-from-human-rights-treaties/.

26 "Derogations by States Parties from Article 21 ICCPR, Article 11 ECHR, and Article 15 ACHR on the Basis of the COVID-19 Pandemic," Laws on the Right Of Peaceful Assembly Worldwide, accessed September 16, 2021, https://www.rightofassembly.info/news/states-begin-to-derogate-from-the-right-of-assembly-owing-to-the-covid-19-pandemic.

27 Emilie M. Hafner-Burton, Laurence R. Helfer, and Christopher J. Fariss, "Emergency and Escape: Explaining Derogations from Human Rights Treaties," *International Organization* 65, no. 4 (October 2011): 680.

28 Article 2(3) of the Hungary-Russia BIT provides that "[t]*his Agreement shall not preclude the application of either Contracting Party of measures, necessary for the … protection of … public health.*" Agreement between the Government of the Republic of Hungary and the

One of the key questions relevant to both concepts is whether and to what extent they are self-judging and how much deference should be given to a State's internal decision-making processes when faced with a crisis. To what extent should hindsight play a role when scrutinizing these decisions *ex post facto*, especially when many of them were based on scientific data that was far from perfect?

A number of recent arbitration tribunals were tasked with scrutinizing the legal consequences of the exercise of host States' regulatory discretion in the health context. For example, in *Philip Morris v. Uruguay*,[29] the claimant argued that Uruguay's anti-smoking campaign was devaluing its investments in the country and pursued a claim under the Uruguay-Switzerland BIT. It alleged that Uruguay's actions constituted indirect expropriation, a breach of the fair and equitable treatment standard and arbitrary, discriminatory and unreasonable measures.

Uruguay argued that the measures it took "were adopted in compliance with [its] international obligations, including the BIT, for the single purpose of protecting public health."[30] The tribunal accepted Uruguay's defence on these grounds and emphasized that investment tribunals "should pay deference to governmental judgments of national needs in matters such as the protection of public health."[31]

Importantly, the tribunal noted that the concept of the "margin of appreciation" as enshrined in Article 1 of the Protocol to the ECHR "is not limited to the context of the ECHR but 'applies equally to claims arising under BITs,' at least in contexts such as public health."[32] Referring to a number of previous

---

Government of the Russian Federation for the Promotion and Reciprocal Protection of Investments (Hungary-Russian Federation BIT), entered into force May 29, 1996, UNCTAD Investment Policy Hub, https://investmentpolicy.unctad.org/international-investment-agreements/treaties/bilateral-investment-treaties/1895/hungary---russian-federation-bit-1995-, accessed September 16, 2021. Similarly, Article 6.16 of the Peru-Singapore FTA provides that "*Nothing ... shall limit the authority of a Party to determine the level of protection it considers necessary for the protection of, inter alia, human health or safety, animal or plant life or health. In pursuance of this, each Party retains all authority to interpret its laws, regulations and administrative provisions.*" Free Trade Agreement between Singapore and Peru, entered into force August 1, 2009, Organization of American States Foreign Trade Information System, accessed September 16, 2021, http://www.sice.oas.org/TPD/PER_SGP/Final_Texts_PER_SGP_e/index_e.asp.

29 *Philip Morris Brands Sàrl, Philip Morris Products S.A. and Abal Hermanos S.A. v. Oriental Republic of Uruguay*, ICSID Case No. ARB/10/7.

30 *Id. at* para. 13.

31 *Id. at* para. 399.

32 *Id.*

decisions on this point, the *Philip Morris* tribunal emphasized the importance of respecting the "discretionary exercise of sovereign power not made irrationally and not exercised in bad faith [...] involving many complex factors."[33]

In other words, the *Philip Morris* decision suggests that unless a claimant can show that a State's decision was manifestly irrational, States enjoy a very wide level of discretion to enact legislation and to take steps designed to safeguard public health. This is likely to be the case even if a host State's actions materially and adversely affect certain foreign investments.

In *Chemtura v. Canada*, a tribunal was tasked with weighing the apparent health benefits of a ban on lindane-based products with the commercial interests of a US manufacturer of agricultural pesticide products. Having evaluated Canada's decision-making process, the tribunal found that the ban had been motivated by "scientific and public policy considerations"[34] rather than driven by an improper motive.

Given the far-reaching actions of governments worldwide in the face of the pandemic, future courts and tribunals will almost certainly be tasked with weighing health-related measures with the detrimental economic effects suffered by foreign investors in the hospitality sector as a result of these measures.

While each case will of course turn on its own facts and the precise wording of the applicable national and international legal instruments, legal challenges will have to overcome a threshold of almost complete deference to national policy. This will especially be the case where governments' decisions were taken quickly and in circumstances where scientific data relating to the spread of the virus may have been unavailable, incomplete or unreliable. The *Chemtura v. Canada* tribunal placed significant weight on the fact that the measures taken were "based on valid science."[35] One can easily envision many hundreds of pages of written advocacy expended on what constitutes "*valid*" science when viewed in connection with a virus as complex and dangerous as COVID-19.

3.3 *The State of Necessity as a Circumstance Precluding Wrongfulness*

The customary international law defence of necessity was codified in Article 25 of the International Law Commission's Draft Articles on State Responsibility.[36]

33 *Id.* (Internal quotation marks and citations omitted).

34 *Chemtura Corporation v. Canada*, Final Award, ICGJ 464 (PCA 2010), August 2, 2010, paragraph 123.

35 *Id. at* para. 254.

36 *Report of the International Law Commission to the General Assembly*, "Draft articles on Responsibility of States for Internationally Wrongful Acts with commentaries 2001," UN Doc A/56/49(Vol. I)/Corr.4.

Its practical application is contingent on the State being able to satisfy a number of very strict conditions. The condition relevant to the present discussion is that the State needs to show that the measures in question were the only way for the State to safeguard an essential interest against a grave and imminent peril. This is a high threshold to meet. It also requires courts and tribunals faced with a plea of necessity to engage in a substantive analysis of the measures in question and to evaluate whether other, less restrictive avenues were open to the State to achieve the same objective.

In practice, this means that it is very difficult for States to invoke this defence successfully.[37] Demonstrating that the breach in question was the only way to safeguard the essential interest at stake is particularly challenging.[38]

Furthermore, the successful invocation of a state of necessity does not necessarily prevent the respondent State from having to compensate the Claimant for any damage that may have resulted from the measure in question during the period of necessity.[39] This may therefore be of limited use to States seeking to excuse the non-performance of their international obligations *vis-à-vis* actors in the hospitality sector.

The defence is also not entirely self-judging. In the *von Pezold v Zimbabwe* case, the tribunal was tasked with considering whether Zimbabwe's national declaration of a state of emergency gave it the automatic right to rely on the state of necessity defence under public international law, thereby excusing the alleged breaches of the treaties in question. The tribunal disagreed. It concluded that "the international law analysis is not affected by the domestic

37 As is well-known, the concept received a significant amount of coverage in the aftermath of the Argentinian financial crisis around 1999, when a rapid devaluation of the national currency and a number of other legislative measures severely harmed many foreign investors' investments in the country. The plea of necessity was accepted in the following cases: *LG&E Energy Corp., LG&E Capital Corp., and LG&E International, Inc. v. Argentine Republic*, ICSID Case No. ARB/02/1, *Continental Casualty Company v. The Argentine Republic*, ICSID Case No. ARB/03/9; *Total S.A. v. The Argentine Republic*, ICSID Case No. ARB/04/01; *Urbaser S.A. and Consorcio de Aguas Bilbao Bizkaia, Bilbao Biskaia Ur Partzuergoa v. The Argentine Republic*, ICSID Case No. ARB/07/26.

38 See CMS *v. Argentina*, where the tribunal concluded "*that the measures adopted were not the only steps available.*" It did so, recognising that to determine "[w]*hich of* [the] *policy alternatives would have been better is a decision beyond the scope of the Tribunal's task, which is to establish whether there was only one way or various ways and thus whether the requirements for the conclusion of wrongfulness have or have not been met.*" *CMS Gas Transmission Company v. Argentine Republic*, ICSID Case No. ARB/01/8, Award, 12 May 2005, para. 323–324.

39 *Report of the International Law Commission to the General Assembly*, *supra* note 36, at article 27(b).

test."[40] Accordingly, a domestic declaration of a state of emergency will likely be only one of many factors in a tribunal's analysis as to whether a necessity defence is successfully made out.

4 To What Extent Does the WHO's Designation of COVID-19 as a "Pandemic" Enable States to Evade Their Legal Obligations *vis-à-vis* Third Parties?

In addition to a declaration of an emergency under national law, the categorisation of the spread of COVID-19 as a "pandemic" by the World Health Organization (the "WHO") in March 2020 may be another relevant factor in an enquiry as to whether a State's non-performance of its international obligations can or cannot be excused.

In *Philip Morris*, the fact that the anti-smoking measures taken by Uruguay were based on the recommendations of the WHO was an important factor in the tribunal's decision.[41] In fact, the WHO even submitted an *amicus curiae* brief to the arbitral tribunal in support of Uruguay's position on this point.[42]

Of the countries which derogated from the International Covenant on Civil and Political Rights, at least 12 referred to the WHO's designation of COVID-19 as a pandemic and/or the WHO's recommendations as to public health measures in their notifications to the UN Secretary-General.[43] At least four of the ten countries who notified the Council of Europe of their intention to invoke Article 15 ECHR also referred to the WHO's designation by way of justification.

The WHO's classification is also relevant outside the realm of human rights. Commentators have suggested that COVID-19 has a greater chance of being considered a *force majeure* event in the context of contracts following the designation of the virus as a pandemic by the WHO.[44] Future *force majeure* clauses

---

40 *Bernhard von Pezold and Others v. Republic of Zimbabwe*, ICSID Case No. ARB/10/15, para. 624.

41 *Philip Morris Brands Sàrl, Philip Morris Products S.A. and Abal Hermanos S.A. supra* note 29, at para. 306.

42 See *Philip Morris Brands Sàrl, Philip Morris Products S.A. and Abal Hermanos S.A. v. Oriental Republic of Uruguay*, ICSID Case No. ARB/10/7, Written Submission (Amicus Curiae Brief) by the WHO and the Secretariat of the Tobacco Control Convention, January 28, 2015, https://www.italaw.com/cases/460.

43 See notifications issued in relation to Treaty IV.4 (the ICCPR) at "Depositary Notifications (CNs by the Secretary-General," United Nations Treaty Collections, accessed July 16, 2021, https://treaties.un.org/Pages/CNs.aspx?cnTab=tab2&clang=_en).

44 See Peter de Verneuil Smith, Adam Kramer, and William Day, "COVID-19: force majeure, frustration and illegality in English law: a detailed guide," Practical Law, April 20, 2021,

may even expressly refer to the WHO as the authoritative body in determining the commencement and the end of a pandemic as a *force majeure* event.

Resolutions, recommendations, and designations issued by the WHO are not legally binding instruments. They do however represent a degree of consensus between the member states of the WHO. The World Health Assembly, the decision-making body of the WHO is composed of delegates from all member states.[45] Decision-making is carried out by simple majority (one State, one vote), but virtually all decisions are adopted by consensus. As such, reference to the WHO's designation of COVID-19 as a pandemic can be interpreted as a reference to the common understanding of 194 countries.[46]

Arguably, in the same way that a national declaration of a state of emergency may serve as evidence of the existence of a state of necessity under customary international law,[47] a reference to the WHO's designation of COVID-19 as a "pandemic" will serve as persuasive evidence that an emergency clause in an investment agreement has been invoked in good faith.

5 Is There a Broader Duty to Compensate?

Neither the derogation clauses in human rights instruments nor the emergency clauses in investment agreements directly address the impact on the level of compensation otherwise due where an investor suffers economic damage as a result of genuine emergency measures. Whether compensation is due and, if so, the level of damages owed will therefore depend on the language of the treaty or treaties pursuant to which the claim in question is pursued. Is the defensive mechanism an exception, *i.e.*, does it limit the substantive scope of a party's obligation, or is it a complete defence, *i.e.*, does it preclude the wrongfulness of the party's action altogether?

In the latter case, there is arguably no right to compensation at all because no legal obligation has been breached in the first place. In the former case, the obligation to compensate and the level of damages are subject to legal debate.

https://uk.practicallaw.thomsonreuters.com/w-024-6685?transitionType=Default&contextData=(sc.Default)&firstPage=true.

45 "Governance," World Health Organization, accessed July 16, 2021, https://www.who.int/about/governance.

46 "Countries," World Health Organization, accessed July 16, 2021, https://www.who.int/countries.

47 See *Bernhard von Pezold and Others, supra* note 40.

For example, an international court or tribunal could reasonably conclude that despite a State successfully relying on the pandemic as a justification for its breach of a treaty obligation *vis-à-vis* a foreign investor in the hospitality sector, compensation to that investor for the breach should still be due. A basis for this approach can also be found in certain national laws. For example, the UK Compensation (Defence) Act 1939 recognizes the right of the executive branch of government to take certain measures in a time of emergency but specifies that when such measures involve the expropriation of private property, compensation must be paid to the property owner nonetheless.[48]

By contrast, US law provides that where the government has imposed a regulation which effectively expropriates an individual's property, the government is not expected to compensate that individual when the regulation imposed is designed to prevent a public nuisance.[49] This debate is ongoing in the context of investment treaty arbitrations, with some commentators arguing that the right to regulate in the public interest and investors' rights should be balanced at the remedies stage of an arbitration, and not just at the merits stage.[50]

In the UK, it has so far proven difficult for hospitality companies to secure compensation for government actions taken during the pandemic. In a recent English case, the court found that two hospitality executives were not eligible to be compensated by the English government for a mandatory five-week pub closure on the basis that the government measures in question had been taken on the basis of the "*best scientific evidence available at the time.*"[51]

6 Conclusion

The significant duration, scope, and human and economic consequences of the pandemic have resulted in governments applying the widest possible

---

48 UK Compensation (Defence) Act, 1939, Section 1.

49 Alison Giest, *supra* note 13, citing to Vicki Been & Joel Beauvais, "The Global Fifth Amendment? NAFTA's Investment Protections and the Misguided Quest for an International 'Regulatory Takings' Doctrine," 78 New York University Law Review 78 (2003): 30, 31, at para. 94, citing *Lucas v. South Carolina Coastal Council*, 505 U.S. 1003, 1029 (1992).

50 Margaret B Devaney, "Remedies in Investor-State Arbitration: A Public Interest Perspective," IISD, March 13, 2013, https://www.iisd.org/itn/en/2013/03/22/remedies-in-investor-state-arbitration-a-public-interest-perspective/.

51 (*On the Application of Sacha Lord and Hugh Osmond*) *v Secretary of State for Health and Social Care*. *See* "Hospitality bosses lose court battle over indoor opening," BBC, May 3, 2021, https://www.bbc.co.uk/news/business-56974835.

discretion in the way they have framed their legal, political, and economic responses. In implementing wide-ranging emergency measures, States have often had no choice but to derogate from their international legal obligations.

Actors in the hospitality industry who were – and remain – adversely affected by the implementation of these measures will need to find creative legal solutions to challenge the exercise of this considerable governmental discretion, both under national and international law. This is particularly so given that the scientific data relating to the pandemic is vast, complex, and likely imperfect.

Courts and tribunals will be faced with the difficult task of scrutinizing governments' decision-making processes and thereby imposing – with the benefit of hindsight – a final set of checks and balances on the *prima facie* unfettered decision-making powers available to governments when dealing with this unprecedented global health crisis.

PART 2

Introduction: Construction Disputes

Katherine Simpson

The ability to adapt to changing circumstances and find solutions to emerging problems are characteristics that the construction industry and the alternative dispute resolution sector share. Throughout the pandemic, each demonstrated its resilience and ability to adapt and thrive.

During the pandemic, parts of the construction sector were publicly declared to be "essential," meaning that work was required to continue despite "lockdowns" and other governmental restrictions that prevented most individuals from leaving their homes. Construction professionals built, maintained, and repaired essential public infrastructure at a time when nearly all other work stopped.

While never publicly declared as such, the alternative dispute resolution sector demonstrated that it is, indeed, "essential" to the continued functioning of the legal system. The so-called "court" of arbitration was the only court that was open and resolving disputes throughout the pandemic. While state courts shuttered, arbitrators around the world were actively engaged in lawfully resolving disputes with final effect, using virtual, telephonic, or other means. Mediators, too, broke new ground by assisting disputants in finding agreed solutions to pressing problems, likewise using virtual means. Labor mediators even helped unions and employers reach new agreements, using the same Internet-based technology that made virtual arbitration hearings a success.

During the pandemic, alternative dispute resolution proved itself to be the safest, most predictable, and reliable means of dispute resolution, and this remains true today. Meeting virtually, arbitration and mediation participants shielded themselves from external threats and variables, including those related to weather, pandemic-related and other illness, and venue-related issues. Arbitrators proved able to render fully enforceable awards and decisions, in a timely manner, following private and confidential hearings that included witness examination. Lawyers and court-reporters alike thrived in the virtual setting, performing at least as well if not better than they had in the "in person" world.

Virtual and remote procedures were so beneficial that, following the pandemic, many businesses and governments have discovered that, even when work is "in person," they prefer to be online. Virtual dispute resolution's

 | DOI:10.1163/9789004514874_009

flexibility lets relevant witnesses testify as needed, rather than letting each hearing day cost the entire team one day's work, as had been the case when in-person hearings were the norm.

Similarly, some aspects of the construction sector have changed permanently. Some governmental permit offices, for example, require electronic rather than paper submission of building proposals, and some require telephonic meetings or email, rather than in-person communications.

The pandemic has changed how the construction industry and the alternative dispute resolution sector conduct business. Of course, in the alternative dispute resolution sector, none of this was possible without agreements that called for arbitration of disputes, and without party willingness to engage in virtual or "not in person"-proceedings. It remains to be seen how these procedures might be adopted in the construction industry.

The ability to resolve complex construction disputes through a flexible, neutral, and enforceable dispute resolution process has proven valuable to the international construction and engineering firms, owners, employers, and financiers alike. Construction contracts often rely on alternative dispute resolution and contain multi-tier dispute resolution mechanisms, involving a standing dispute resolution board, mediation, and then arbitration. These strict mechanisms and their in-person requirements may have prevented the construction sector from taking full advantage of the technology now available to assist parties in resolving disputes. Indeed, the resolution of some construction disputes was undoubtedly delayed by an inability to agree on alternative dispute resolution mechanisms that could function in a "lockdown" society. These claims could be filed in the coming months or years.

By some estimates, the construction sector represents approximately 13% of the world's Gross Domestic Product and employs an estimated 7–8% of the global workforce. This industry confronted every issue that one could expect to arise from a pandemic with global lockdowns: labor shortages, supply shortages, transportation delays, contractor insolvency, and dramatic changes in law that either prevented their work or required that work continue. The potential for investor-state arbitration in response to these conflicting demands on specific construction projects, and in relation to the field generally, remains a possibility.

While the large scale "lockdowns" associated with the COVID-19 pandemic are hopefully over, the full extent of dispute resolution in respect of matters affecting the construction sector from March 2020 onward may not be truly clear for years. Indeed, as of the drafting of this introduction, the March 2020 start of the COVID-19 pandemic and its related closures is still within the statutory limitations period for claims arising in a variety of jurisdictions. The world could be at the pre-dawn or even dawn of COVID-related construction claims. The following chapters enable the reader to envision the myriad ways and fora where these cases may present in the near future.

CHAPTER 7

Abeyance to Resuscitation – Construction Arbitration in the Post-COVID Era

Gautam Mohanty and Yasaschandra Devarakonda

1 Introduction

The international construction industry has been one of the most impacted sectors because of the COVID-19 pandemic. Global supply networks, which are quintessential for equipment, materials, plants, and personnel were disrupted due to various restrictive governmental measures, including lockdowns, quarantines, and other related measures. Such disruptions inevitably resulted in disputes which required an in-depth examination of the general principles governing such global supply networks. The expected impacts of COVID-19 on the construction industry must be examined through the lens of dispute resolution, especially arbitration. As government-imposed restrictions became a reality, it is imperative to assess whether COVID-19 will result in a paradigm shift in disputes arising out of construction projects. It is likely that the disputes emanating from disruptions caused by COVID-19 will be premised on the delay, procurement, and execution phases of construction projects. This will inevitably also include claims relating to costs in execution and cash flow, as it is a fairly common practice to make payments to contractors subject to the achievement of predetermined milestones or various other metrics of progress defined in the agreement.

Considering impairments caused by COVID-19, claims for extensions of time, the prolongation of costs, additional payments, and/or a levy of liquidated damages for the delay in completion of contractual milestones were amplified. Among many recourses available, including potential claims invoking "change in law" provisions triggered by government-imposed COVID-19 restrictions, claims for commercial impracticability of contractual performance and the resulting reliance on either the civil law remedy of hardship and adaptation *via* selective application of the Convention on International Sale of Goods or the common law remedy of impossibility of performance, and *force majeure* are few recourses, the application of which will add another layer of complexity. An in-depth analysis of the expected impacts of COVID-19 on construction arbitration is thus imperative.

 | DOI:10.1163/9789004514874_010

Specifically, there should first be a general overview of the measures adopted in several countries concerning the construction industry. Next, there should be a discussion on contractual and extra-contractual defenses, which will likely have significance in the resolution of disputes by arbitration, such as change in law, hardship, *force majeure*, and other related defenses. Lastly, there should be an analysis regarding the possible impacts of COVID-19 on arbitration and how arbitration in the construction industry must adapt considering the challenges presented by COVID-19, especially when recourse and reliance upon virtual technologies are enhanced.

2 Lockdown Measures in the Construction Industry

In response to the COVID-19 crisis, and with an aim to limit the spread of the pandemic, the construction industry witnessed almost immediate preventive measures adopted by governments. China, which was the pandemic's epicentre, imposed strict regional lockdowns and quarantine measures[1] and international travel bans and border closures.[2] However, construction projects deemed essential for public functioning (public utilities) and combating the pandemic (production of medical equipment) were allowed to continue. In India, the central government imposed a three-week nationwide lockdown from March 24, 2020, and later extended it through till June 8, 2020.[3] After the initial three-week lockdown, however, construction of essential projects was allowed from April 15, 2020[4] - and from June 8, 2020, even non-essential construction projects

1 On January 1, 2020, the Chinese government took the first measure in response to COVID-19 by closing the seafood market that was identified as the suspected source of the virus. *See* Du Juan, "Wuhan Wet Market Closes Amid Pneumonia Outbreak," China Daily, January 1, 2020, https://www.chinadaily.com.cn/a/202001/01/WS5e0c6a49a310cf3e35581e30.html; China officially notified the WHO of an outbreak in Wuhan. See "Timeline of WHO's Response to COVID-19," World Health Organization, last modified April 7, 2021, https://www.who.int/emergencies/diseases/novel-coronavirus-2019/interactive-timeline#!; see also Lili Kuo, "Coronavirus: Panic and Anger in Wuhan as China Orders City into Lockdown," The Guardian, January 23, 2020, https://www.theguardian.com/world/2020/jan/23/coronavirus-panic-and-anger-in-wuhan-as-china-orders-city-into-lockdown.

2 China Briefing, "Q&A: China's Travel Ban Policy and Visa Issues for Foreigners," March 15, 2021, https://www.china-briefing.com/news/faqs-china-travel-ban-policy-visa-issues-foreigners/.

3 Elizabeth Puranam, "India Lifts Lockdown Measures Despite COVID-19 Surge," Al Jazeera News, June 8, 2020, https://www.aljazeera.com/videos/2020/6/8/india-lifts-lockdown-measures-despite-covid-19-surge.

4 Kanika Verma, "Ministry of Home Affairs Releases List of Exempted Activities During Lockdown," Invest India, April 17, 2020, https://www.investindia.gov.in/team-india-blogs/ministry-home-affairs-releases-list-exempted-activities-during-lockdown; see "New

were allowed to resume subject to adherence to strict social distancing rules and mandatory thermal screening.

In contrast, in Japan, the government relied on voluntary compliance with recommended measures;[5] therefore, it was possible for construction projects to continue. Interestingly, Singapore enacted the COVID-19 (Temporary Measures) Act 2020[6] to provide relief to businesses unable to perform their contractual obligations due to COVID-19 lockdown measures. Notably, the Act suspended claims for liquidated damages for delays in performance or non-performance.

In Europe, the construction industry was severely impacted when the World Health Organization ("WHO") declared Europe as the pandemic's epicentre in March 2020.[7] Italy imposed strict measures on construction activities, except for essential projects, such as national defense projects and public utilities,[8] while France effectively halted all construction projects by prohibiting all non-essential travel. The Eurosat survey highlights that construction activity in France witnessed a decline of 32.6% in April 2020.[9] Spain, one of the countries

Lockdown Guidelines: Here's a List of Economic Activities That Will Be Allowed After April 20," The Economic Times, April 20, 2020, https://economictimes.indiatimes.com/news/politics-and-nation/heres-a-list-of-economic-activities-that-will-be-allowed-after-april-20-2020/articleshow/75152409.cms; see also "Government Allows Resumption of Some Construction Projects in India," Design Build Network, April 22, 2020, https://www.designbuild-network.com/comment/construction-india-covid-19/.

5 Leika Kihara, "Japan State of Emergency Mutes Nightlife but Cities Still Open as Infections Rise," Reuters, April 9, 2020, https://www.reuters.com/article/us-health-coronavirus-japan-total-idUSKCN21R0JN; Joel Rush, "No Lockdown in Japan: Request-Based Emergency Measures Having Limited Effect in Reducing Crowds," Forbes, April 12, 2020, https://www.forbes.com/sites/joelrush/2020/04/12/no-lockdown-in-japan-request-based-emergency-measures-having-limited-effect-in-reducing-crowds/?sh=429a 65c230e9.

6 COVID-19 (Temporary Measures) Act 2020 (No. 14 of 2020), April 20, 2020.

7 "WHO Director-General's Opening Remarks at the Media Briefing on COVID-19," World Health Organization,March 11, 2020, https://www.who.int/director-general/speeches/detail/who-director-general-s-opening-remarks-at-the-media-briefing-on-covid-19---11-march-2020.

8 "Coronavirus: How Lockdown Is Being Lifted Across Europe," BBC, July 2, 2020, https://www.bbc.com/news/explainers-52575313; see "Coronavirus travel rules: European countries' border restrictions and travel measures explained," Euronews, July 6, 2020, https://www.euronews.com/travel/2020/10/21/which-european-countries-have-opened-their-borders-ahead-of-the-summer-holiday-season.

9 ILO Sectoral Brief, "Impact of COVID-19 crisis on the construction sector," International Labour Organisation, January 2021, https://www.ilo.org/wcmsp5/groups/public/---ed_dialogue/---sector/documents/briefingnote/wcms_767303.pdf.

most affected by COVID-19, declared a state of emergency on March 14, 2020, and all construction activity was automatically shut down.[10]

Perhaps the most diverse approach in the construction industry *vis-à-vis* lockdown measures was witnessed in the United States, where on March 11, 2020, the federal government imposed travel restrictions and issued non-binding guidance on the measures that should be adopted, and additionally notified the categories of workers which were to be deemed essential.[11] In response, construction activity was prohibited in Michigan and Pennsylvania, while in the District of Columbia, Florida, and Texas construction activity continued without any restrictions.[12]

3 Global Response and Impact on the Industry

The peculiar nature of the construction industry meant that COVID-19 related restrictions impacted the sector in a unique manner. Most commonly, these restrictions affected two lifelines of the construction industry – the supply chain, both internationally and domestically, and transportation and labor. For example, China, a significant supplier of raw and manufactured construction materials to the global supply chain, experienced a severe shortage of materials because of the stringent lockdown measures imposed, leading to factories either slowing down or completely shutting down due to financial hardships.[13] Local lockdowns impacted the movement of vehicles, and the delivery of internationally transported raw materials disrupted the supply chain of many construction projects, resulting in an unprecedented halting of progress. Restrictions on the transportation of workers due to lockdowns meant that they were unable to be present on-site to carry on the work. In the context of international construction projects, the importation of manpower

---

10 "Royal Decree-Law 10/2020," State Agency Official State Bulletin, March 29, 2020, https://www.boe.es/buscar/doc.php?id=BOE-A-2020-4166.

11 See, *e.g.*, Cybersecurity & Infrastructure Security Agency ("CISA"), "Guidance on the Essential Critical Infrastructure Workforce: Ensuring Community and National Resilience in COVID-19 Response," US Department of Homeland Security, August 10, 2021, https://www.cisa.gov/publication/guidance-essential-critical-infrastructure-workforce.

12 Todd Wetmore and Simon Elliot, "Chapter 12: COVID-19 and Construction Disputes," in *International Arbitration and the COVID-19 Revolution*, eds. Maxi Scherer, Niuscha Bassiri, and Mohamed S. Abdel Wahab (Kluwer Law International, 2020), 203–230.

13 See Ross Mew, "Possible Impacts of COVID-19 on Construction Markets," SNC Lavalin, April 2020, https://www.snclavalin.com/en/beyond-engineering/possible-impacts-covid-19-on-construction-markets.

for both skilled and non-skilled work was severely affected. In some situations, workers had to be repatriated to their countries of origin. The lockdown restrictions especially hampered the use of "fly-in-fly-out" workers who specialize in construction projects.[14] Unlike most of the sectors, which were quick to adopt a work-from-home lifestyle, the construction industry was on the backfoot due to the nature of work not being conducive to an online work culture.

Generally, all ongoing projects were divided into two types – essential and non-essential.[15] Critical construction projects were some of the first economic activities to resume operations. The partial relaxation of restrictions related to those projects, although a respite, led to delays owing to only the partial deployment of the workforce because of on-site COVID-19 protocols. This delay in the procurement and execution phases of various projects led to an unclear landscape when dealing with potential claims and damages arising out of a failure to perform,[16] delayed deliveries,[17] and defective performance,[18] in addition to similar forms of breaches of contract. Ordinarily, contract drafting would include negotiations on potential safeguards to protect the interests of the parties against foreseeable and unforeseeable circumstances, which

14 Wetmore and Elliot, *supra* note 12.

15 In Asia, China and India allowed construction projects which were deemed essential. *E.g.*, Public utilities, biotech – biopharma projects, and renewable energy projects, respectively. Singapore enacted a specific legislation allowing only essential construction works. See *id.* at 6. Europe also restricted construction activities to only essentials such as national defence projects. cf. Japan did not impose any similar explicit restriction on construction projects. Saudi Arabia had considered construction to be non-essential in principle but allowed permission on a case basis while UAE allowed all constructions as essential subject to health measures.

16 Chapter 7 of the UNIDROIT Principles of International Commercial Contracts 2016 ("UPICC") enunciates the principle of contractual non-performance and the consequent remedies thereof. Art. 7.3.1 gives the parties the right to terminate the contract if the act or omission amounts to a fundamental non-performance, and further illustrates acts which amount to fundamental non-performance. In the post COVID-era, based on the facts of each potential dispute, subject to the applicable laws in their contracts, Art. 7.3.1 (2) (a)/(e) of UPICC or an equivalent principle based on the applicable law of the contract, may be used by parties to argue rightful termination due to non-performance.

17 Art. 7.1.5 (3) of UPICC partially exempts non-fundamental delayed performance at the discretion of the aggrieved party. Additional time may be granted at the end of which, the contract may be terminated.

18 Art. 7.1.1 of UPICC includes defective performance in the definition of non-performance and Art. 7.2.3 gives the right to repair, replacement or other cure of defective performance. cf. nonconformity principle under the CISG, albeit inapplicable in the context of construction contracts, is akin to defective performance. Section II of CISG – Arts. 35 to 44 elaborates upon the principle of nonconformity of delivery, seller and buyer remedies and rights respectively.

may or may not be beyond the sphere of control of the parties. In construction contracts, which are often long-term in nature, there are common forms of legal remedies available, such as claims of changes in law, adaptations, hardship clauses, and *force majeure* clauses.

3.1 *Change in Law*

Change in law clauses in construction contracts seek to absolve a contractor's potential liability arising out of a change in the applicable law affecting the construction activity on-site. Typically, these would include a change in building regulations, environmental regulations, and local municipal laws in the jurisdiction where the construction activity is being carried out. In the context of COVID-19, the restrictions that limited contractors' options led to supply chain disruptions, and transportation and labor shortages must qualify as "changes in law," giving effect to the remedies available in the contract. Anecdotal reports suggest that change in law provisions that provide for monetary compensation will be the most commonly used remedy by contractors. Notably, in the International Federation of Consulting Engineers ("FIDIC") forms, a change in the laws of the country gives leeway to both an adjustment of the contract price and an extension of time.[19]

Notwithstanding the above, it is evident that contractors will have a solid legal ground for claims for a change in law in countries where the government-introduced measures led to delays in the achievement of construction milestones. However, in countries that did not impose binding legal restrictions on construction projects, such as the United Kingdom ("UK") and Japan, contractors might have found it challenging to rely on change in law provisions and instead might have had to rely on other contractual doctrines.[20] The crucial factor in ascertaining whether the change in law provision was applicable depended upon the terms of the change in law provision in the contract.

---

19 See Sub-Clause 13.7 of the 1999 Red Book, Yellow Book, Silver Book, and Pink Book forms; see also Sub-Clause 13.6 of the 2017 Red Book, Yellow Book, Silver Book, Emerald Book, and Gold Book; see also Clause 2.15 of the 2016 JCT Design and Build Contract, 2016 JCT Intermediate Building Contract, and 2016 JCT Intermediate Building Contract with Contractor's Design forms; Clause 10.5 of the 2016 JCT Major Project Construction Contract form; Clause 2.17 of the 2016 JCT Standard Forms (with and without Quantities); Clause 2.12.2.1 of the 2016 JCT Design and Build Sub-Contract; see also Option X2 of the NEC4 Engineering and Construction Contract, NEC Term Service Contract, and NEC4 ECC Subcontract.

20 Wetmore and Elliot, *supra* note 12. See Sub-Clause 8.5 of the 1999 Red Book, Yellow Book, Silver Book, and Pink Book forms; see also Sub-Clause 8.6 of the 2017 Red Book, Yellow Book, Silver Book, and Emerald Book forms; see also Sub-Clause 9.4 of the Gold Book.

Ultimately, parties faced difficulties to argue that lockdown measures introduced by the government constituted a "change in law."

Contrary arguments could have been made to suggest that these restrictions did not qualify as "law," since many of them were non-binding guidelines, and thus fell outside the scope of "law" as defined in the contract. Nonetheless, it was likely reasonable to consider these restrictions as a "changes in law" because the peculiar nature of COVID-19 required contractors to comply with these guidelines to protect workers' health and safety. In the absence of a mutual understanding of what constituted a "change in law," a poorly drafted contract could inhibit the contractor from invoking a genuine change in law circumstance.

3.2 *Adaptation*

The second most common remedy potentially arising out of contract disputes involved with the COVID-19 pandemic was 'adaptation.' The legal concept of adaptation is implicitly recognized in Section 79 of the Convention on Contracts for the International Sale of Goods ("CISG"). Adaptation is a common feature in long-term contracts aimed to protect the interests of the parties against unforeseen events.[21] Adaption refers to the power to modify and vary the terms of a contract considering an impediment beyond the parties' control. From a common law perspective, the concept of adaptation can be found in *force majeure* clauses or legal provisions exempting impossible performance.[22] This power to adapt or modify the contract is often vested in the hands of a judge or an arbitrator and follows the principle of synchronized competence of judges and arbitrators, since both of them are legally recognized forms of dispute resolution processes.[23] The legal concept of adaptation

21 United Nations Convention on Contracts for International Sale of Goods 1980, UN Doc A/CONF.97/8 (adopted on 11 April 1980, entered into force 01 January 1988) 1489 UNTS 3, art. 79.

22 In common law, the principle of Sanctity of Contracts is given primacy. Departure from strict interpretations of contractual performance began with the famous Coronation case. See *Krell v. Henry*, 2 KB, 740 (EWCA 11 August 1903). In arbitrations, *ICC Case No. 1512/1971* confirmed the strict application of the frustration doctrine. In the US, the principle of commercial impracticability, to be intended as an extreme and unreasonable hardship, has been recognised by courts and legislators. See *Mineral Park Land v. P.A. Howard*, 172 Cal 289, 294 (Cal. Mar. 13, 1916) and Section 2–615(a) of the UCC. See also sec. 454 Restatement (First) of Contracts and sec. 261 Restatement (Second) of Contracts. Cf. *Northern Illinois Gas v. Energy Co-operative*, 461 NE 2d, 1049 (Ill. App. Ct. Mar. 27, 1984) (where the application of impracticability doctrine was justified based on foreseeability).

23 However, there exists a procedural limitation to the power of adaptation despite the recognition of the principle of synchronized competence. The power of an arbitrator to adapt a contract is a procedural arbitrability matter which must not be expressly barred

implicitly recognized in CISG takes the form of an "adaptation clause" in a contract. Adaptation is a remedy which begins with renegotiations in good faith and can proceed to the intervention of third parties to the contract, such as arbitrators or judges.[24] In long-term contracts and contracts between parties dealing in an uncertain business environment, legally and economically, adaptation clauses are a standard feature. Depending on the nature and the duration of the contract, adaption can take the form of either a price review clause or a hardship clause.[25] Price review clauses allow parties to revise or update the cost and selling price of the good or service per the prevailing market costs and global economic conditions. Ordinarily, this involves renegotiation of the price. A hardship clause, on the other hand, recognizes the distress of one of the parties caused by an impediment that was beyond the control of the parties and exempts performance of contract, either in full or in part. Arbitrations over adaptation clauses often entail the latter, with a disputed "hardship" event, while the former is ordinarily resolved via good faith negotiations.

Adaptation is also a common extra-contractual remedy relied upon by businesses that are affected by unforeseen events. In the absence of an adaptation clause in the contract, especially the lack of clauses regarding COVID-19 due to its sudden emergence, enforcing a remedy such as adaptation has two potential implications. First, the dispute of adaptation must be considered arbitrable under the applicable procedural laws; second, the substantive law must recognize adaptation in its legal system, along with conditions for

---

by mandatory provisions of the *lex arbitri*. An additional challenge thus lies in ensuring that the chosen *lex arbitri*'s mandatory provisions do not bar adaptation. See J.G. Frick, *Arbitration and Complex International Contracts* (Kluwer Law International, 2001), 193–194. Cf. K.P. Berger, *International Economic Arbitration* (Kluwer Law and Taxation, 1993), 86, where, if arbitration law does not provide for the relevant rules on the issue of power of adaptation, reliance must be placed on the rules of the competent court which may allow for such power. Further, if not found in the court rules, last resort must be the substantive law which serve as an indicator for contract adaptation.

24 Norbert Horn, "Procedures of Contract Adaptation and Renegotiation in International Commerce," in *Adaptation and Renegotiation of Contracts in International Trade and Finance* (Antwerp, Boston, London, Frankfurt AM: Kluwer Law International, 1985), 173.

25 A "price review clause" aims to adapt the price to the current market conditions when they change, compared to those existing at the time of the conclusion of the contract. The aim is to either restore the original equilibrium by the change in prices or to find a new equilibrium based on the new market conditions. See George von Mehren, "The Arbitrator's Role," in *Gas Price Arbitration*, 1st edition, ed. Mark Levy (Globe Law and Business, 2014), 94. Cf. the principle of hardship and onerousness of performance of contract is statutorily recognised in Articles 6.2.1 and 6.2.2 of the UNIDROIT Principles and in Art. 6:111 of the Principles of European Contract Law.

its enforcement and potential remedies for the parties, because the power of adaptation must be expressly vested in the hands of the arbitrator to ensure that there exists jurisdictional, procedural, and substantive arbitrability in the hands of the arbitral tribunal.

In the context of construction arbitrations and claims arising from the COVID-19 pandemic, although CISG does not cover construction contracts obligating the performance and completion of construction activity, the Convention is highly relevant in terms of supply chain management and delivery of raw materials across borders.[26] In the absence of an express mandate in the contract empowering the arbitrator to alter the terms of the contract, to consider the renewed interests of the parties owing to an impediment, and/or to restore the economic equilibrium envisaged by the parties at the time of entering into the contract, the parties are left at the mercy of the applicable legal system to their dispute.

Concomitant to the understanding of the legal concept of adaptation *vis-à-vis* COVID, it is crucial to peruse through the various legal systems that have, in some form or another, recognized adaptation as a form of remedy. The non-existence of adaptation clauses in current construction contracts poses a significant challenge regarding the governing law of the contract. Legal systems may be selected based on their acceptance of adaptation or modification of contracts after the occurrence of an event that was unprecedented and which has made contractual performance onerous. Conservative legal systems, such as the French,[27] the Belgian,[28] or the Swiss systems,[29] do not provide the power of adaptation to arbitrators or courts, giving preference to the idea of the primacy of the contract – *pacta sunt servanda*. The Italian legal system is an

---

26 Art. 1 of the CISG defines the scope of application of the convention to contracts for sale of goods between parties whose places of business are in different contracting states. Although construction contracts do not fall under the exclusions listed in Art. 2 of the convention, CISG is not directly applicable in a construction contract owing its nature being that of performance of a certain work.

27 French procedural law does not allow judges and arbitrators to adapt contracts. The Civil Code, too, does not provide any reference to any kind of *imprevision*. See Article 1134.1 of the French Civil Code.

28 Article 1134 of the Civil Code affirms the principle of execution of contracts in good faith. A statutory exception provided in Article 1231 allows a judge to reduce a penalty if it is manifestly excessive. See D. Philippe, "CESL: change of circumstances and prescription," in *The Draft Common European Sales Law: Towards an Alternative Sales Law?: A Belgian Perspective*, ed. Ignace Claeys (UK: Intersentia Publishers, 2013), 299 et seq.

29 Swiss law does not allow adaptation, but it discharges the obligations of a party that are excessively onerous due to the occurrence of an impediment. See Article 119 of the Swiss Code of Obligations.

example of a system that partially recognizes the concept of hardship and the possibility that the parties can adapt the contract under circumstances that are not in the control of the parties, but it does not recognize the power of the courts or arbitrators to adapt contracts.[30] On the other hand, modern legal systems, such as Germany's[31] and the Netherlands',[32] expressly recognize the power of adaptation by courts and, because of the synchronized competence principle, to arbitrators as well. Such power is conferred upon courts based on the concept that the performance of contract terms that became unreasonable upon the occurrence of an unforeseen event is contrary to the principle of contract negotiation in good faith, thus necessitating adaptation by courts. The new context and conditions of performance of the contract must not obligate onerous performance. The traditional approach of renegotiation on good faith is relatively similar to the understanding of modern legal systems, that onerous performance of the contract is contrary to good faith. The limitation with the former model is that there exists no remedy in case of a failure to renegotiate. Jurisprudentially and legislatively, courts and tribunals cannot intervene in a contract between two private parties. At best, the impossibility of performance would render the contract null and void, perhaps to the benefit of neither party.

Thus, from a procedural perspective, the applicable law would be the deciding factor that determines the potential adaptation of a contract. In international arbitrations, the complexity of the various applicable laws and their interaction with adaptation is exasperated by the party's choice of law provisions, which can conflict on the issue of adaptation. If the law of the place of

30 See Article 2908 of the Italian Civil Code, which entitles judges and arbitrators to create, modify, or extinguish legal relationships via constitutive decisions, which includes the adaptation of contracts. This is, however, in case of an express provision in law, *e.g.*, Article 1384 of the Civil Code, granting the judge the power to equitably reduce the amount of the penalty provided by the parties in case of a breach of contract; Articles 1657 and 1660 of the Civil Code regard the determination of the price and the variations to the original project of construction contracts and contracts for the supplying of services.

31 Art. 313 of the German Civil Code (BGB) establishes a course of action upon occurrence of unforeseen events, based on the principle of good faith provided in Art. 242 of the BGB. See P. Oertmann, *Geschaftsgrundlage – Ein neuer Rechtsbegriff* (Deichert, 1921). The German Federal Supreme Court ("Bundesgerichtshof"), on January 16, 1953, and October 14, 1992, as cited in H. Beale et al., *Cases, Materials and Text on Contract Law* (Hart Publishing, 2010), 1127, 1142, 1144, reaffirmed the principle of adaptation of contracts in light of doctrine of the collapse of the contract's foundation and of the principle of good faith.

32 Art. 6:258 of the Civil Code, which deals with unforeseen circumstances authorises arbitrators under Art. 1020 of the Code of Civil Procedure with the authority to adapt. See *ICC Case No. 8486/1996*, 1999 XXIV YBCA, 162 (1996). The approach is similar in international arbitration as well. See *ICC Case No. 1512/1971*, Collection of ICC Arbitral Awards 1974–1985, 3 (1971).

arbitration and *lex arbitri* were to differ on the jurisprudence of adaptation, this would create issues that can be resolved by looking at the intention of the parties[33] and resorting to the principle of good faith.[34]

This assumes the absence of an express adaptation clause in the contract. If a contract provides an adaptation clause, either in the substantive part of the contract or in the arbitration clause, then arbitrators and courts, when the award is challenged, will give effect to the express agreement between the parties.[35] This supersedes the procedural and substantive limitations of the applicable law, unless the bar on adaption is a part of the mandatory provision of the *lex arbitri*.[36] Although complex issues may arise when the adaptation clause does not expressly provide for the power to adapt, the general approach of international arbitration is in line with the principles of *pacta sunt servanda* and party autonomy.

3.3 *Hardship and Force Majeure Clauses*

Hardship and *force majeure* are contractual defenses commonly invoked in international contracts, in scenarios where an unforeseen event has occurred, making the performance of the contractual obligations impossible or extremely onerous. Pertinently, in a case where the performance of the contract becomes impossible, the defense of *force majeure* is invoked, which would ultimately relieve the affected party from performance of the contract. In contrast, in cases where the performance of the contract becomes extremely onerous, the defense of hardship would be applicable, where the party subject to hardship in certain cases would be able to renegotiate the contract in light of the changed circumstances.[37]

---

33 Parties choosing a *lex arbitri* which does not allow the power of adaptation goes a long way to suggest their intention. The analysis must therefore involve an analysis of pre-contractual negotiations and post contractual conduct to ascertain the intention of the parties.

34 Good faith must also be resorted to, when parties choose a procedural and substantive law which conflict on the issue of adaptation as well. See Oertmann, *supra* note 31.

35 *Atlantic LNG Company of Trinidad and Tobago v. Gas Natural Aprovisionamentos* unpublished (final arbitration award 17 January 2008). ICC has in various instances dealt with similar questions of adaption and the power to do so. See *ICC Case No. 9812/1999*, 2009 20 ICC Int'l Ct Arb Bull 69, 69–70 (1999); *ICC Case No. 13504/2007*, 2009 20 ICC Int'l Ct Arb Bull, 93, 94–95 (2007).

36 J.G. Frick, *Arbitration and Complex International Contracts* (Kluwer Law International, 2001), 193–194.

37 Fabio Bortolotti and Dorothy Ufot, "Introduction," in *Hardship and force majeure in international commercial contracts: dealing with unforeseen events in a changing world*, eds. Fabio Bortolotti and Dorothy Ufot (Paris: ICC Services Publications Department, 2018), 8–10.

Hardship[38] and *force majeure* are general consequences of the concept of adaptation and are exemptions in the law. Hardship's scope is limited to impediments and events which fundamentally alter the economic equilibrium of the contract.[39] The requirements to establish *force majeure* and hardship are different. According to the general contract principles and prevalent model hardship clauses, such as the ICC Hardship Clause,[40] *force majeure* requires an impediment to performance, while hardship requires equivalency distortion.[41] This distinction is of immense importance to understand the causation of the exemption. Since *force majeure* requires an impediment to performance, the non-performance "due to" the impediment causes the *force majeure* event. On the contrary, the performance of the contract becoming excessively onerous "because of" a change in circumstance triggers the remedy of hardship. The critical prerequisites to both defenses require a supervening event after the creation of the contract,[42] which could not have been overcome[43] as it was beyond the sphere of control of the parties.[44]

Force majeure is perhaps the most popular and well-known defense that contractors will rely upon for their case because of the COVID-19 pandemic. A few countries have already declared COVID-19 as a *force majeure* event,[45]

38 Hardship clauses (Hardship is used as a contractual defence in civil law jurisdictions, such as France – French Civil Code, Art. 1195; Egypt – Egyptian Civil Code, Art. 147; Algeria – Algerian Civil Code, Art. 107(3); Switzerland – Swiss Federal Act on the Amendment of the Swiss Civil Code – Part Five: The Code of Obligations, Art. 373 B; the Netherlands – Dutch Civil Code (BW), Art. 6:258; and Germany Civil Code – Bürgerliches Gesetzbuch (BGB), sec. 313) are civil law creations that allow for renegotiating stipulated contractual obligations in exceptional circumstances. The fundamental plinth of the defense of hardship is premised on good faith and it is usually invoked on the occurrence of an exceptional or unforeseeable event which alters the circumstances under which the parties had initially entered into the contract.

39 *Scafom International v Lorrain Tubes*, Decision of the Cour de Cassation, 19 June 2009.

40 "ICC Force Majeure And Hardship Clauses," International Chamber of Commerce, March 2020, https://iccwbo.org/news-publications/icc-rules-guidelines/icc-force-majeure-and-hardship-clauses/.pdf.

41 Occurrence of events fundamentally alter the equilibrium of the contract either because the cost of a party's performance has increased or because the value of the performance a party receives has diminished. See Art. 6.2.2 UPICC; Art. 6.111(1), (2) PECL; ICC Hardship Clause 2003, para. 2(a); TLDB-Principle VIII1(a)(iii).

42 Art. 6.2.2(a) UPICC; see also ICC Hardship Clause 2003, Note d; ICC Publ. No. 650 at 17.

43 Art. 7.1.7(1) UPICC; Art. 8:108(1) PECL.

44 Art. 7.1.7(1) UPICC; Art. 8:108(1) PECL.

45 Eg., France and India have declared COVID-19 as a *force majeure* event. See French Government Regulation No. 2020–306, 25 March 2020. Office Memorandum No.F. 18/4/2020, Department of Expenditure, Ministry of Finance, Government of India, 19 March

and it should come as no surprise that contractors are relying upon *force majeure* clauses in defense for non-compliance with their contractual obligations. Generally, construction contracts entail elaborate *force majeure* clauses which are descriptive of the events that qualify as *force majeure*.[46] It is highly probable that contracts created before the onset of the pandemic will not refer to pandemics as a *force majeure* event; nevertheless, the party invoking *force majeure* may be able to satisfy the prerequisites of *force majeure*, depending upon the jurisdiction in which it is invoked.

Neither hardship nor *force majeure* provide for financial entitlement, but rather for the termination of the contract or a suspension of obligations.[47] Parties will likely rely on these defenses either in addition to, or as an alternative to, financial remedies. These defenses are extremely fact dependent, and the use of these defenses should be considered with respect to the specific contracts involved and the impact of COVID-19 on the construction project in question. Whichever remedy the parties and the legal representatives choose to pursue, there must exist a universal understanding that COVID-19 caused a rise in disputes, the impact of which might trigger the specific thresholds to qualify for a variety of remedies on a case-by-case basis.

A corollary to the principle of the fundamental alteration of the equilibrium of contract is "frustration of purpose," recognized in civil and common law, where the receiver of performance argues its inadequacy and substantial decline.[48] In arbitration, the doctrine of changed circumstances, *i.e.*, hardship, has been recognized as a general principle of law.[49] In a construction dispute, depending on the nature of the claim and the legal background of the parties,[50] the remedy of hardship or *force majeure* may be chosen subject to the

2020. According to the China Council for the Promotion of International Trade, China has issued 4,811 *force majeure* certificates as of March 3, 2020, due to the epidemic.

46 See Sub-Clause 19.1 of the 1999 Red Book, Yellow Book, Silver Book, and Pink Book forms; see also Sub-Clause 18.1 of the 2017 Red Book, Yellow Book, Silver Book, Emerald Book. FIDIC forms define *force majeure* events as events or circumstances which: (i) are beyond a party's control; (ii) the party could not reasonably have provided against before entering the contract; (iii) having arisen, the party could not reasonably have avoided or overcome and (iv) are not substantially attributable to the other party.

47 Wetmore and Elliot, *supra* note 12.

48 Günter Heinz Treitel, *Frustration and force majeure* (Sweet & Maxwell, 1994), 309, para. 7–001.

49 *Questech, Inc. v. Ministry of National Defence of the Islamic Republic of Iran*, Award in Case No. 59, 9 Iran-US CTR at 122–23, YB Com Arb 1986, 283–89; *Rockwell International Systems, Inc. v. The Government of the Islamic Republic of Iran* (The Ministry of National Defence), Award in Case No. 430 YB Com Arb 1990, 239, 243.

50 Civil law systems follow the rule of "limit of sacrifice," subject to which a party can bear higher risk of performance. See Georg Gruber and Hans Stoll, in *Commentary on*

provisions of the contract governing them. Parties must note that while proving hardship is difficult, owing to the high legal threshold of proving onerous circumstances, relying on *force majeure* has its own set of problems, the most pertinent of which is satisfying the test of foreseeability and mitigation.

4 Construction Disputes in Context: Ramifications of Contractual and Extra-contractual Defenses

Construction contracts often provide for a multi-tier dispute resolution mechanism that involves a dispute resolution board, mediation, and then arbitration. A boilerplate construction contract usually will stipulate optional or mandatory mediation or conciliation. Given the varied options presented to the parties, it can be concluded that parties have numerous alternative dispute resolution ("ADR") methods at their disposal to resolve disputes arising post-COVID-19. Additionally, in the post-COVID-19 era, it is likely that all ADR methods will involve online hearings and the extensive use of technology, *inter alia*, the use of drones for virtual inspections of project sites. Hence, it is imperative that all involved parties are well-versed and well-equipped with technology to resolve their disputes, especially because it is advisable that parties resolve their disputes on their own, as the alternatives might be non-conducive in a financially crippled post-COVID-19 era, given the rising costs of arbitration.

The arbitration community has embraced virtual hearings as the apparent solution to recommence the arbitral process post-COVID-19. The previously limited use of technology in arbitration proceedings has now transitioned to a full-fledged technological process, where counsels and arbitrators conduct online arbitrations without delays. Notably, in a 2018 survey, while 60% of the participating arbitration community used videoconferencing frequently, 64% of the community had never used virtual hearing rooms.[51] One of the positives

the UN-Convention on the International Sale of Goods (CISG), 2nd edition, eds. Peter Schlechtriem and Ingeborg Schwenzer (Oxford University Press, 2005), Art. 79 CISG para. 32. Common law system follows the principle of commercial impracticability. For the US, see *Florida Power & Light Co. v. Westinghouse Electric Corp*, 510 So. 2d 899 (Fla. 1987). For the UK, see *British Movietonenews Ltd. v. London District Cinemas* [1952] AC 166. cf. *Davis Contractors Ltd. v. Fareham Urban District Council*, [1956] AC (HL) 696 (where the HOL denied application of the doctrine of impracticability in a case where labour shortage led to delayed construction of a project, which led to an overall increase in costs by 23%).

51 White and Case LLP, "2018 International Arbitration Survey: The Evolution of International Arbitration," Queen Mary University of London, accessed September 24, 2021, https://arbitration.qmul.ac.uk/research/2018/.

emerging from the pandemic is the high level of flexibility and adaptability of the arbitration community. Arbitral institutions have issued guidelines regarding virtual hearings[52] and have collaborated with service providers for virtual hearings.[53] In particular, arbitral institutions have illustrated a great degree of adaptability in the context of the arbitration proceedings. Generally, arbitral institutions have removed the requirement of filing a request for arbitration in hard copy. The International Chamber of Commerce (ICC) now mandates the filing of requests for arbitration in electronic form.[54] The ICC Guidance Note on Possible Measures Aimed at Mitigating the Effects of the COVID-19 Pandemic ("Guidance Note") is worth noting.[55] The Guidance Note has four significant guidelines: (1) the Guidance Note urges arbitrators to examine the dispute and the issues involved therein to ascertain whether the dispute can be resolved solely based on documentary evidence without a hearing; (2) the Guidance Note empowers the parties to agree on electronic notifications of awards and orders, subject to the requirements of the mandatory law; (3) the Guidance Note advises tribunals to consult the parties before conducting virtual hearings and obtain consent from them to counter any possible issues that may arise during the enforcement of the award. Regarding virtual hearings, the Guidance Note advises the tribunals to consider time zones while scheduling arbitration hearings and to ensure that each party is provided a full opportunity to present its case. Lastly, the Guidance Note, by way of annexes, provides a valuable protocol for setting up virtual hearings and a compilation of suggested clauses for cyber-protocols.

---

52 See *e.g.*, "ICC Guidance Note on Possible Measures Aimed at Mitigating the Effects of the COVID-19 Pandemic," International Chamber of Commerce, April 9, 2020, https://iccwbo.org/news-publications/arbitration-adr-rules-and-tools/icc-guidance-note-on-possible-measures-aimed-at-mitigating-the-effects-of-the-covid-19-pandemic/; see also "AAA-ICRD Model Order and Procedures for a Virtual Hearing via Videoconference," American Arbitration Association, July 30, 2020, https://go.adr.org/rs/294-SFS-516/images/AAA270_AAA-ICDR%20Model%20Order%20and%20Procedures%20for%20a%20Virtual%20Hearing%20via%20Videoconference.pdf; "Enhanced COVID-19 Measures," Singapore International Arbitration Centre, April 6, 2020, https://www.acerislaw.com/wp-content/uploads/2020/04/SIAC-Enhanced-COVID-19-Measures.pdf; "Guidance Note on Remote Dispute Resolution Proceedings," The Chartered Institute of Arbitrators, May 30, 2021, https://www.ciarb.org/media/8967/remote-hearings-guidance-note.pdf.

53 See *e.g.*, "Australian Disputes Centre Virtual," Australian Disputes Centre, accessed September 24, 2021, https://www.disputescentre.com.au/adc-virtual/; "Virtual Hearing Experience at Maxwell Chambers," Maxwell Chambers, May 30, 2021, https://www.maxwellchambers.com/2020/05/12/the-virtual-hearing-experience/.

54 See *e.g.*, International Chamber of Commerce, *supra* note 52.

55 *Id.*

Regarding construction arbitration proceedings, virtual hearings might prove to be cumbersome. Construction arbitrations involving multiple parties and considerable volumes of documents can be challenging to comprehend, especially for the arbitral tribunals, for numerous reasons. The complexity and multifaceted nature of the issues, fatigue due to extensive online hearings, and information being lost in translation are some of the issues in construction arbitrations. However, tribunals can adopt some measures to ensure that construction arbitrations are conducted well. First, ensuring that evidence is filed in scanned copies and hard copies can ease the navigation and reference process during the hearing. Second, tribunals should draft and provide the counsel with guidelines regarding the mode of conduct during the virtual hearings. For example, besides for the arbitral tribunal and the respective legal representatives, all cameras and audio should be switched off. Third, tribunals and counsel should limit their hearings to a few hours at the maximum to avoid screen fatigue from staring at the screens for an extended duration. Tribunals may also want to consider the guidelines and suggestions in the Guidance Note, which can to some degree address the concerns emanating from virtual hearings. As the restrictions owing to the pandemic resulted in enormous financial strain, it is possible that the parties resort to third-party funding, which may further give rise to complex questions regarding the admissibility of claims, the jurisdiction of the claimant, and the amount of control of the third-party funder over the arbitration proceedings. Interestingly, the China Council for the Promotion of International Trade, in anticipation of *force majeure* claims, issued *force majeure* certificates to Chinese companies from February 2020.[56]

Construction disputes in the post-COVID-19 era are likely to increase in number, although the type of disputes is likely to remain the same. As the number of disputes increases, the spotlight will be on the legal remedies provided to parties, such as adaptation, hardship, impossibility of performance, or *force majeure*. As the world recovers from the impact of the pandemic and the prolific rise of virtual hearings, it remains to be seen whether the resolution of construction disputes will undergo a paradigm shift, especially in the context of the technological revolution that the pandemic has imposed on the arbitration community.

56 Alison Frankel, "Chinese force majeure certificates presage complexity of resolving post-crisis disputes," Reuters, March 16, 2020, https://www.reuters.com/article/us-otc-covid19-idUSKBN2133MQ.

CHAPTER 8

Investor-State Arbitration and the International Construction Sector

R. Zachary Torres-Fowler, Jamey Collidge, and Cindy Lee

International commercial arbitration is among, if not the, most common form of dispute resolution within the international construction industry.[1] The ability to resolve complex construction disputes through a flexible, neutral, and enforceable dispute resolution process has proven to be a boon to international construction and engineering firms as well as owners/employers around the globe. However, while international commercial arbitration will likely remain the principal form of dispute resolution for international construction projects, many overlook the role investor-state arbitration plays within this sector.

After years of weathering the COVID-19 pandemic, governments around the world continue to confront substantial macroeconomic challenges stemming from, among other things, global economic uncertainty, armed conflict, and climate change.[2] These challenges have caused, and will likely continue to cause, governments around the world to take actions (whether rightfully or wrongfully) that are adverse to the interests of foreign direct investors, including actors within the international construction industry. While risk allocation provisions in construction agreements commonly contemplate changes in law, *force majeure*, and other government actions, these provisions still place at least one party at the mercy of a sovereign government. Thus, what recourse do members of the construction industry have against unfair treatment by sovereign governments?

In many cases, the answer may lie in a network of international investment treaties between governments around the world that grant foreign investors

1 *See generally* Queen Mary University of London and Pinsent Masons, "International Arbitration Survey – Driving Efficiency in International Construction Disputes: How can international construction disputes be resolved more efficiently whilst maintaining fairness and access to justice?" CAM Santiago, November 2019, accessed October 13, 2022, https://www.camsantiago.cl/minisites/informativo-online/2019/NOV/docs/international-arbitration-survey-november-2019.pdf.

2 International Monetary Fund (IMF), "World Economic Outlook Update: Gloomy and More Uncertain," IMF, July 2022, accessed October 13, 2022, https://www.imf.org/en/Publications/WEO/Issues/2022/07/26/world-economic-outlook-update-july-2022.

 | DOI:10.1163/9789004514874_011

certain basic protections against expropriation, unfair treatment, and discrimination. Most significantly, these international investment treaties also afford foreign investors the right to sue a sovereign government to recover their losses through investor-state arbitration.

Indeed, over the last half-decade, the number of investor-state arbitrations arising out of international construction projects has steadily increased, and the construction industry now makes up one of the most significant economic sectors for investor-state arbitral institutions.[3] As the ramifications of COVID-19 continue to percolate up through dispute-resolution procedures and as government entities continue to invest in infrastructure projects around the world, it is very likely that current trends will continue into the foreseeable future.

Given the role the international construction industry plays and will continue to play in the field of investor-state arbitration, this chapter provides a survey of some of the most salient investment arbitration matters involving the international construction industry. Importantly, the field of investor-state arbitration is nuanced. As a result, it is beyond the scope of this chapter to cover every possible facet of construction-related investor-state arbitrations. Instead, this chapter covers some of the core concepts related to investor-state arbitration and illustrates how arbitral tribunals have addressed these issues as they arise in connection with an international construction project.

This chapter is structured in three parts. First, the authors provide a very brief introduction into international investment treaties and investor-state arbitration. Second, the authors discuss how arbitral tribunals have addressed jurisdictional questions concerning the existence of an "investor" and "investment" in the context of a pair of construction-related arbitration awards. Third, the authors summarize the most common substantive treaty claims that arise in connection with investor-state arbitrations involving the international construction industry.

1 Introduction to International Investment Treaties and Investor State Dispute Settlement

International Investment Treaties ("IIT"), or International Investment Agreements, are treaties between sovereign states that, in broad strokes, seek

3 International Centre for Settlement of Investment Disputes (ICSID), "The ICSID Caseload – Statistics," ICSID 2022, accessed October 13, 2022, 12, https://icsid.worldbank.org/sites/default/files/publications/The_ICSID_Caseload_Statistics_2022-2_ENG.pdf.

to promote foreign investment between the signatory countries.[4] These treaties include terms that cover a wide array of international trade matters. Most critically, they ensure that foreign investors (individuals and companies) from a signatory state (i) receive guarantees of specific protections against state actions like expropriation, discrimination, or unfair treatment from the treaty counterparty, and (ii) retain the ability to pursue claims against the host state's government in an investor-state arbitration.[5] In doing so, these sovereign governments are willing to waive sovereign immunity in exchange for increased foreign direct investment.[6]

The term "International Investment Treaty" is broadly defined and encompasses both Bilateral Investment Treaties ("BIT") and Multilateral Investment Treaties ("MIT").[7] BITs are IITs between *two* countries while MITs, like the Energy Charter Treaty and the now defunct North American Free Trade Agreement, are IITs made between multiple countries.[8]

The origins of IITs date back to the late 1700s, when the United States began to enter into bilateral treaties with foreign countries to foster international commercial relations.[9] The framework for the modern IIT, which focuses on the promotion of foreign direct investment, originated following World War II.[10] During this period, the major economic powers focused their efforts on

4 Eustace Chikere Azubuike, "The Place of Treaties in International Investment," *Annual Survey of International & Comparative Law* 19, no. 1 (2013): 190.

5 *See generally* Scott Miller and Gregory N. Hicks, "Investor-State Dispute Settlement: A Reality Check," CSIS, January 2015, accessed October 13, 2022, 1–6, https://csis-website-prod.s3.amazonaws.com/s3fs-public/legacy_files/files/publication/150116_Miller_InvestorStateDispute_Web.pdf; Robert Echandi, "Bilateral Investment Treaties and Investment Provisions in Regional Trade Agreements: Recent Developments in Investment Rulemaking," in *Arbitration Under International Investment Agreements: A Guide to the Key Issues*, ed. Katia Yannaca-Small, 2nd ed. (Oxford: OUP, 2018); Campbell McLachlan, Laurence Shore, and Matthew Weinger, *International Investment Arbitration: Substantive Principles* (Oxford: OUP, 2017), paras. 1.32–1.52, 2.21.

6 A substantial debate exists, however, on whether international investment treaties actually promote foreign direct investment. See Jonathan Bonnitcha, "Assessing Impacts of Investment Treaties: Overview of the evidence," IISD, September 2017, accessed October 13, 2022, https://www.iisd.org/system/files/publications/assessing-impacts-investment-treaties.pdf.

7 Julien Chaisse, "The Treaty Shopping Practice: Corporate Structuring and Restructuring to Gain Access to Investment Treaties and Arbitration," *Hastings Business Law Journal* 11 (2015): 231.

8 *See generally* Miller and Hicks, *supra* note 5; Echandi, *supra* note 5.

9 *See* Kenneth J. Vandevelde, "A Brief History of International Investment Agreements," *U.C. Davis Journal of International Law & Policy* 12, no. 1 (2005): 158–161.

10 *Id.* at 161–175.

liberalizing trade and sought to normalize relations with many economically underdeveloped countries that recently obtained newfound independence.[11] The 1960s saw a further increase in the number of IITs as countries executed these investment treaties to promote foreign direct investment. However, as globalization expanded throughout the 1980s and beyond, the number of IITs exploded.[12] Today, there have been nearly 2,800 BITs, and over 3,000 investment treaties, executed worldwide.[13]

Critically, most IITs contain dispute resolution provisions that afford foreign investors the right to pursue claims against a sovereign government (*i.e.*, the host state) through a process known as investor state dispute settlement ("ISDS") that often calls for disputes to be ultimately resolved through investor-state arbitration. While the precise framework and procedures associated with an investor-state arbitration are beyond the scope of this chapter, investor-state arbitrations share many (though not all) of the procedural features of a more conventional international commercial arbitration.

Claims brought in an investor-state arbitration are commonly resolved by three-arbitrator tribunals that retain the authority to, among other things, order the host state to compensate the foreign investor for its losses in the event the tribunal concludes the host state violated one or more of the IIT's protections. Tribunals that oversee these arbitration proceedings are not bound by precedent or prior tribunal decisions (though they may rely on prior decisions as persuasive authority). Further, while investor-state arbitration procedures vary depending on the applicable treaty, investor-state arbitrations are commonly conducted under the auspices of established international arbitration institutions such as the International Centre for Settlement of Investment Disputes (ICSID), the International Chamber of Commerce (ICC), the Stockholm Chamber of Commerce (SCC), or pursuant to the United Nations Commission on International Trade Law ("UNCITRAL") Arbitration Rules.[14]

---

11 *Id.* at 161–167.

12 *Id.*

13 *See* United Nations Conference on Trade and Development (UNCTAD), "International Investment Agreements Navigator," UNCTAD, accessed October 13, 2022, https://investmentpolicy.unctad.org/international-investment-agreements.

14 ICSID, "About ICSID," ICSID, accessed October 6, 2022, https://icsid.worldbank.org/about; International Court of Arbitration (ICC), "ICC International Court of Arbitration," ICC, accessed October 6, 2022, https://iccwbo.org/dispute-resolution-services/icc-international-court-arbitration/; Arbitration Institute of the Stockholm Chamber of Commerce (SCC), "SCC Institute," SCC, accessed October 6, 2022, https://sccarbitrationinstitute.se/en; United Nations Commission on International Trade Law (UNCITRAL), "UNCITRAL Arbitration Rules," UNCITRAL, accessed October 6, 2022, https://uncitral.un.org/en/texts/arbitration/contractualtexts/arbitration.

2 Jurisdictional Issues – "Investors" and "Investments"

Among the most fundamental features of investor-state arbitration are the concepts of the "investor" and an "investment."[15] Indeed, the purpose of investor-state arbitration is to provide *investors* with a forum to adjudicate disputes arising from acts that adversely affected their *investment* in a host state.[16] Thus, for an arbitral tribunal to retain jurisdiction over an investor-state arbitration, a protected *investor* must assert a claim against the host state arising out of a qualifying *investment*.[17] Absent one of these two factors, an arbitral tribunal must decline to exercise jurisdiction over the case.[18] However, because a specific treaty may define "investor" and "investment" differently, outcomes concerning these questions can vary and are often subject to the peculiar language of the treaty and the facts.

Under most IITs, an "investor" must be a national of a signatory state that makes an investment in another signatory state (often referred to as the host state).[19] IITs only protect investments made by *foreign* investors – *i.e.*, investors that retain a different nationality from the state in which it made the investment (the host state).[20] Investors that share the same nationality as the host state may not avail themselves of treaty protections and will only have recourse to local courts of the host state.[21] Likewise, a foreign investor whose nationality is not that of a signatory state may not (in theory) avail itself of those particular treaty protections (*but see* discussion of Most Favored Nation Clauses in Section 3.4).[22]

15 Organisation for Economic Co-operation and Development (OECD), "Definition of Investor and Investment in International Investment Agreements," in OECD, *International Investment Law: Understanding Concepts and Tracking Innovations: A Companion Volume to International Investment Perspectives* (Paris: OECD Publishing, 2008).

16 *Id.*

17 *See generally* Katia Yannaca-Small, "Who is Entitled to Claim? Nationality Challenges," in *Arbitration Under International Investment Agreements*, ed. Katia Yannaca-Small, 2nd ed. (Oxford: OUP, 2018), 211–242; Katia Yannaca-Small, "Definition of 'Investment': An Open-Ended Search for a Balanced Approach," in *Arbitration Under International Investment Agreements*, ed. Katia Yannaca-Small, 2nd ed. (Oxford: OUP, 2018), 243–269.

18 *Id.*

19 OECD, *supra* note 15, at 10.

20 *Id.* at 12.

21 *Id.*

22 *See generally* Yannaca-Small, "Who is Entitled to Claim? Nationality Challenges," *supra* note 17; *see also* Abby Cohen Smutny and Lee Steven, "The MFN Clause: What are its Limits?," in *Arbitration Under International Investment Agreements*, ed. Katia Yannaca-Small, 2nd ed. (Oxford: OUP, 2018), 351–381.

Questions commonly arise regarding the nationality of an investor when multiple corporate forms are involved in the underlying dispute. For example, under some IITs, the "nationality" of an investor may be determined by virtue of the country in which the investor was formed or incorporated.[23] In other instances, the applicable treaty may require more stringent criteria, such as having actual business activity in the contracting state, or determine nationality according to the party who actually exercises control over the investor.[24] This issue is particularly significant for international construction projects where it is common for firms to use various corporate forms like subsidiaries, joint ventures, and consortiums to share risk and comply with local regulations.

The concept of an "investment" is even more fraught. Indeed, notwithstanding just how fundamental the concept of an "investment" is to investor-state arbitration, there is much debate over precisely what an investment actually constitutes.[25] Very often, IITs contain broad, non-exclusive language that helps to define the concept of an investment. Although treaties inevitably vary, commonly recognized forms of investment include: "an enterprise;" "shares, stock, and other forms of equity participation in an enterprise;" "turnkey, construction, management, production, concession, revenue-sharing, and other similar contracts;" and "intellectual property rights," to name just a few.[26]

In other instances, a definition of an investment is more elusive. To the extent an IIT refers disputes to ICSID arbitrations, Article 25 of the ICSID Convention – the multilateral treaty governing ICSID arbitrations – only affords tribunals jurisdiction to hear disputes "arising directly out of an investment" but does not actually define the term "investment."[27] This has led ICSID arbitral tribunals to apply what is known as the "double keyhole" or "double barrel" test that requires the tribunal to determine whether the investment qualifies under both the applicable IIT *and* Article 25 of the ICSID Convention.[28]

---

23 See, *e.g.*, *Tokios Tokelés v. Ukraine*, ICSID Case No. ARB/02/18, Decision on Jurisdiction, (29 April 2004), para. 38.

24 Roland Ziadé and Lorenzo Melchionda, "Structuring and Restructuring of Investment in Investment Treaty Arbitration," in *Contemporary Issues in International Arbitration and Mediation: The Fordham Papers 2014*, ed. Arthur W. Rovine (Brill, 2015).

25 OECD, *supra* note 15, at 8.

26 UNCTAD, "Model Bilateral Investment Treaty, U.S., 2012," UNCTAD, accessed October 13, 2022, https://investmentpolicy.unctad.org/international-investment-agreements/model-agreements.

27 ICSID, "ICSID Convention, Regulations and Rules," ICSID, April 2006, accessed October 13, 2022, Article 25, https://icsid.worldbank.org/sites/default/files/ICSID%20Convention%20English.pdf.

28 Filippo Fontanelli, *Jurisdiction and Admissibility in Investment Arbitration: The Practice and the Theory* (Brill, 2018), 11–14.

However, because the ICSID Convention does not define investment, tribunals have implemented varying standards to assess whether a particular asset qualifies as an investment.[29] One such standard is known as the "*Salini* test," which holds that to qualify as an investment under Article 25 of the ICSID Convention, the asset must (i) be a contribution; (ii) for a certain duration; (iii) retain an element of risk; and (iv) contribute to the host state's economic development.[30] Critically, however, the *Salini* test is not uniformly followed and has been roundly criticized for being too narrow and unsupported by the text of the ICSID Convention.[31]

Notwithstanding the above, for purposes of construction projects, there appears to be a general consensus that construction contracts that require substantial investment of manpower, resources, and time constitute an "investment."[32] The following cases illustrate the types of jurisdictional challenges that arise in the context of an investor-state arbitration concerning a construction industry dispute.

2.1 *Garanti Koza LLP v. Turkmenistan*

In *Garanti Koza v. Turkmenistan*, Garanti Koza LLP ("**GK LLP**"), a limited liability partnership formed in the United Kingdom and partially owned by the Turkish firm, Garanti Koza Insaat ("**Garanti Insaat**"), entered into a contract with an arm of the Turkmenistan government, Turkmenavtoyollary ("**TAY**"), for the construction of 28 highway bridges throughout Turkmenistan.[33] During the course of construction, a series of disputes arose in connection with the parties' payment and invoicing procedures and GK LLP's performance on the projects. TAY ultimately terminated the underlying construction contracts[34] and commenced proceedings before the local Turkmenistan courts.[35] Within

29 Alex Grabowski, "The Definition of Investment under the ICSID Convention: A Defense of Salini," *Chicago Journal of International Law* 15, no. 1 (2014): Article 13.

30 *Salini Costruttori S.p.A. and Italstrade S.p.A v. Kingdom of Morroco*, ICSID Case No. ARB / 00/4, Decision on Jurisdiction, (July 23, 2001), para. 52.

31 Laurence Burger, "The Trouble with Salini (Criticism of and Alternatives to the Famous Test)," *ASA Bulletin* 31, no. 3 (2013).

32 *See Salini Costruttori S.p.A., supra* note 30; *see also Borkowski and Rasia FZE v. Armenia*, ICSID Case No. ARB/18/28, (2018); *Way2B ACE v. State of Libya*, ICC Case No. 20971/MCP/DDA, (May 24, 2018).

33 *Garanti Koza LLP v. Turkmenistan*, ICSID Case No. ARB/11/20, Objections to Jurisdiction, (Dec. 19, 2016), para. 4.

34 *Id.* at paras. 45–147.

35 *Id.* at para. 142.

a matter of weeks, TAY received an order from the local courts attaching GK LLP's assets and awarding TAY approximately $15 million in damages.[36]

GK LLP, thereafter, initiated an ICSID arbitration pursuant to the Treaty for the Promotion and Protection of Investments concluded between the United Kingdom of Great Britain and Northern Ireland and the Government of Turkmenistan (the "**U.K.-Turkmenistan BIT**").[37] According to GK LLP, Turkmenistan's actions violated the various treaty protections contained in the U.K.-Turkmenistan BIT, including protections against expropriation and unfair and inequitable treatment.[38]

The Turkmenistan government challenged the tribunal's jurisdiction to hear GK LLP's claims and asserted that GK LLP had not made a qualifying investment within the meaning of Article 25 of the ICSID Convention and the U.K.-Turkmenistan BIT.[39] In support of its position, Turkmenistan raised three substantive arguments.

- First, GK LLP's construction activities were akin to a traditional commercial transaction that fell outside the scope an "investment" as required by both Article 25 of the ICSID Convention and the U.K.-Turkmenistan BIT.[40]
- Second, for jurisdiction to exist under the U.K.-Turkmenistan BIT, the specific language of the BIT required an "investment" to be made by a "national or company" of the U.K. Here, any investment that was made in Turkmenistan was done by GK LLP's Turkish parent company Garanti Insaat, not GK LLP, and, as a result, there could be no "investment" as defined by the BIT.[41]
- Third, GK LLP's claims were purely contractual claims, not claims related to the violation of the BIT, and, as a result, should be subject to jurisdiction of the local Turkmenistan courts.

The tribunal rejected each of the Turkmenistan government's arguments and found that GK LLP had indeed made an investment under the U.K.-Turkmenistan BIT.

The tribunal first concluded that GK LLP made an investment in Turkmenistan pursuant to the U.K.-Turkmenistan BIT.[42] Specifically, according

36 *Id.* at paras. 141–147.
37 *Id.* at para. 1.
38 *Id.* at para. 249.
39 *Id.* at paras. 154–177.
40 *Id.* at paras. 161–166.
41 *Id.* at paras. 171–176.
42 *Id.* at para. 234.

to Article 1(a) of the U.K.-Turkmenistan BIT, "investment" included "every kind of asset" and provided a non-exhaustive list of examples, including:

> "Moveable and immoveable property and any other property rights such as mortgages, liens, or pledges;"
>
> "Claims to money or to any performance under contract having a financial value;" and
>
> "Intellectual property rights, goodwill, technical processes, and know-how."[43]

The tribunal found that, based on the language of the BIT, GK LLP made an investment in Turkmenistan because GK LLP "negotiated a contract to build bridges for TAY in Turkmenistan, put resources into the country, and actually built a number of bridges."[44] According to the tribunal, this was "an investment of equipment and material resources – moveable property – while carrying out in Turkmenistan at least a portion of the obligations it undertook to perform under a contract having a financial value – USD 100 million in gross value."[45] The tribunal determined that these activities satisfied the BIT's definition of "investment."[46] Thereafter,[47] the tribunal also concluded that by satisfying the definition of investment in the U.K.-Turkmenistan BIT, GK LLP's activities in Turkmenistan also satisfied the definition of investment under Section 25 of the ICSID Convention.[48]

The tribunal also rejected the argument that the investment was only made by GK LLP's Turkish parent, Garanti Insaat, and, therefore, could not be an "investment" pursuant to the terms of the BIT.[49] In rejecting the government's arguments, the Tribunal first acknowledged that the U.K.-Turkmenistan BIT did not define "investor." However, the U.K.-Turkmenistan BIT protected "investments of nationals or companies of the other Contracting Party."[50] Accordingly, without a definition of a qualifying "investor," the tribunal focused

43 *Id.* at para. 228.

44 *Id.* at para. 232.

45 *Id.* at para. 234.

46 *Id.*

47 Importantly, in doing so, the tribunal declined to apply the *Salini* test that other investment arbitration tribunals have used to define an investment under the ICSID Convention. *Id.* at para. 239.

48 *Id.* at paras. 235–242.

49 *Id.* at paras. 221–224.

50 *Id.* at para. 219.

on (i) the definition of "companies" under the U.K.-Turkmenistan BIT, and (ii) the meaning of "investments."[51]

The Tribunal found that the U.K.-Turkmenistan BIT broadly defined "company" and essentially required *only* that a business be organized under the laws of the U.K – as was the case for GK LLP.[52] Contrary to the government's position, the BIT did not require a claimant to have actual operations in the U.K.[53] Moreover, the tribunal found that TAY clearly knew it was contracting with a U.K. company because, among other reasons, (i) the contract identified GK LLP as TAY's counterparty, (ii) the Central Bank of Turkmenistan released payments to GK LLP, and (iii) the Turkmenistan government's announcement of the contract award referenced GK LLP and its U.K. nationality.[54]

Last, the tribunal rejected Turkmenistan's argument that GK LLP's claims arose out of contract, not the BIT, and therefore must be referred to the local courts and not arbitration pursuant to the BIT.[55] The tribunal acknowledged that if GK LLP had, in fact, only referred claims for breach of contract, the tribunal would lack jurisdiction to hear the dispute.[56] However, the tribunal explained that "[a]ll that is required to confer on this Tribunal jurisdiction to consider the Claimant's treaty claims is for one of the Claimant's claims to arise under the BIT" and concluded that GK LLP's claims for expropriation, denial of fair and equitable treatment, *etc.* all fell within the scope of the BIT.[57] In doing so, the tribunal explained that regardless of the merits of GK LLP's treaty claims, to confer jurisdiction to the tribunal, all that mattered was that GK LLP properly alleged a claim arising under the BIT.[58]

2.2 *Strabag SE v. Libya*

In *Strabag SE v. Libya*, the claimant, Strabag SE, asserted various treaty claims against the Libyan government due to losses stemming from the 2011 Libyan civil war. Strabag SE is an Austrian company and a large international construction firm.[59] Strabag SE's German subsidiary, Strabag International Ltd. ("Strabag Intl.") entered into several large road and infrastructure projects

51 *Id.* at paras. 219–220, 228.
52 *Id.* at para. 220.
53 *Id.* at para. 222.
54 *Id.* at paras. 220–225.
55 *Id.* at paras. 243–247.
56 *Id.* at para. 244.
57 *Id.* at para. 247.
58 *Id.* at para. 246.
59 *Strabag SE v. Libya*, ICSID Case No. ARB(AF)/25/1, Objections to Jurisdiction, (June 29, 2020), paras. 2–4.

with the Libyan Investment and Development Company ("LIDCO"), a Libyan governmental organization.[60] Strabag Intl. and LIDCO subsequently created a joint venture named Al Hani Construction Co. ("Al Hani") to carry out the contracts.[61] Strabag SE indirectly owned 60% of Al Hani through its 100% ownership of Strabag Intl. During construction, Al Hani experienced substantial losses and witnessed the destruction of its equipment as a result of the 2011 Libyan conflict.[62] Strabag SE alleged that those losses were the product of multiple violations by Libya of the Agreement between the Republic of Austria and the Great Socialist People's Libyan Arab Jamahiriya (the "Austria-Libya BIT") and elected to pursue its claims against Libya under the Austria-Libya BIT pursuant to the ICSID Additional Facility Rules.[63]

During the course of the arbitration, the tribunal considered a series of jurisdictional questions, the most salient of which include: (i) whether the claimant had made a qualifying "investment," (ii) whether the claimant was an "investor" under the Austria-Libya BIT; and (iii) whether Strabag SE retained standing to recover the losses suffered by a local subsidiary.[64]

2.2.1 Did Strabag SE Make an Investment?

Libya first argued that Strabag SE did not have a qualifying "investment" as required by the Austrian-Libya BIT and the ICSID Additional Facility Rules because Strabag SE's activities did not retain the essential characteristics of an "investment" as defined by the *Salini* test.[65] First, Strabag SE had not assumed any investment risk because Al Hani had contractual guarantees that it would be paid for its work.[66] Second, Strabag SE had not made any significant capital contribution to its activities in Libya because, according to Libya, Strabag SE funded its work through advance payments from Libyan entities and regular payments to Al Hani for completed work.[67] Third, Strabag SE's series

---

60 *Id.* at paras. 57–58.

61 *Id.*at para. 59.

62 *Id.* at paras. 75–84.

63 *Id.* at paras. 1, 9.

64 Libya also objected to the tribunal's jurisdiction to hear Strabag SE's contractual claims and argued that Strabag SE was required to resolve those claims through the Libyan courts. The tribunal ultimately rejected Libya's argument on the ground that an umbrella clause contained in Article 8(1) of the Austria-Libya BIT afforded the tribunal jurisdiction. The concept of and application of umbrella clauses are discussed in greater detail *infra* Section 3.5.

65 *Strabag SE*, *supra* note 59, at para. 104.

66 *Id.*

67 *Id.*

of limited-term construction contracts were of insufficient duration to be an investment.[68] Fourth, Strabag SE did not make sufficient contribution to Libya's economic development.[69]

The tribunal rejected each of the government's arguments and concluded that Strabag SE made a protected investment within the meaning of the applicable BIT and the ICSID Additional Facility Rules for a variety of reasons.[70]

First, the tribunal explained that Article 1(2) of the Austria-Libya BIT defined "investment," in relevant part, as: "*every kind of asset* ... owned or controlled, directly or indirectly" by an investor.[71] The tribunal concluded that Strabag SE's construction activities in Libya squarely fit within the definition of investment in the Austria-Libya BIT.[72] As the tribunal explained, Strabag SE indirectly owned a 60% majority of Al Hani through its 100% ownership of Strabag Intl. Al Hani was a substantial joint venture that held significant contracts and carried out major construction activities, owned real property, and had a prolonged physical presence in Libya.[73]

Second, the tribunal quickly dispatched each of the four arguments Libya raised to assert that Strabag SE's activities did not retain the essential characteristics of an "investment."[74] As the tribunal explained, Strabag SE "committed significant human and material capital to its investment over a period of several years, acquiring property in Libya, building large facilities, and importing large quantities of heavy equipment, including material such as rock crushers that only made economic sense in the context of a long term presence in Libya."[75] Strabag SE's venture "was hardly free from risk" and "provided a social benefit to [Libya] in the form of roads that were significantly improved."[76] Although the tribunal did not decide whether the *Salini* test should be applied, the tribunal concluded that there was no real question that Strabag SE's activities in Libya qualified as an investment by nearly any standard.[77]

68 *Id.*

69 *Id.* at paras. 103–104.

70 *Strabag SE* was initiated pursuant to the Additional Facility Rules whereby none of the ICSID Convention provisions apply. Because the *Salini* test was derived from an interpretation of the ICSID Convention, the tribunal concluded that the *Salini* test should not apply here.

71 *Strabag SE*, *supra* note 59, at paras. 99, 108.

72 *Id.* at para. 108.

73 *Id.* at paras. 108–110.

74 *Id.* at para. 110.

75 *Id.*

76 *Id.* at paras. 108–110.

77 *Id.* at para. 109.

2.2.2 Was Strabag SE an Investor?

The Libyan government also disputed that Strabag SE was an "investor" under the Austria-Libya BIT.[78] The government primarily argued that Strabag SE's "investment" was made indirectly through multiple layers of subsidiaries, including Strabag Intl., which owned 60% of Al Hani.[79] The government claimed that Strabag SE needed to have made a direct investment without using intermediate entities to be an "investor."[80]

The tribunal rejected this argument as well.[81] Based on article 1(2) of the BIT, an "investment" includes assets "owned or controlled … indirectly" by an investor. With little discussion, the tribunal determined that Strabag SE had clearly made an investment through its wholly owned subsidiary. Indeed, nothing in the Austria-Libya BIT required that Strabag SE make a direct investment to qualify as an investor.[82]

2.2.3 Did Strabag SE Have Standing as a Shareholder?

Last, Libya also challenged the jurisdiction of the tribunal to hear Strabag SE's claims on the ground that Strabag SE had no authority to assert claims on behalf of and collect funds that belonged to a separate juridical entity, Al Hani.[83] As explained above, Strabag SE operated in Libya as a 60% shareholder in Al Hani.

As the tribunal explained, prior investment arbitration cases have found that a claimant has standing to recover compensation based on the diminution of value of its shareholding interests in a locally incorporated entity.[84] However, the tribunal acknowledged that this case was distinct because Strabag SE sought to collect compensation based on a pro-rata share of the damage incurred by Al Hani directly, such as unpaid payment certificates, costs for additional works, and costs for delays.[85] In other words, instead of calculating its losses based on the loss of value to its shares in Al Hani, Strabag SE sought 60% of the compensation it contended that Libya owed Al Hani.

The tribunal disagreed with Libya's challenge. Based on Article 1(2) of the BIT, investment included: "investment by an investor of a Contracting

78 *Id.* at para. 113.
79 *Id.* at paras. 113–115.
80 *Id.* at paras. 113–116.
81 *Id.* at para. 119.
82 *Id.* at paras. 117–119.
83 *Id.* at paras. 121–122.
84 *Id.* at para. 125.
85 *Id.* at para. 126.

party, *owned or controlled, directly or indirectly*, by an investor of the other Contracting Party."[86] The tribunal also concluded that based on the available evidence, Al Hani was, in fact, controlled and directed by Strabag SE in all practical respects.[87] As a result, "[t]he investment here included a variety of assets, in addition to Strabag's 60% interest in Al Hani, that were owned or controlled, directly or indirectly, by Claimant."[88]

3 Substantive Treaty Claims in Investor-State Arbitration

As explained above, IITs provide foreign investors certain basic protections against expropriation, unfair or inequitable treatment, or discrimination by host states. The breadth of these protections, and whether they are provided for at all, depend very much on the precise language of each individual IIT. More significantly, however, a violation of any one of these protections will entitle the investor to assert specific "treaty claims" against the host state. While treaty claims take many shapes and forms, as explained in greater detail below, some of the most common types of treaty claims include: (i) direct/indirect expropriation claims; (ii) fair and equitable treatment claims; (iii) full protection and security claims; (iv) most favored nation claims; and (v) umbrella clause claims.[89]

The following section discusses each of these substantive treaty claims and provides examples of how these claims arise and have been addressed in connection with construction industry disputes.

3.1 *Direct and Indirect Expropriation*

Expropriation claims are among the most common forms of treaty claims and, in basic terms, occur when a host state takes property from its owner.[90] However, international law does not dictate that all forms of expropriation

86 *Id.* at para. 127.

87 *Id.* at paras. 131–134.

88 *Id.* at para. 135.

89 *See, e.g.*, George Town Law, "Legal Provisions most Invoked in Disputes," Center for the Advancement of the Rule of Law in the Americas, accessed October 6, 2022, https://isdslac.georgetown.edu/legal-provisions-most-invoked-in-disputes/ (listing most common treaty claims amongst Latin American countries).

90 Tim R. Samples, "Winning and Losing in Investor-State Dispute Settlement," *American Business Law Journal* 56, no. 1 (2019): 168 ("A more recent study illustrates the greatest portion of ISDS activity consists of indirect expropriation claims[.])."

are wrongful.[91] Indeed, expropriations that serve a public purpose, are not discriminatory, and result in just compensation for the investor are not inherently problematic.[92] As a result, most IITs only prohibit expropriations that are wrongful or unlawful.[93]

Notwithstanding the above, what constitutes "expropriation" is heavily dependent on the specific language contained in the relevant IIT and is evaluated on a case-by-case basis.[94] Most often, expropriation takes one of two forms: (i) direct expropriation and (ii) indirect or creeping expropriation.[95]

Direct expropriation consists of a mandatory legal transfer of title to property (often by virtue of some form of legal decree) or physical seizure without just compensation.[96] As one arbitral tribunal explained: "[r]ecognizing direct expropriation is relatively easy: governmental authorities take over a mine or a factory, depriving the investor of all meaningful benefits of ownership or control."[97]

On the other hand, indirect expropriation involves the deprivation of use, management, and/or control of the investor's property in a meaningful way without necessarily transferring title of the property.[98] This type of expropriation typically involves "covert or incidental interference with the use of property which has the effect of depriving the owner, in whole or in significant part, of the use or reasonably-to-be-expected economic benefit of the property even if not necessarily to the obvious benefit of the state."[99] For example, in the case of *Metalclad*, the Mexican government revoked a permit that enabled the claimant to operate a hazardous waste plant based on alleged concerns over environmental protection, but the ICSID arbitral tribunal concluded that the acts of the Mexican government constituted an act of expropriation.[100]

---

91 *See generally* Caroline Henckels, "Should Investment Treaties Contain Public Policy Exceptions?" *Boston College Law Review* 59, no. 8 (2018): 2825; UNCTAD, "Expropriation: UNCTAD Series on Issues in International Investment Agreements II," UNCTAD, 2012, accessed October 13, 2022, https://unctad.org/system/files/official-document/unctaddiaeia2011d7_en.pdf.

92 *See generally id.*

93 *See generally id.*

94 *See generally* UNCTAD, *supra* note 91.

95 *See id.*

96 *See, e.g., Metalclad Corporation v. United Mexican States*, ICSID Case No. ARB/97/1, Award, (Aug. 30, 2000).

97 *Marvin Roy Feldman Karpa v. United Mexican States*, ICSID Case No. ARB(AF)/99/1, Award, (Dec. 16. 2002), 36.

98 *See, e.g., Metalclad Corporation*, *supra* note 96, at para. 103.

99 *Id.* at 28.

100 *Id.*

Separately, the concept of a "creeping expropriation" refers to a series of actions by the host state that, over an extended period, cumulatively deprives the claimant of the value of its investment.[101]

In the context of construction disputes, expropriations can take a variety of forms ranging from the physical seizure of assets to government interference that deprives the investor of the value of the investment. However, tribunals have also made clear that a state actor's decision to terminate a construction agreement or seize a party's assets by virtue of a contractual right or through proper legal channels will not necessarily constitute expropriation. The following cases illustrate how tribunals have addressed expropriation claims in connection with construction projects and when certain conduct may (and may not) give rise to valid claims of expropriation.

3.1.1 Alpha Projektholding GmbH v. Ukraine

In *Alpha Projektholding*, a real estate development company based in Villach, Austria known as Alpha Projektholding GmbH ("Alpha") asserted a variety of treaty claims against the government of Ukraine in connection with the reconstruction and renovation of several floors of a hotel in Kyiv, Ukraine.[102] The hotel was owned and operated by an arm of the Ukrainian government.[103] Although the facts that gave rise to the arbitration are complex, in essence, during the course of construction, hotel authorities encountered difficulties financing the project and, alongside Ukrainian government officials, engaged in a series of protracted negotiations that sought to restructure the underlying payment terms of the construction agreements.[104] Ultimately, after several years, the Ukrainian authorities ceased payment altogether and attempted to revoke the underlying construction agreements through legal actions filed with the Ukrainian courts.[105] After several failed efforts to resolve the dispute, Alpha initiated an arbitration against the Ukrainian government pursuant to the Agreement for the Promotion and Reciprocal Protection of Investments between the Republic of Austria and Ukraine (the "Austria-Ukraine BIT")

101 *Starrett Housing Corp v. the Government of the Islamic Republic of Iran*, Award No. ITL 32-24-1, 4 Iran–US C.T.R. 162, 1983, 115; *see also Crystallex international Corp. v. Bolivarian Republic of Venezuela*, ICSID Case No. ARB(AF)/11/2, Award, (Apr. 4, 2016).

102 *Alpha Projektholding GmbH v. Ukraine*, ICSID Case No. ARB/07/16, Award, (Nov. 8, 2010), paras. 1, 103.

103 *Id.* at para. 97.

104 *Id.* at paras. 44–100.

105 *Id.* at paras. 125, 404.

alleging, among other things, that Ukraine's denial of payment constituted an indirect expropriation.[106]

Alpha argued that the Ukrainian authorities' extended efforts to renegotiate the payment terms of the underlying construction agreements over the course of several years and the ultimate cessation of payment constituted a form of creeping expropriation.[107] For its part, Ukraine argued that the contract renegotiation efforts and the ultimate cessation of payment (i) were actions of the hotel's management, not the Ukrainian government; (ii) did not deprive Alpha of value of its investment because Alpha could enforce the contracts in the courts; and (iii) were commercial decisions unrelated to any exercise of sovereign power of the Ukrainian government.[108]

The tribunal found in favor of Alpha and concluded that Ukraine had, in fact, indirectly expropriated Alpha's investment.[109] The tribunal explained, "[i]t is well established that a government action need not amount to an outright seizure or transfer of title to amount to an expropriation under international law."[110] Thus, according to the tribunal, the underlying investment would be expropriated if the contracts were rendered useless by the actions of the Ukrainian government.[111] Applying this standard, the tribunal concluded that Ukraine clearly expropriated Alpha's investment. There was no dispute that Alpha had been deprived of the value of the contracts because the Ukrainian authorities ceased payment and never intended to resume making payments.[112]

The tribunal rejected Ukraine's arguments to the contrary.[113] Specifically, the tribunal found that the Ukrainian authorities' actions caused the cessation of payments, not hotel management.[114] Further, the tribunal concluded that the right to enforce the contracts in the local Ukrainian courts was not relevant to the question of whether Alpha had been denied the value of its investment. All that mattered was that there was no prospect that Ukraine would ever resume payment, even if the contracts may be nominally enforceable in the local courts.[115] Last, while the tribunal questioned the relevance of drawing

106 *Id.* at para. 404.

107 *Id.* at paras. 404–406.

108 *Id.* at para. 407.

109 *Id.* at paras. 407–412.

110 *Id.* at para. 408.

111 *Id.* at para. 408.

112 *Id.* at paras. 409–410.

113 *Id.* at paras. 411–412.

114 *Id.* at paras. 372–373.

115 *Id.* at para. 411.

a distinction between "sovereign" and "commercial" actions, the tribunal concluded that, in any event, the Ukrainian government exercised an outsized role in the management of the underlying construction contracts such that the state itself caused the ultimate breach of the commercial agreements.[116]

3.1.2 Garanti Koza LLP v. Turkmenistan

In *Garanti Koza*, GK LLP argued that Turkmenistan *directly* expropriated its investment when Turkmenistan (i) seized GK LLP's factory in Turkmenistan, sold GK LLP's equipment, and expelled GK LLP employees from GK LLP's factory in Turkmenistan; (ii) terminated the underlying construction contract between GK LLP and TAY; and (iii) secured the Turkmenistan judgments that attached GK LLP's assets and awarded TAY approximately $15 million.[117]

In addition, GK LLP argued that Turkmenistan *indirectly* expropriated its investment because the government engaged in a series of actions that, taken together, substantially deprived GK LLP of "the use, enjoyment, and economic benefits of its investment without paying fair compensation."[118] GK LLP emphasized that the government (i) repudiated the lump sum pricing structure originally dictated by the underlying construction contract; (ii) failed to pay sums due to GK LLP; (iii) wrongfully imposed delay penalties; and (iv) failed to notify GK LLP of the actions taken before the Turkmenistan courts.[119]

The tribunal denied both GK LLP's claims of direct and indirect expropriation.[120]

According to the tribunal, although it was true the Turkmenistan government seized GK LLP's factory and equipment, *it did so as a result of GK LLP's default under the parties' contract*.[121] "A seizure of property by a court as a result of normal domestic legal processes does not amount to expropriation under international law unless there was an element of serious and fundamental impropriety about the legal process."[122] Based on the tribunal's review of the evidence, it did not find that Turkmenistan departed from the normal legal process to unfairly prejudice GK LLP.[123] The tribunal also determined that because GK LLP's indirect expropriation claim was based on the same allegations used

116 *Id.* at para. 403.
117 *Garanti Koza LLP*, *supra* note 33, at paras. 253–255.
118 *Id.* at paras. 253–258.
119 *Id.* at para. 258.
120 *Id.* at paras. 364–370.
121 *Id.* at para. 364.
122 *Id.* at para. 365.
123 *Id.* at para. 369.

to support its direct expropriation claim, a finding that the government did not directly expropriate GK LLP's investment meant that Turkmenistan did not *indirectly* expropriate GK LLP's investment as well.[124]

3.1.3 Malicorp Limited v. Arab Republic of Egypt

In *Malicorp Limited v. Arab Republic of Egypt*, the claimant, a U.K. based-company named Malicorp Limited ("Malicorp"), entered into a contract with the Egyptian government to construct the Ras Sudr International Airport on the basis of a "Build, Operate, Transfer" ("B.O.T.") concession contract.[125] A B.O.T. contract is unique in that the contracting partner, not the owner, bears the responsibility of financing the project.[126]

Malicorp's bid was accepted by the Egyptian government and the contract was signed in November 2000.[127] According to the contract, Malicorp was obligated to undertake a number of administrative actions quickly, including establishing an Egyptian company capable of doing business in Egypt and providing Egypt with a series of bank guarantees to secure Malicorp's performance.[128] Malicorp, however, allegedly did not complete these administrative tasks within the contractual timeline.[129] Indeed, beginning as early as December 2000, Egypt placed Malicorp on notice of non-performance and requested that the company cure the alleged breaches.[130] After numerous notices and meetings between party representatives, in August 2001, Egypt terminated Malicorp's contract for non-performance.[131]

In light of Egypt's termination, Malicorp initiated ICSID arbitration against the Egyptian government pursuant to the Agreement for the Promotion and Protection of Investments between the United Kingdom of Great Britain and Northern Ireland, and the Arab Republic of Egypt ("U.K.-Egypt BIT").[132] Malicorp alleged the Egyptian government's unilateral termination of the contract without compensation amounted to, among other things, expropriation in violation of Article 5 of the U.K.-Egypt BIT.

Article 5 of the UK-Egypt BIT provides as follows:

---

124 *Id.* at paras. 370–371.

125 *Malicorp Ltd. v. Arab Republic of Egypt*, ICSID Case No. ARB/08/18, Claims of Expropriated Compensation, (Feb. 7, 2011), para. 93.

126 *Id.* at paras. 93, 132.

127 *Id.* at para. 15.

128 *Id.* at para. 17.

129 *Id.* at paras. 18–22.

130 *Id.* at para. 18.

131 *Id.* at para. 33.

132 *Id.* at para. 74.

> Investments of nationals or companies of either Contracting Party shall not be nationalised, expropriated or subjected to measures having effect equivalent to nationalization or expropriation (hereinafter referred to as 'expropriation') in the territory of the other Contracting Party except for a public purpose related to the internal needs of that Party and against prompt, adequate and effective compensation. [sentence 2] Such compensation shall amount to the market value of the investment expropriated immediately before the expropriation itself or before there was an official government announcement that expropriation would be effected in the future, whichever is the earlier, shall be made without delay, be effectively realizable and be freely transferable. The national or company affected shall have a right, under the law of the Contracting Party making the expropriation, to prompt review, by a judicial or other independent authority of that Party, of whether the expropriation is in conformity with domestic law and of the valuation of his or its investment in accordance with the principles set out in this paragraph.[133]

Upon review of the evidence and the applicable treaty provisions, the tribunal concluded that Egypt had not expropriated Malicorp's investment by virtue of Egypt's decision to terminate the contract.[134] Although Malicorp alleged that Egypt's decision to terminate the underlying agreement was pre-textual, the tribunal did not find Malicorp's argument compelling.[135] Instead, as the tribunal explained, Malicorp had breached its obligations under the contract, including the requirement to form an Egyptian company within 90 days, and that, as a matter of law, Egypt was entitled to terminate the agreement.[136] This form of rescission, "justified in fact and in law," was not an "expropriatory measure."[137]

3.2 *Fair and Equitable Treatment Claims*

Fair and equitable treatment ("FET") claims, like expropriation claims, are commonly invoked in investor-state arbitrations. Nevertheless, there is no uniform definition of "fair and equitable treatment" amongst IITs.[138] In some

133 *Id.* at para. 123.
134 *Id.* at para. 137.
135 *Id.* at para. 129.
136 *Id.* at paras. 130–142.
137 *Id.* at para. 143.
138 UNCTAD, "Fair and Equitable Treatment: UNCTAD Series on Issues in International Investment Agreements II," UNCTAD, 2012, accessed October 13, 2022, 2–3, https://unctad.org/system/files/official-document/unctaddiaeia2011d5_en.pdf.

instances, IITs draft FET clauses with reference to customary international law[139] while others provide more prescriptive definitions for the concept of "fair and equitable treatment."[140] Regardless, in basic terms, the FET standard is intended to protect investors from arbitrary, discriminatory, or abusive conduct by host states.[141]

The evaluation of an FET claim is a fact-specific analysis. Tribunals commonly assess a number of factors to determine whether a host state's conduct was either unfair or inequitable. Most often, however, FET claims arise out of a common set of scenarios where an investor was either (i) denied justice and due process; (ii) the victim of arbitrary or discriminatory decision making; (iii) subject to abusive, coercive, or harassing conduct by the host state; or (iv) deprived of its legitimate expectations concerning the legal/business environment in the host state.[142]

In the context of construction projects, actions such as the failure to process or arbitrary revocation of permits,[143] unexpected and significant changes in legislation,[144] and unreasonable interference in the administration of the underlying contracts,[145] among others, all constitute breaches of the FET standard. The following case studies illustrate how the administration of construction contracts by government authorities give rise to FET claims.

3.2.1 Garanti Koza LLP v. Turkmenistan

In addition to GK LLP's expropriation claims, GK LLP also alleged that the Turkmenistan government's actions violated the U.K.-Turkmenistan BIT's fair and equitable treatment protections. GK LLP advanced its FET claim based on a number of allegations.[146] The most significant of those allegations were (i) that the Turkmenistan Ministry of Finance, an arm of the Turkmenistan government, insisted that GK LLP follow invoicing procedures that were fundamentally different from those required under GK LLP's contract with TAY and (ii) that the Turkmenistan government unfairly harassed GK LLP after

139 *See id.* at 6–8.

140 *See, e.g.*, the Comprehensive Economic and Trade Agreement (CETA), E.U.-Canada, October 30, 2016.

141 *See* UNCTAD, *supra* note 138, at 31.

142 *Id.* at 29–32.

143 *Metalclad Corporation*, *supra* note 96, at para. 74.

144 *MTD Equity Sdn. Bhd. and MTD Chile S.A. v. Republic of Chile*, ICSID Case No. ARB/01/7, Award, (May 25, 2004), para. 107.

145 *Garanti Koza LLP*, *supra* note 33.

146 *Id.* at para. 267.

termination of the project contracts through tax assessments, legal proceedings, and an improper assessment of USD 3 million in delay penalties.[147]

Article 2(2) of the U.K.-Turkmenistan BIT, like many other BITs, provides no definitive definition for "fair and equitable treatment."[148] Instead, it simply provides: "Investments of nationals or companies of each Contracting Party shall at all times be accorded fair and equitable treatment."[149] To fill this gap, the tribunal looked to prior arbitral decisions concerning FET claims and sought to determine:

- whether the shock or surprise occasioned to an impartial tribunal leads, on reflection, to justified concerns as to the judicial propriety of the outcome;
- whether there has been a willful disregard of due process of law, an act which shocks, or at least surprises, a sense of judicial propriety; and
- whether there has been inconsistency of action between two arms of the same government vis-à-vis the same investor, that is, has the government acted coherently and applied its policies consistently.[150]

Based on its review of the evidence, the tribunal determined that GK LLP successfully asserted a claim of unfair treatment.[151] Specifically, as GK LLP explained, during the course of construction, TAY delayed payment to GK LLP after GK LLP failed to utilize a project reporting and cost accounting procedure common to post-Soviet countries known as "*smeta*" (also spelled CMETA).[152] Problematically for Turkmenistan, the concept of *smeta* was not incorporated in the underlying construction contract and would adversely affect the value of progress payments GK LLP would receive during the work.[153] To circumvent the adverse impact on progress payments and still comply with *smeta*, GK LPP would have been required to misreport its costs on the underlying invoices.[154] As the tribunal explained, the different treatment of GK LLP's invoices by two Turkmenistan governmental agencies effectively forced GK LLP to decide between two untenable choices: (i) submit accurate invoices based on the new procedure and receive less compensation than it contracted for; or (ii) submit false invoices to receive full compensation.[155]

147 *Id.* at paras. 263–270.
148 *Id.* at para. 264.
149 *Id.* at para. 379.
150 *Id.* at para. 381.
151 *Id.* at para. 382.
152 *Id.*
153 *Id.* at para. 349.
154 *Id.* at para. 383.
155 *Id.* at para. 383.

According to the tribunal, the use of governmental power to force an investor to choose between receiving less than what it bargained for or certifying false information is so fundamentally unfair that it amounted to a denial of fair and equitable treatment.[156]

The tribunal did not, however, find that GK LLP met its burden to establish that the Turkmenistan government unfairly harassed GK LLP after the termination of the contracts.[157] Specifically, although GK LLP complained that the Turkmenistan authorities imposed substantial fines for alleged tax infractions and improperly assessed delay penalties for GK LLP's performance, the tribunal pointed out that GK LLP did not allege that it actually paid those fines and penalties.[158] Further, the tribunal was unpersuaded that the legal proceedings advanced in the Turkmenistan courts departed from the normal procedures of Turkmenistan law and, therefore, could not give rise to a cognizable FET claim.[159]

3.2.2 ADF Group Inc. v. USA

In *ADF Group Inc. v. USA*, the claimant, ADF Group, Inc. ("ADF Group") a Canadian structural steel fabrication company, pursued an FET claim against the United States pursuant to the now obsolete North American Free Trade Agreement ("NAFTA").[160]

The dispute arose out of a subcontract agreement between ADF Group's subsidiary, ADF International, Inc. ("ADF Intl.") and Shirley Contracting Corporation ("Shirley") wherein ADF Intl. agreed to supply Shirley with all structural steel components for a major highway interchange project in Virginia approximately 20 kilometers south of Washington, D.C.[161] ADF Intl. agreed to use U.S.-produced steel for the project, but advised Shirley that it wished to fabricate the steel at ADF Group's facilities in Canada.[162] Shirley advised the Virginia Department of Transportation of ADF Intl.'s intentions and, in response, the department notified ADF Intl. that fabricating even U.S.-produced steel in Canada violated the upstream contract (the "prime contract") between Shirley and the Virginia Department of Transportation.[163] Specifically,

156 *Id.* at paras. 379–390.
157 *Id.* at paras. 386, 390.
158 *Id.* at paras. 267, 386, 389.
159 *Id.* at para. 387.
160 *ADF Grp. Inc. v. United States of America*, Case No. ARB(AF)/00/1, Claims of Unfair Treatment, (Jan. 9, 2003), paras. 1, 59.
161 *Id.* at para. 44.
162 *Id.* at para. 49.
163 *Id.* at para. 50.

the prime contract incorporated, by reference into the subcontract, certain *Buy America* provisions that required the steel to be produced and fabricated in the U.S.[164] ADF Intl. and Shirley attempted to convince the Virginia Department of Transportation and the Federal Highway Authority that the Buy America Act permitted the non-domestic fabrication of American-produced steel, but the Federal Highway Authority rejected ADF Intl.'s reading of the act.[165] As a result, ADF Intl. had to subcontract with five different U.S. fabrication facilities at significant additional cost to fulfill its obligations under the subcontract.[166]

According to ADF Group, the Federal Highway Authority's insistence that the *Buy America Act* required the steel materials to be 100% produced and fabricated in the U.S. was "*per se* unfair and inequitable within the context of NAFTA."[167]

NAFTA Article 1105(1), titled The Minimum Standard of Treatment Obligation, provided as follows:

> Each party shall accord to investments of investors of another Party treatment in accordance with international law, including fair and equitable treatment and full protection and security.[168]

The tribunal ultimately rejected ADF Group's unfair treatment claim for a variety of reasons.[169]

First, the tribunal concluded that measures like the *Buy America Act* were not unfair or inequitable because similar requirements are common amongst procurement contracts in the United States, as well as Canada, Mexico, and other countries around the world.[170] Thus, the tribunal explained that ADF Group could not reasonably maintain that the United States' *Buy America Act* was so arbitrary or idiosyncratic to give rise to a violation of Article 1105(1).[171]

Second, the tribunal rejected the argument that the Federal Highway Administration, in enforcing the Buy America Act's provisions, violated Article 1105(1) because its interpretation of the act and decisions were inconsistent with applicable law.[172] As the tribunal explained, the law on which

164 *Id.* at para. 52.
165 *Id.* at para. 51.
166 *Id.* at para. 55.
167 *Id.* at para. 71.
168 *Id.* at para. 68.
169 *Id.* at paras. 187–192.
170 *Id.* at para. 188.
171 *Id.*
172 *Id.* at paras. 189–190.

ADF Group relied was subject to differing interpretations and the U.S. Federal Government's decision to reject ADF Group's reading of applicable law was not unfair or arbitrary.[173] Without more, the tribunal concluded, ADF Group could not prove a violation of Article 1105(1).[174]

Third, the tribunal dismissed ADF Group's argument that the United States violated the FET standard set forth in Article 1105(1) because the United States allegedly breached its duty under customary international law to perform its obligations in good faith.[175] According to the tribunal, the question of whether the United States acted in good faith was of "only negligible assistance."[176] In truth, questions of "fair and equitable treatment" required the investor to prove that the United States either acted arbitrarily, purposefully discriminated against ADF Group, and/or unfairly imposed extraordinary costs on ADF Group.[177] According to the tribunal, ADF Group failed to meet its burden.[178]

3.3 *Full Protection and Security*

Most IITs include certain minimum guarantees of "Full Protection and Security."[179] These guarantees, in general terms, aim to ensure that the host state takes reasonable measures, as it would for its own nationals, to prevent the physical destruction of an investment, in particular, where the protective measures fell within the normal exercise of government functions.[180]

Full protection and security claims can arise in a number of different scenarios. For example, in *APPL v. Sri Lanka*, the arbitral tribunal concluded that Sri Lanka violated the relevant BIT's full protection and security guarantees when Sri Lankan military forces destroyed the investor's shrimp farm and killed several of the investor's employees as part of a military campaign by Sri Lankan authorities to combat militia groups in the region.[181] In other cases, some tribunals have extended the full protection and security guarantees to

173 *Id.*

174 *Id.* at paras. 189, 192.

175 *Id.* at para. 191.

176 *Id.*

177 *Id.*

178 *Id.* at para. 192.

179 Helge Elisabeth Zeitler, "Full Protection and Security," in *International Investment Law and Comparative Public Law*, ed. Stephen W. Schill (Oxford: OUP, 2010), 383.

180 *AAPL v. Republic of Sri Lanka*, ICSID Case No. ARB/87/3, Award, (June 27, 1990); *Am. Mfg. & Trading v. Republic of Zaire*, ICSID Case No. ARB/93/1, Award, (February 21, 1997); *Wena Hotels Ltd. v. Arab Republic of Egypt*, ICSID Case No. ARB/98/4, Award, (December 8, 2000).

181 *AAPL*, *supra* note 180.

guarantees of adequate legal/judicial protection of the rights of foreign investors beyond just protection against physical harm.[182]

Given that many international construction projects are executed in remote jurisdictions, often with limited resources and infrastructure, security protections can be significant for construction firms. The following cases illustrate how tribunals have addressed claims related to full protection and security clauses.

3.3.1 American Manufacturing & Trading v. Zaire

In *American Manufacturing v. Zaire*,[183] a U.S. based manufacturing firm called American Manufacturing & Trading Corporation ("AMT") with operations in Zaire (now the Democratic Republic of the Congo) asserted treaty claims against Zaire for violations of the Bilateral Treaty concluded between the United States of America and the Republic of Zaire concerning the Reciprocal Encouragement and Protection of Investment (U.S.-Zaire BIT).[184]

According to AMT, in September 1991, an industrial complex that AMT owned and operated was looted by members of Zaire's armed forces.[185] AMT claimed that the soldiers broke into the complex and destroyed, damaged, and stole various forms of goods and raw materials found on the premises.[186] Although AMT reopened the complex in February 1992, the complex was looted once again approximately a year later and permanently closed thereafter.[187] According to AMT, Zaire was liable for AMT's losses because Zaire breached its full protection and security obligations under Article II of the U.S.-Zaire BIT.[188] Article II states as follows:

> *Investment of nationals and companies of either Party shall at all times be accorded fair and equitable treatment and shall enjoy protection and security in the territory of the other party. The treatment, protection, and security of investment shall be in accordance with applicable national laws, and may not be less than that recognized by international law … Each Party*

182 *Siemens A.G. v. Argentine Republic*, ICSID Case No. ARB/02/8, Award, (February 6, 2007).

183 The authors acknowledge that *American Manufacturing v. Zaire* does not directly arise out of a construction and engineering project; however, the facts and circumstances described in the arbitration award are equally as applicable to the conditions encountered on international construction projects.

184 *Am. Mfg. & Trading, Inc., supra* note 180.

185 *Id.* at para. 3.04.

186 *Id.*

187 *Id.*

188 *Id.* at para. 3.07.

> *shall observe any obligation it may have entered into with regard to investment of nationals or companies of the other party.*[189]

In response, Zaire offered no evidence to establish that it afforded AMT any form of protection or security.[190] Instead, Zaire cited a provision of the Zairian Ordinance law that excused the government from liability for losses or injuries suffered as a result of riots or insurrections.[191] Relying on this provision of Zairian law, Zaire argued that that it could not be responsible for AMT's losses because its obligations to provide full protection and security would only extend as far as permitted by local law.[192]

The tribunal disagreed.[193] As the tribunal explained, the U.S.-Zaire BIT created "an obligation of vigilance, in the sense that Zaire as the receiving State of investments made by AMT, an American company, shall take all measures necessary to ensure the full enjoyment of protection and security of its investment *and should not be permitted to invoke its own legislation to detract from any such obligation.*"[194] Based on the available evidence (or lack thereof), the tribunal concluded that Zaire "breached its obligation by taking *no measure whatever* that would serve to ensure the protection and security of the investment in question."[195]

3.3.2 Strabag SE v. Libya

As explained in detail above, in *Strabag SE*, the 2011 Libyan conflict led to the loss and destruction of a significant amount of Al Hani's equipment and other material resources in Libya.[196] Among Strabag SE's treaty claims was that Libya violated its obligations to provide full protection and security under the Austria-Libya BIT.

Specifically, Article 3(1) of the Austria-Libya BIT requires each contracting party to accord investments by investors of the other state "full and constant protection and security."[197] Strabag SE argued that Libya violated Article 3(1) because the state allegedly failed to provide reasonable measures of protection

189 *Id.* at para. 6.04.
190 *Id.* at para. 3.12.
191 *Id.*
192 *Id.*
193 *Id.* at paras. 6.02–.08.
194 *Id.* at para. 6.05 (emphasis added).
195 *Id.* at para. 6.08 (emphasis added).
196 *Strabag SE*, *supra* note 59, at paras. 75–84.
197 *Id.* at para. 229.

against physical harm. Strabag also denied that a lack of resources could serve as an excuse for the host state.[198]

The Tribunal detailed at some length the widespread 2011 Libya conflict and the resulting violence and civil disorder.[199] However, notwithstanding the substantial physical harm suffered by Strabag SE, the Tribunal ultimately determined that Libya did not breach its treaty obligations.[200] More specifically, the tribunal concluded that it was not reasonably possible for the Libyan government to take all full and consistent measures to protect Strabag SE's investments.[201] Indeed, international law affords a host country deference in relation to its duty to protect.[202] Ordinarily, a "State will only breach its obligations if what was done shows such a degree of negligence, defective administration of justice or bad faith, that the procedure falls below the standards of international law."[203] A state's exercise of diligence must be evaluated in the context of the surrounding circumstances and, in the context of the 2011 Libya conflict, the Libyan government's actions did not fall below that standard.[204]

3.4 *Most Favored Nation Status*

IITs commonly contain provisions known as "most favored nation" ("MFN") clauses that ensure the host state may not treat one foreign investor's investment any differently than an investor from another foreign country. While the language of these MFN provisions can vary, the concept is generally well accepted.[205] These provisions aim to provide investors "a guarantee against certain forms of discrimination by host countries, and … [to establish] equality of competitive opportunities between investors from different foreign countries."[206] Most favored nation clauses can be particularly valuable provisions because they allow investors of one state to be afforded protections the host state offers to investors of other countries under an entirely separate IIT.[207] The

198 *Id.* at paras. 230–231.
199 *Id.* at paras. 75–84.
200 *Id.* at paras. 234–236.
201 *Id.*
202 *Id.*
203 *Id.* at para. 232.
204 *Id.* at paras. 234–236.
205 *See* OECD, "Most-Favoured-Nation Treatment in International Investment Law: OECD Working Papers on International Investment 2004/02," OECD, September 2004, accessed October 13, 2022, https://www.oecd-ilibrary.org/docserver/518757021651.pdf?expires=1665652589&id=id&accname=guest&checksum=655AA00B9ADFB1611CDA191F5865213D.
206 UNCTAD, "Most Favored-Nation Treatment," UNCTAD, 1999, accessed October 13, 2022, 1, https://unctad.org/system/files/official-document/psiteiitd10v3.en.pdf.
207 *See* OECD, *supra* note 205, at 1.

following case of *ATA Construction v. Jordan* illustrates how MFN provisions are used in connection with construction-related investor-state arbitrations.

3.4.1 ATA Construction, Industrial and Trading Company v. The Hashemite Kingdom of Jordan

At issue in *ATA Construction v. Jordan* was the question of whether the Kingdom of Jordan ("Jordan") violated an MFN clause under the Agreement between the Kingdom of Jordan and Republic of Turkey Concerning the Reciprocal Promotion and Protection of Investment ("Jordan-Turkey BIT").[208]

In 1998, ATA Construction, Industrial and Trading Company ("ATA") and Arab Potash Company ("APC") entered into a form construction contract for APC to construct a dike at a site on the Dead Sea.[209] The contract was governed by the laws of Jordan and contained an arbitration clause.[210] Once the dike was constructed, APC took possession of the dike and filled it with water.[211] During the filling process, a section of the dike collapsed.[212] A dispute arose between the parties concerning who was liable for the collapse.[213]

APC commenced commercial arbitration proceedings against ATA pursuant to the parties' contract. On September 30, 2003, the arbitral tribunal concluded that ATA was not at fault.[214] In addition, the arbitral tribunal upheld, in part, ATA's counterclaim and awarded compensation to ATA.[215]

Less than a month later, on October 29, 2003, APC applied to the Jordanian Court of Appeal to have the final award annulled under the Jordanian Arbitration Law.[216] Approximately three years later, on January 24, 2006 the Jordanian Court of Appeals annulled the award principally because the arbitral tribunal allegedly failed to correctly apply the Jordanian Civil Code to decide the merits of the case.[217] ATA subsequently appealed this annulment to the higher Jordan Court of Cassation, but the Court of Cassation upheld the annulment.[218]

---

208 *ATA Constr., Indus. and Trading Co. v. The Hashemite Kingdom of Jordan*, ICSID Case No. ARB/08/2, Claims of MFN Clause Violations, (May 18, 2010), para. 88.
209 *Id.* at para. 31.
210 *Id.* at paras. 61–62.
211 *Id.* at para. 32.
212 *Id.*
213 *Id.*
214 *Id.* at para. 33.
215 *Id.* at para. 32.
216 *Id.* at para. 35.
217 *Id.* at para. 46.
218 *Id.* at paras. 48–54.

In order to resolve the underlying dispute, APC commenced suit before the Jordanian courts instead of arbitration.[219] APC did so because, in 2001, just after the parties' executed the contract but before the arbitral tribunal issued its final award, Jordan enacted the Jordanian Arbitration Law that, pursuant to Article 51 of the statute, extinguished the right to arbitration if an arbitral award was annulled.[220] As a result, following the annulment of the final award, ATA no longer had the ability to pursue its claims through arbitration as required by the parties' underlying contract.[221]

After the Court of Cassation's decision, ATA brought a claim under the Jordan-Turkey BIT alleging a violation of the MFN clause.[222] Specifically, as ATA explained, Jordan was obligated, by virtue of Article II(2) of the Turkey-Jordan BIT, to provide ATA's investment with protections no less favorable than that accorded in similar situations to investments of investors of any third country.[223] Those protections included guarantees of fair and equitable treatment and treatment required by customary international law, by virtue of similar protections contained in Jordan's other BITs.[224] ATA argued that the annulment of the arbitration award and extinguishment of ATA's right to arbitration amounted to a denial of justice and that the denial of justice constituted a violation of both the fair and equitable treatment standard and customary international law.[225] Accordingly, ATA concluded that the Jordanian courts' decisions to annul the arbitration award and extinguish ATA's right to arbitration constituted a violation of the MFN clause contained in the Turkey-Jordan BIT.

The tribunal agreed with ATA's interpretation and application of the MFN clause contained in the Turkey-Jordan BIT and sought to determine whether Jordan's actions denied ATA's right to fair and equitable treatment.[226] While the tribunal disagreed with the assertion that the Jordanian court's decision to annual the final award constituted a violation of the FET standard, the tribunal

219 *Id.* at para. 55.

220 *Id.* at paras. 81–82.

221 *See id.* at paras. 35–36.

222 As the tribunal in *ATA Construction* acknowledged, the preamble of the Turkey-Jordan BIT also made reference to a "fair and equitable treatment" standard. However, because no FET provision was specifically incorporated into the provisions of the Turkey-Jordan BIT, ATA relied on the MFN to ensure it could avail itself of FET protections.

223 *ATA Constr., Indus. and Trading Co.*, *supra* note 208, at para. 79.

224 *Id.* at para. 73. For example, ATA pointed to what it viewed as more favorable protections the Jordanian government afforded under treaties with the U.K., Spain, Croatia, and the U.S.

225 *Id.* at paras. 73–74.

226 *Id.* at paras. 121–125.

found that the Jordanian Arbitration Law did.[227] Specifically, the tribunal reasoned that a right to arbitration is a right to legitimate performance related to an "investment."[228] By depriving ATA any recourse after the Court of Cassation extinguished ATA's right to arbitration, the tribunal found that Jordan violated the Jordan-Turkey BIT by denying ATA a vital contractual right to arbitration.[229]

3.5 *Umbrella Clauses*

An "umbrella clause" is a provision found in many IITs that provides additional protections to investors.[230] In general terms, an umbrella clause ensures that breaches of investment contracts entered into between the host state and a foreign investor amount to a breach of the umbrella clause contained in a BIT.[231] In theory, an umbrella clause therefore allows an investor to elevate contractual claims to the level of treaty violations.[232] However, there is substantial uncertainty over how tribunals should interpret and apply umbrella clauses in investor-state arbitrations.[233] The case of *Garanti Koza* illustrates the application of an umbrella clause.

3.5.1 Garanti Koza LLP v. Turkmenistan

In *Garanti Koza*, GK LLP also alleged that TAY's various breaches of the parties' contract were not only breaches of that agreement, but also breaches of the U.K.-Turkmenistan BIT pursuant to an umbrella clause within the applicable treaty. Specifically, Article 2(2) of the U.K.-Turkmenistan BIT provided, in relevant part, that the contracting states agreed to "observe any obligation it may have entered into with regard to investments of nationals or companies of the other Contracting Party."[234] Turkmenistan opposed GK LLP's interpretation of the umbrella clause and argued, "a breach of a purely commercial contract should not become an international wrong within the reach of an investment treaty simply because one party to the contract could be considered an organ of the state."[235]

---

227 *Id.* at paras. 124–132.

228 *Id.* at para. 117.

229 *Id.* at paras. 121–129.

230 *See* Jarrod Wong, "Umbrella Clauses in Bilateral Investment Treaties: Of Breaches of Contract, Treaty Violations, and the Divide Between Developing and Developed Countries in Foreign Investment Disputes," *George Mason Law Review* 14 (2006): 138–39.

231 *Garanti Koza LLP*, *supra* note 33, at para. 328.

232 *See* Wong, *supra* note 230, at 149.

233 *See id.* at 138–139.

234 *Garanti Koza LLP*, *supra* note 33, at para. 328.

235 *Id.* at para. 330.

The tribunal acknowledged that umbrella clauses could not elevate all contractual breaches to the status of a treaty violation.[236] As the tribunal put it, "[a] failure by a government agency to pay for a box of pencils delivered pursuant to an agreement to provide office supplies, for example, would not come within the reach of [the BIT], because it would have nothing to do with an investment."[237] However, "an act of an organ of a state that results in the breach of a contractual obligation *relating to an investment* of a national or company of the other state party to the BIT," according to the tribunal, "does seem to come within the reach of [the umbrella clause]."[238] Upon its review of the facts, the tribunal concluded that the contract breaches at issue in *Garanti Koza* fell into the latter category of breaches and, therefore, would constitute a treaty violation.[239]

More precisely, the tribunal agreed that Turkmenistan breached its obligations under the BIT when it refused to comply with the invoicing standards dictated by the underlying contract and, instead, demanded that GK LLP apply the *smeta* project reporting and cost accounting procedure.[240] According to the tribunal, Turkmenistan's breach of the invoicing requirements set out in the underlying construction agreement deprived GK LLP of a substantial portion of its investment.[241] These failures thus constituted a violation of the umbrella clause of the U.K.-Turkmenistan BIT.[242]

4 Conclusion

Much more can be said about the dozens of different investor-state arbitration awards that arise out of international construction and engineering project disputes. However, the survey of cases above introduces readers to many of the concepts and problems these arbitrations present. As is apparent from international commercial arbitrations, large-scale international projects raise issues and disputes that are truly unique to the construction sector. The same logic applies, in varying degrees, to *investor-state* arbitrations involving construction

236 *Id.*
237 *Id.*
238 *Id.*
239 *Id.* at para. 330.
240 *Id.* at paras. 338, 346–354.
241 *Id.* at para. 346.
242 *Id.* at para. 397.

projects. As construction continues to become an increasingly more significant sector for investor-state arbitration, expect that the issues raised in these arbitrations will become increasingly more nuanced, complex, and common.

CHAPTER 9

Expedited Arbitration as an Alternative to Dispute Boards during the Course of International Construction Projects

Pierre-Yves Gunter and Anya Marinkovich

1 Introduction

Construction projects inherently imply long-term contractual relationships, with a myriad of risk factors that lend themselves to claims and disputes arising between the employer/owner and contractor. It is in both parties' interests to resolve these disputes as expeditiously as possible, especially during the life of the project, to enable the parties to have the necessary clarity on questions of cash-flow, risk allocation, and allocation of project resources to complete the works. The need to resolve disputes in real-time during the course of a construction project is reflected in the claims procedures under the Fédération Internationale des Ingénieurs Conseils ("FIDIC") standard form contracts, according to which claims must be notified "as soon as practicable" and no later than 28 days after the claiming party has or should have become aware of the claim, failing which means the claim is (in principle)[1] time-barred.

To address the need for real-time dispute resolution during large construction projects, dispute boards have become prominent in the past half-century in the construction industry (albeit the concept of industry-specific dispute resolution mechanisms (such as trade-specific commercial courts) date back much longer than that).[2]

Since their introduction in US infrastructure projects in the 1970s, dispute boards have become a standard feature of international construction contracts

1 As noted by Philip Norman and Leanie van der Merwe, whether such strict time-bar defenses are upheld may depend on the governing law of the contract. See Philip Norman and Leanie van der Merwe, "Chapter 11: Claims Resolution Procedures in Construction Contracts," in *Guide to Construction Arbitration*, eds. Stavros Brekoulakis and David Brynmor Thomas (London: Law Business Research Ltd, 2019), 152–153.

2 See *e.g.*, Michael Mortimer-Hawkins, "Clause 20, Dispute Resolution," FIDIC, accessed April 26, 2022, https://fidic.org/sites/default/files/24%20CLAUSE%2020,%20DISPUTE%20RESOLUTION.pdf.

 DOI:10.1163/9789004514874_012

that are seen as providing efficient and cost-effective dispute resolution during the life of construction projects and preventing recourse to arbitration.[3] Indeed, according to one analysis of the data of the use of dispute boards from 1975 to 2006, in 1,532 projects, 92.4% of disputes were settled, and only 2.8% of disputes were referred to binding dispute resolution procedures.[4] However, another study concerning the use of dispute boards on the Central Artery/ Tunnel project in Boston found that, out of 86 construction contracts associated with that project, 46 used dispute review boards and 40 did not, and "a greater percentage of [contracts using dispute review boards] as opposed to [contracts not using dispute review boards] had unresolved claims/disputes" after the project's substantial completion.[5] Moreover, the majority of respondents to the 2019 Queen Mary University of London survey concerning international construction arbitration stated that parties "infrequently" comply with pre-arbitral decisions (such as decisions from a dispute board),[6] and while 71% of respondents reported using international commercial arbitration to resolve construction disputes, only 36% reported having used dispute boards.[7] With the large number of disputes that end up in arbitration (often despite having gone through the dispute board process), the question arises whether parties would not be better served by a process of expedited arbitration, which is now provided for under most institutional arbitration rules, and which results in a final and binding – and immediately enforceable – arbitral award.[8]

---

3 See *e.g.*, Albert Bates and Zach Torres-Fowler, "Dispute Boards: An Approach to the Efficient Resolution of Disputes in the Construction Sector," *Dispute Resolution Magazine* 26, no. 3 (September 2020).

4 Donald Charrett, "Dispute Boards and Construction Contracts," FIDIC, October 20, 2009, para. 12, https://fidic.org/sites/default/files/3%20charrett09_dispute_boards.pdf.

5 Kathleen M. Harmon, "Case Study as to the Effectiveness of Dispute Review Boards on the Central Artery/Tunnel Project," *Journal of Legal Affairs and Dispute Resolution in Engineering Construction* 1, no. 1 (February 2009): 18–31. (It is nevertheless noted that the study in question does not consider the type of dispute board put in place or the applicable procedures, nor did it consider whether there was any eventual recourse to litigation or arbitration for these "unresolved" claims and disputes).

6 Pinsent Masons, "International Arbitration Survey – Driving Efficiency in International Construction Disputes," Queen Mary University of London, accessed April 26, 2022, 12, http://www.camsantiago.cl/minisites/informativo-online/2019/NOV/docs/international-arbitration-survey-november-2019.pdf.

7 22% reported having used "dispute boards" and 14% having used "standing dispute boards." *Id.* at 8.

8 The question of how best to address disputes during the life of a construction project was also recently discussed by eminent arbitrator Sally Roe at her keynote speech for the Global Arbitration Review (GAR) Live: Construction Disputes conference held on September 23, 2021. Ms. Roe opined that another possible alternative to the typical dispute board-to-arbitration mechanism would be the process of expert determination (see Cosmo Sanderson, "Is

This chapter will explore the essential facets of dispute boards under a number of institutional rules, including the International Chamber of Commerce ("ICC") Dispute Board Rules, the Chartered Institute of Arbitrators ("CIArb") Dispute Board Rules, the American Arbitration Association ("AAA") Dispute Resolution Board Guide Specifications, and the dispute resolution provisions contained in FIDIC standard form contracts, which will then be compared with the process of expedited arbitration in terms of their applicability under the leading institutional arbitration rules, the length and scope of the process, the choice and appointment of arbitrators, and the enforceability of the resulting determination. Finally, the advantages and disadvantages of these two forms of dispute resolution will be analyzed in the context of four main types of disputes that arise in international construction projects, namely technical/factual disputes (site conditions, material defects, *etc.*), legal/contractual disputes (rights and obligations under the law, contract interpretation), disputes arising from project delays, and financial disputes (relating to payment mechanisms, performance bonds, insurance, *etc.*). Through this analysis, this chapter will give some insight as to whether expedited arbitration is better suited to resolve certain types of disputes, and/or whether dispute boards provide the most efficient mechanism to prevent and resolve disputes during the life of a project.

2 The Use of Dispute Boards on International Construction Projects

2.1 *The Concept*

Dispute boards are intended to assist the parties with contemporaneous dispute resolution and project management. Ideally, the use of a dispute board results in dispute avoidance, or at least minimizes recourse to litigation or arbitration, with associated time and cost implications.

Therefore, the use of a dispute board is typically agreed in the construction contract itself, *i.e.*, at the outset of the parties' contractual relationship.[9] In concrete terms, this is done through the inclusion of a multi-tiered arbitration agreement that defines the requirements and time limits for notifying a claim to the other party, referring the dispute to the dispute board, and in the event

expert determination a 'third way' for construction disputes?," Global Arbitration Review, September 23, 2021, https://globalarbitrationreview.com/expert-determination-third-way-construction-disputes). What is clear is that users are not entirely satisfied with the dispute board-to-arbitration approach and that alternatives do exist.

9 That is not to say that parties to a construction contract could not decide at a later stage, or even at the time when a dispute arises, to refer the matter to a dispute board.

a party is unsatisfied with the outcome of the dispute board proceeding, referring the matter to arbitration.

The two main types of dispute boards are the dispute adjudication board (DAB), who issues binding decisions, and the dispute review board (DRB), who issues recommendations. Dispute boards can either be standing (*i.e.*, constituted at the beginning of the project and retained until completion of the works) or *ad hoc* (*i.e.*, appointed if and when a dispute arises).[10] It is widely acknowledged that standing dispute boards are more effective in achieving the purposes of project management and dispute avoidance because standing boards are able to become familiar with the project and the parties.[11] Indeed, for large, on-site construction projects, standing dispute boards are recommended.[12] Standing dispute boards conduct regular site visits, can be consulted when an issue arises, and can assist the parties in agreeing on a solution before it becomes adversarial.[13] However, standing dispute boards are likely (but not always)[14] a more expensive option.

Where a contractual dispute resolution clause requires referral of claims to a dispute board before they can be referred to arbitration, a decision from the dispute board acts as a condition precedent to arbitration.[15] Thus, any dispute – no matter how big or small – must undergo the dispute board procedure before it can be finally determined by a court or arbitral tribunal.

2.2 *Standard Rules and Procedures*

To assess the utility of a dispute board in relation to specific types of construction disputes, it is necessary to have a view of the common attributes of dispute board rules and procedures. Questions of timing and cost must be carefully considered, as this will determine whether using a dispute board makes sense for the nature or value of a dispute.

There are two main sources of rules that would apply to the dispute board: the terms of the parties' contractual agreement to use a dispute board and the specific dispute board rules that the parties agree to apply (if any).

---

10 Lindy Patterson and Nicholas Higgs, "Chapter 12: Dispute Boards," in *Guide to Construction Arbitration*, eds. Stavros Brekoulakis and David Brynmor Thomas (London: Law Business Research Ltd, 2019), 156–157.

11 Charrett, *supra* note 4, at para. 14; Patterson & Higgs, *supra* note 10, at 157.

12 Mortimer-Hawkins, *supra* note 2.

13 In the same vein, it should be noted that the 2017 revision of the FIDIC Yellow Book now refers to the "Dispute Avoidance/Adjudication Board" (DAAB), highlighting that a main function of a dispute board should be the avoidance of disputes.

14 Patterson & Higgs, *supra* note 10, at 157; see also *supra* note 9.

15 Patterson & Higgs, *supra* note 10, at 160.

Either the contract or the applicable rules, or both, will address issues such as the appointment of dispute board members, how and by which party the dispute board fees are paid, whether the dispute board's decision is binding, and the modalities of notices and referrals.

An example of a contractual clause regarding the use of dispute boards, and probably one of the most common examples, can be seen in Clause 20 of the FIDIC Yellow Book (1999). According to Clause 20.1, contractor claims must be notified to the employer/owner within 28 days of (actual or constructive) knowledge of the event giving rise to a claim, followed within 42 days by the submission of the detailed particulars of the claim, upon which the Engineer must then make a determination within another 42 days (in accordance with Clause 3.5 FIDIC Yellow Book). Only then can a dispute be referred to the dispute board, which is then given 84 days to issue a decision that is immediately binding on the parties. Either party may, however, file a notice of dissatisfaction with the dispute board's decision within 28 days from receipt and refer the matter to arbitration.

There are also several rules and regulations that have been developed specifically for dispute board proceedings, such as the ICC Dispute Board Rules, CIArb Dispute Board Rules, and the AAA Dispute Resolution Board Guide Specifications.

Under the ICC Dispute Board Rules, the establishment of a standing dispute board is the general rule.[16] Provisions are made for three types of dispute boards: dispute review boards (who issue non-binding recommendations),[17] dispute adjudication boards (who issue binding decisions),[18] and combined dispute boards (who can issue both recommendations and decisions where specifically requested by a party).[19] In all cases, the dispute board "shall establish a schedule of meetings" (and/or site visits).[20] The powers of the dispute

16 Art. 3(1) ICC Dispute Board Rules ("*Unless otherwise agreed, the Parties shall establish the [dispute board] at the time of entering into the Contract*"). It is also stated in the Foreword to those rules that a dispute board is a "standing body," and Art. 7, "Appointment of the DB Members," states that DB member(s) shall be appointed within 30 days from the signing of the Contract. As agreements to use dispute boards are usually included in the project contract, this would mean that a dispute board is established at the beginning of the project. Of course, the parties to an ongoing project could however conclude their "Contract" to appoint a dispute board at any stage, which would be more akin to an *ad hoc* dispute board, even if governed by the ICC Dispute Board Rules. "Dispute Board Rules," ICC, Art. 3(1).

17 *Id.* at Art. 4.

18 *Id.* at Art. 5.

19 *Id.* at Art. 6.

20 *Id.* at Art. 12.

board include ordering the production of documents, deciding upon procedural matters, questioning the parties and/or any representatives or witnesses, and – with agreement of the parties – appointing an expert.[21] Users of international arbitration will recognize many of these same powers as being those granted to arbitral tribunals under typical arbitration rules. Importantly, an additional power of dispute boards under the ICC Dispute Board Rules is set out in Article 16, according to which:

> [i]f at any time, in particular during meetings or site visits, the [dispute board] considers that there may be a potential Disagreement between the parties, the [dispute board] may raise this with the Parties with a view to encouraging them to avoid the Disagreement on their own.

In terms of notification and time limits, under the ICC Dispute Board Rules, the referral of a dispute to the dispute board takes the form of a Statement of Case (Article 19), upon receipt of which the responding party has 30 days to submit its Response (Article 20). Article 21 states that hearings should in principle be held 15 days after receipt of the Response. Finally, Article 22 states that the dispute board shall issue its recommendation or decision "promptly and, in any event, within 90 days of the Date of Commencement" (*i.e.*, the date of receipt of the Statement of Case: see Article 19(2)).

The CIArb Dispute Board Rules are very similar in essence to the ICC Dispute Board Rules, particular in terms of timing and procedures. Under both rules, approximately three months will elapse from the referral of the dispute to the dispute board to the issuance of the board's recommendation or decision. The AAA Dispute Resolution Board Guide Specifications are slightly different, as they provide only for the issuance of recommendations by the dispute board, and the overall timing of the procedural steps is less defined. For instance, while the time limit for the response to the initial statement of case is 28 days, a hearing will be "generally be conducted at the time of the next regularly scheduled Site visit," after which the dispute board has only 14 days to issue its recommendation.[22]

---

21 *Id.* at Art. 15.

22 See "AAA Dispute Resolution Board Guide Specifications," AAA, December 1, 2000, Rules C.3, D.1 and I.1, https://www.adr.org/sites/default/files/document_repository/AAA%20Dispute%20Resolution%20Board%20Guide%20SPECIFICATIONS.pdf.

The AAA also has a specific and separate set of rules concerning the organization of site visits and progress reports by the dispute board[23] and another set of rules concerning the organization of hearings and taking of evidence.[24] Certain aspects of these rules highlight the unique nature of construction disputes that need to be taken into consideration in the dispute avoidance and resolution process, such as the need for having up-to-date knowledge of the progress of the works[25] and of the existence of subcontractors with their own potential related claims.[26]

2.3 *Enforceability*

As mentioned, dispute board proceedings result in either a decision (in the case of a DAB) or a recommendation (in the case of a DRB).[27] DAB decisions are binding on the parties and therefore the parties must immediately comply, but they are not final, as either party can issue a notice of dissatisfaction and refer the dispute to arbitration. DRB recommendations are neither final nor binding, and are really intended to assist the parties in coming to agreement regarding the settlement of the dispute.

Even where a dispute board decision has become final, as when neither party has submitted a notice of dissatisfaction, the parties might not voluntarily comply. In such cases, the dispute as to compliance is a question of breach of contract (*i.e.*, breach of the parties' dispute resolution agreement) and must itself be referred to the dispute board for determination, or – depending on the terms of the applicable dispute resolution procedures set out in the contract – referred directly to arbitration or litigation.[28] It should be noted that the ICC Dispute Board Rules has dispensed with the need for a dispute over

23 "AAA Dispute Resolution Board Operating Procedures," AAA, December 1, 2000, https://www.adr.org/sites/default/files/AAA_Dispute_Resolution_Board_Operating_Procedures.pdf.

24 "AAA Dispute Resolution Board Hearing Rules and Procedures," AAA, December 1, 2000, https://www.adr.org/sites/default/files/AAA_Dispute_Resolution_Board_Hearing_Rules_and_Procedures.pdf.

25 AAA Dispute Resolution Board Operating Procedures, *supra* note 23, at Rule 7.0 "Site Visit Agenda."

26 See AAA Dispute Resolution Board Hearing Rules and Procedures, *supra* note 24, at Rule 14.0 "Disputes involving Subcontractor Claims."

27 Patterson & Higgs, *supra* note 10, at 157. See also the definition of "Decision" and "Recommendation" provided for in the CIArb Dispute Board Rules, at 1–2, and Arts. 3(1) and 4(1) of those rules, which highlight the difference. "Dispute Board Rules," CIArb, August 2014, 1, 4, https://www.ciarb.org/media/3934/ciarb-dispute-board-rules-practice-standards-committee-august-2014.pdf.

28 Patterson & Higgs, *supra* note 10, at 161.

non-compliance with a decision to be referred back to the dispute board by providing, under Article 6(4), that such disputes can be referred directly to arbitration (if arbitration has been agreed as a dispute resolution mechanism), or to any court of competent jurisdiction.

3 Expedited Arbitration under Institutional Arbitration Rules

In response to growing discontent from users as to the length of international arbitration proceedings,[29] the concept of expedited arbitration has taken hold in the past decade as a means of providing more expeditious dispute resolution, especially for smaller-value disputes (although expedited procedures can also be opted into for high-value disputes, such as is often the case with construction disputes). The use of expedited arbitration for construction disputes has gained traction recently, one example being the use of the ICC Expedited Arbitration Rules in the revised FIDIC Green Book standard form contract.

Expedited arbitration is not referring to emergency arbitration or summary adjudication, but rather to a full-blown adversarial procedure within an expedited timeframe.

3.1 *Landscape of Institutional Rules*

Various forms of expedited arbitration are provided in most leading international intuitional arbitration rules, but the rules can differ with respect to some key questions, such as what threshold amount in dispute is taken into consideration for the application of the expedited arbitration provisions and what time limits are given to the parties and the tribunal for main procedural steps like filing submissions and rendering the award.

The most common arbitration rules in the construction industry are the Arbitration Rules of the ICC ("ICC Rules"), most likely due to their reference in the FIDIC standard form contracts. Article 30 of the ICC Rules provides for

29 Average arbitration proceedings administered by some of the leading arbitration institutes have been found to average over a year in length, and in the case of the ICC nearly two years. See Niklas Åstenius & Martin Ågren, "Chapter 3: Time and Cost in Arbitration," in *International Arbitration in Sweden: A Practitioner's Guide*, eds. Annette Magnusson, Jakob Ragnwaldh, and Martin Wallin, 2nd ed. (Kluwer Law International: 2021), para. 8. While this means that arbitration should still be preferred over court litigation, expedited procedures that last in principle for a maximum of six months provide a noticeable difference in terms of timing as compared to standard arbitration proceedings.

mandatory expedited arbitration within the terms set out in Appendix IX, referred to as the "Expedited Procedure Provisions."

The following other arbitration rules also provide for expedited arbitration: the Swiss Arbitration Centre's Arbitration Rules (see Article 42); the Hong Kong International Arbitration Centre ("HKIAC") Arbitration Rules (see Article 42); the Arbitration Institute of the Stockholm Chamber of Commerce ("SCC") (see the Rules for Expedited Arbitrations of the SCC); and the International Arbitration Rules of the International Dispute Resolution Center ("ICDR") (see Articles E1 *et seq.*).

The United Nations Commission on International Trade Law ("UNCITRAL") committee has recently adopted a set of expedited procedures as part of the UNCITRAL Arbitration Rules,[30] which are often used in *ad hoc* arbitrations not administered by an arbitral institution.

One exception are the Rules of Arbitration of the London Court of International Arbitration ("LCIA Rules"), which do not provide for expedited proceedings in the same way as the other rules cited above. Instead, there is the possibility to expedite the appointment of the arbitral tribunal under Article 9A of the LCIA Rules, and for the expedited replacement of an arbitrator under Article 9C, but otherwise no specific rules for expediting the remainder of the arbitral proceedings are included.

The AAA has also developed a set of "Fast Track Procedures" specifically for construction disputes, but their automatic application is limited to disputes between "two parties in which no disclosed claim or counterclaim exceeds $100,000,"[31] which is a low threshold. Parties can opt in to the Fast Track Procedures for any size of dispute, but the time limits under the Fast Track Procedures (being seven days for the filing of the answer and counterclaim,[32] seven days for the parties to agree upon a sole arbitrator[33] (failing which, one will be appointed by the institute),[34] a one-day hearing,[35] and issuance of the

30 See United Nations, Commission on International Trade Law, Report of Working Group II (Dispute Settlement) on the work of its seventy-fourth session (Vienna, 27 September – 1 October 2021), A/CN.9/1085, October 5, 2021.

31 "Construction: Industry Arbitration Rules and Mediation Procedures," AAA, last modified July 1, 2016, Rule R-1(b), https://www.adr.org/sites/default/files/Construction%20Rules.pdf.

32 *Id.* at Rule F-2.

33 Indeed, the Fast Track Procedures only apply where the case can be heard by a sole arbitrator. If the case is to be heard by a three-member panel, the Regular Track Procedures or Large, Complex Case Procedures will be used. See *id.* at Rule F-1, para. 3.

34 *Id.* at Rule F-5(c).

35 *Id.* at Rule F-11.

award fourteen days from the hearing or receipt of the parties' final briefs)[36] would be extremely difficult to apply where there are complex issues or multiple claims.

Another interesting set of rules established by the AAA are the "Supplementary Rules for Fixed Time and Cost Construction Arbitration," which contain Time/Cost Schedules setting out the precise amount of administrative fees, overall time of the arbitration from filing to award, and arbitrator's fees depending on the amount in dispute. For disputes valued up to $500,000, the maximum time limits from filing to award are between three and six months, similar to other expedited arbitration procedures. However, for higher-value claims (*i.e.*, above $1– 5 million), the maximum time from filing to award is up to 360 days. While this timeframe does not immediately appear expeditious, given that large and complex arbitration cases often last for two or more years, the AAA's fixed time arbitration is still relatively fast compared to the average arbitration, and therefore might also be an option for those parties seeking a faster dispute resolution procedure to include in their arbitration agreements.

3.2 *Standard Rules and Procedures*

Expedited arbitration procedures almost always apply in the case of smaller-value disputes where the parties have decided to arbitrate under a set of institutional arbitration rules. The specific threshold value differs from one set of rules to another, and as seen above it can range from approximately $100,000 (for example, under the AAA "Fast Track Procedures") to $3,000,000 (under the ICC Expedited Arbitration Rules). Not all expedited arbitration provisions are incorporated into main institutional rules and automatically apply to certain disputes subject to those main rules, one notable example being the Expedited Arbitration Rules of the SCC, which must be specifically chosen by the parties to govern their arbitration.[37] The German Arbitration Institute (DIS) Arbitration Rules also provide for an opt in expedited procedure following the formation of the arbitral tribunal[38] (and the arbitral tribunal must raise the possibility of using an expedited procedure with the parties at the first case management conference).[39] The 2018 Administered Arbitration Rules of the HKIAC also provide for an opt in expedited procedure, the application of which

36 *Id.* at Rule F-13.

37 See "Rules for Expedited Arbitrations," SCC, January 1, 2017, Preamble, ("SCC Rules for Expedited Arbitration").

38 "2018 DIS Arbitration Rules," German Arbitration Institute, March 1, 2018, Art. 1.4, ("DIS Rules").

39 *Id.* at Art. 27.4(ii).

can be requested by one party prior to the constitution of the arbitral tribunal.[40] Conversely, parties can always opt out of the application of expedited arbitration rules, although the automatic application of expedited arbitration provisions to construction disputes – which are often high-value disputes – is less likely to occur than for other types of contract disputes.

Other common features of most expedited arbitration rules are: by default, the appointment of a sole arbitrator as opposed to a three-member tribunal;[41] only one round of written submissions with shortened time limits;[42] limited time for the issuance of the final award (*e.g.*, three or six months from the start of the procedure).[43] Expedited arbitration procedures also do not make provisions for the production of documents, which is seen to be one of the more time-consuming phases of standard arbitral proceedings.[44]

In general, the attributes of an expedited arbitration procedure are similar to that of dispute boards, especially in terms of the amount of time one can expect to elapse – assuming no major extensions of time are agreed between the parties – from start to finish.[45] That said, expedited arbitration rules tend

40 "Hong Kong International Arbitration Centre Administered Arbitration Rules 2018," HKIAC, November 1, 2018, Art. 42.1, ("HKIAC Rules").

41 "Swiss Rules of International Arbitration (Swiss Rules)," Swiss Arbitration Centre, June 2021, Art. 42(2)(a), ("Swiss Rules"); "China International Economic and Trade Arbitration Commission (CIETAC) Arbitration Rules," China Council for the Promotion of International Trade/China Chamber of International Commerce, January 1, 2015, Art. 58, ("CIETAC Rules"); "International Dispute Resolution Procedures," ICDR, July 1, 2016, Art. E-6, ("ICDR Expedited Procedures"). Some rules go even further and state that the expedited arbitration "shall" be heard by a sole arbitrator. See *e.g.*, Art. 17 of the SCC Rules for Expedited Arbitration. Article 2(1) of the ICC Expedited Procedure Rules also mandates the institution to appoint a sole arbitrator even where the parties have agreed otherwise in their arbitration agreement. "2021 Arbitration Rules," ICC, January 1, 2021, Appendix VI, Art. 2(1), ("ICC Expedited Arbitration Rules").

42 See, *e.g.*, Arts. 57 and 59 of the CIETAC Rules; Art. 42.2(d) of the HKIAC Rules; Art. 3 of Annex 4 of the DIS Rules; Art. 42.2(c) of the Swiss Rules.

43 Art. 62 of the CIETAC Rules (3 months from the formation of the arbitral tribunal); Art. 43 of the SCC 's Rules for Expedited Arbitration (3 months from the transfer of the file to the arbitrator); Art. 42(2)(e) of the Swiss Rules (6 months from the receipt of the file by the arbitral tribunal); Art. 4(1) of the ICC Expedited Arbitration Rules (6 months from the case management conference, to be held 15 days from the transfer of the file to the arbitrator).

44 Christophe Seraglini and Patrick Baeten, "Chapter 2: Expedited Rules and the Possibility of Immediate Measures one a Tribunal is Constituted," in *Expedited Procedures in International Arbitration, Dossiers of the ICC Institute of World Business Law*, eds. Laurent Lévy and Michael Polkinghome (Paris: ICC Services, 2017), para. 32.

45 As indicated in footnote 43, this should be approximately 3 months in the case of dispute board proceedings and 3 to 6 months for expedited arbitration.

to be drafted with more restrictive language than dispute board rules regarding party autonomy in the interest of expeditiousness. The main difference, however, is the finality of the resulting decision.

3.3 *Limitations on Party Autonomy*

As a general rule in arbitration, in line with the fundamental principle of party autonomy, the parties are free to agree upon the arbitrator(s) that will hear their dispute.[46] This is also the case under expedited arbitration rules, although the default rule under some institutional arbitration rules is that expedited cases be heard by a sole arbitrator, even if the parties agreed upon a three-member arbitral tribunal in their arbitration agreement.[47] In this way, expedited arbitration procedures can limit party autonomy by overriding the parties' express choice as to the composition of the arbitral tribunal and the appointment procedure. The parties may also be limited in their means of presenting their case, for instance by restricting the number of written submissions and dispensing with in-person hearings.[48]

These limitations are justified by the need for an expeditious process, and the fact that the parties agreed to arbitrate their disputes under arbitration rules that provide for expedited arbitration with special procedures means that these limitations should not be seen as violating the parties' freedom of choice.[49] Furthermore, parties can often opt out of a restriction by agreement or can even choose to opt out of expedited arbitration provisions entirely.

3.4 *Enforceability*

The most important difference between a dispute board proceeding and an expedited arbitration lies in the finality of the resulting award or decision.

Awards issued from an expedited arbitration are final and binding in the same way as an arbitral award conducted under "normal" procedures. Therefore, except for the limited grounds of appeal that are generally available against arbitral awards (under national arbitration laws or the UN Convention

46 See discussion in Gary B. Born, "Chapter 12: Selection, Challenge and Replacement of Arbitrators in International Arbitration," in *International Commercial Arbitration*, 3rd ed. (Kluwer Law International, 2021), 1767–1788.

47 Art. 17 of the SCC's Rules for Expedited Arbitration; Art. 2(1) of the ICC Expedited Arbitration Rules.

48 Abdel Wahab, "Chapter 6: Expedited Institutional Arbitral Proceedings Between Autonomy and Regulation," in *Expedited Procedures in International Arbitration, Dossiers of the ICC Institute of World Business Law*, eds. Laurent Lévy and Michael Polkinghome (Paris: ICC Services, 2017), 144–146.

49 *Id.* at 150.

on the Recognition and Enforcement of Foreign Arbitral Awards), the expedited arbitration award is immediately enforceable.

As seen above, once parties have agreed to have their disputes heard by a dispute board as a mandatory pre-arbitral step, the failure to first refer a claim to the dispute board is a bar to arbitration. Thus, in the case of a multi-tiered contractual dispute resolution agreement, a pre-requisite to arbitration (expedited or not) would be compliance with the dispute board claims procedure. The Swiss Federal Tribunal has confirmed the mandatory nature of the pre-arbitral step of referring the dispute to the dispute board, failing which an arbitral tribunal would not, in principle and subject to any agreed exceptions, have jurisdiction to hear the dispute.[50] Thus, enforceability of an eventual arbitral award can itself depend on compliance with the dispute board process.

3.5 *A Note on Emergency Arbitration*

Another form of arbitration that is sometimes available to parties that have agreed to arbitrate disputes is emergency arbitration, which might be yet another alternative to dispute board use or even to the use of expedited arbitration for certain issues. A key condition to the availability of emergency arbitration is urgency, and therefore its application would be limited to a much narrower range of disputes. Also, emergency arbitration, as opposed to interim relief, is available in the circumstances where an arbitral tribunal has not yet been constituted for the dispute in question.

A typical example of an emergency arbitrator provision is Article 43 of the Swiss Rules, which provides at sub-clause 43(1) that "a party requiring urgent interim measures pursuant to Article 29 before the arbitral tribunal is constituted may submit to the Secretariat an application for emergency relief proceedings." In principle, the emergency arbitrator (who is appointed by the institution without consultation with the parties) shall issue its decision within 15 days from receiving the case file,[51] and such decision is binding only on a temporary basis (*i.e.*, until the termination of arbitral proceedings for the same matter or a final award has been issued).[52]

As with expedited arbitration, parties can choose to opt out of the emergency arbitration provisions of any given set of arbitration rules, for example by expressly stating in their arbitration agreement that emergency arbitration provisions shall not apply. Due to some national courts refusing to hear requests for interim relief because the parties agreed to arbitrate their disputes

---

50 Tribunal fédérale [TF] [Federal Court] July 7, 2014, 4A_124/2014.

51 Art. 43(7) of the Swiss Rules.

52 Art. 43(10) of the Swiss Rules.

with the option of emergency arbitration being available to the parties,[53] many parties, at least in the UK and US, now expressly opt out of emergency arbitration provisions in their arbitration agreements. However, if not subject to an express opt out, it may be useful for certain disputes to know that emergency arbitration is available if a temporary order to maintain the *status quo* is necessary while a party awaits an arbitral decision.

The question arises, where the parties have agreed to a dispute board as a mandatory pre-arbitral step, whether emergency arbitration would be available at all. It would likely depend on the nature of the urgent relief requested and its connection to a matter already decided by the dispute board and therefore ripe for arbitration.

3.6 *A Note on Summary Procedures and Early Determination*

Expedited arbitration also must be distinguished from summary dismissal procedures (also referred to as early determination) that are expressly provided for under several institutional arbitration rules.[54]

The purpose of summary procedures is the dismissal of a claim without undertaking all standard procedural steps on the grounds that the claim is manifestly unfounded (either in law or in fact). Summary dismissal must be the subject of a specific request from one of the parties and may result in the early dismissal of one or more claims.

Summary dismissal or early determination may take the form of bifurcation of the arbitral proceedings, in the sense that the parties agree (or the tribunal orders) that a preliminary issue of admissibility, jurisdiction, or liability is determined before the other issues on the merits. This does not necessarily entail any gains in expeditiousness, as a full set of pleadings and even hearings may be held on the preliminary issues. Thus, while there is a potential for an early determination to shorten the arbitration, there is also the potential that the request for dismissal on a preliminary issue is rejected and a final decision on the merits of the dispute will then only be obtained after the second phase of the proceedings. Of course, in the end, the overall expeditiousness of the

53 In the UK, the English High Court's decision in *Gerald Metals S.A. v. Timis & Ors*, [2016] EWHC 2327 (CH) was one such case. There, the court rejected a request for urgent relief under Section 44(3) of the English Arbitration Act on the grounds that the requirement of urgency was not met where an expedited tribunal or emergency arbitrator (under the LCIA Rules) could have properly dealt with the matter.

54 See, *e.g.*, Art. 39 of the SCC Rules for Expedited Arbitration; Art. 23 of the ICDR Expedited Procedures; Art. 43 of the HKIAC Rules. While Chapter IV of the CIETAC Rules is titled "Summary Procedure," this in fact relates to a form of expedited arbitration for disputes under RMB 5,000,000 and not the summary dismissal of a claim.

process also depends on the parties' willingness to have short time limits and to limit the number of submissions.

Finally, summary procedures can be used within expedited arbitration proceedings, as for example expressly set out in Article 40 of the SCC's Rules for Expedited Arbitration.

4 Tailoring the Dispute Resolution Mechanism to the Case at Hand

Dispute boards are often helpful, and even essential, for the proper functioning of construction projects, especially large international projects. However, the situation is becoming increasingly frustrating due to the dispute board process becoming too adversarial and with too many dispute board decisions being taken to arbitration. The arbitral process can even be complicated by the fact that only certain disputes – but perhaps not all related matters – have been taken to the dispute board and by parties confounding the arbitral process with a review of the dispute board decisions (therefore relying heavily on the submissions and procedures of the dispute board), whereas the arbitral tribunal must decide the dispute on its merits (and thus should hear the dispute *de novo*).

These issues beg the question whether there are circumstances in which it would be more appropriate to have immediate recourse to expedited arbitration rather than having a dispute first referred to a dispute board. It depends largely on the nature of the dispute and size of the dispute. There are four major types of disputes that arise in construction projects that merit consideration.

The first major category of disputes are those concerning technical and factual matters. These are the disputes that most benefit from the use of a (standing) dispute board that has knowledge of the project specifications and conditions, and which will more likely be made up of members with technical expertise in the field rather than legal expertise.

The second category of construction disputes are those related to the applicable law and contract interpretation. Here, there may be a good argument that this category of disputes lends itself to expedited and final determination in expedited arbitration proceedings in the interest of providing the parties with the contractual certainty required to carry out their obligations during the construction works. However, considering the high stakes involved when questions of risk allocation under the contract are in dispute, parties may be reluctant to have such issues decided in an expedited proceeding and may wish to keep the option to opt out of expedited proceedings where the issues in dispute are complex and require more time.

Another category of disputes in construction that cannot be overlooked are those relating to delay and requests for extensions of time. It is extremely important for the contractor to know its entitlement to an extension of time (or not) at the time of project execution, as this enables it to take acceleration measures when necessary to attempt to mitigate the effects of delays with a view to the planned date of completion (as extended). This may be a reason that expedited arbitration could better suit these types of disputes. At the same time, a contractor will have an obligation to mitigate delays, and issues of causation and concurrency of delays over the course of the project lean against expediting a final determination of delay disputes in favor of having these disputes first heard by a dispute board. Moreover, a standing dispute board will likely have a better idea of the real causes of delay because of its contemporaneous involvement with the parties and the project.

Finally, financial disputes – *i.e.*, disputes over late payments, performance bonds and guarantees, and other sureties often arise in construction projects and may have important implications on the contractor's available cash-flow during the life of the project and its ability to carry out the works on time. Financial disputes are more limited with respect to the factual and technical issues involved, and in light of the need for expeditious and final determination on questions of financing and cash flow, these types of disputes may be more appropriately dealt with directly in expedited arbitration proceedings rather than undergoing the dispute board process.

It is often difficult to place a dispute in only one of the four categories mentioned above. Delay issues may be intimately related to payment and financing issues or to the technical and factual issues on the ground, and legal issues such as risk allocations under the contract are often intimately tied to factual issues such as the site ground conditions.

For this reason, the choice of expedited arbitration as a replacement for dispute boards would, in most circumstances, not be easy or even beneficial. At the very least, parties to construction projects should be encouraged to opt in to expedited arbitration procedures when or if disputes are eventually referred to arbitration, especially if the dispute has already been hashed out in front of the dispute board and more time during the arbitral process encourages a "leave no stone unturned" legal approach that increases costs and uncertainty for the parties rather than efficient and practical resolution.

Another innovative solution might be found in combining the power of these two dispute resolution mechanisms to address construction disputes more efficiently. This could be spelled out in the agreed dispute resolution provision in the following manner:

The parties agree at the onset of the project to appoint a standing dispute board of either one or three members with the necessary technical expertise as well as a panel of either one or three arbitrators with legal expertise, subject to expedited arbitration rules. The chosen arbitrator(s) will remain the same for any dispute that arises during the project.[55]

The dispute board's jurisdiction will be limited to technical matters with a specific time-limit to issue: (1) a recommendation (on such technical matters only) and (2) a final and binding decision on those technical matters in the event a party submits a Notice of Dissatisfaction. This decision will not be subject to arbitration or appeal.

Disputes relating to the interpretation of the contract or of the applicable law will be subject to expedited arbitration.[56]

Site visits will be conducted by the dispute board, with the arbitral panel member(s) in attendance.

When deciding a dispute, the arbitral panel will be allowed to consult with the dispute board and vice-versa as necessary. However, to ensure due process and the parties' right to be heard, the consultation process shall always be done in a transparent manner.[57] Moreover, the parties must always have the opportunity to know the content of these discussions and to take positions thereon.[58]

---

55 This eliminates the inefficiencies relating to the constitution of an arbitral tribunal and from having multiple panels made up of different arbitrators.

56 Under one of the institutional procedural rules discussed above, and thus decided within a maximum of 3 to 6 months, depending on under which rules the parties wish to agree.

57 Indeed, a fair amount of debate exists in the context of arbitral tribunals' use of tribunal-appointed experts in this regard, as an expert normally should not take part in the tribunal's deliberations. As noted by certain authors, "there are serious risks associated with allowing the expert to be present in meetings with the tribunal without the parties also being present. […] If a tribunal were to listen to additional input from the expert during a meeting or deliberations without giving the parties the opportunity to comment on that input before taking it into account, this would undoubtedly breach rules of natural justice." Roman Khodykin and Carol Mulcahy, "Appendix 1 Commentary on the IBA Rules on Evidence, Article 6 Tribunal-Appointed Experts," in *A Guide to the IBA Rules on the Taking of Evidence in International Arbitration*, ed. Nicholas Fletcher (Oxford University Press, 2019), para. 9.121.

58 The idea here is that the tribunal and/or the dispute board could – upon consultation and with the participation of the parties – pose questions to each other to ensure a full

It could be argued that having standing dispute board and arbitral panels at the same time over the life of the project will have substantial cost implications; however, the potential for cost-saving by avoiding massive, years-long arbitration procedures would also be substantial. As an additional motivation to both the contractor and the employer to cooperate with the procedures, all costs associated with the dispute board and expedited arbitration proceedings should be split equally between the parties until a final decision on the allocation of these costs is issued after project completion.

5 Conclusion

Effective resolution in construction disputes requires both structure and flexibility. An ideal structure should anticipate the type of issues that arise on construction projects and have the proper mechanism to address those issues in a way that will provide finality and certainty to the parties so that the works can progress smoothly. The structure should also be adaptable to the needs of any dispute. The potential to avoid dispute escalation by addressing disagreements early, in a final and binding way, also merits consideration. Thankfully, there is no limit to the number of dispute resolution mechanisms available to the parties, and these mechanisms can always be tailored to the circumstances. Knowing what mechanisms are out there and how to use them effectively is the first step in the right direction.

---

understanding of the relevant issues. Using such an approach, the dispute board and the expedited arbitration panel could work hand-in-hand to have more consistent decisions.

CHAPTER 10

To What Port You Sail: Make Your Call on Demand Guarantees

Martina Magnarelli

1 Introduction: Navigating the Options for Injunctive Relief on Demand Guarantees

"If a man knows not to which port he sails, no wind is favorable."[1] This ancient quote is quite fitting for the applicant of an on-demand guarantee and the different fora (the ports) where he could seek interim relief. In any construction project, there are issues of contractor delay, contractor failure to perform, and many other known and unknown risks to owners. In domestic and international construction projects, it is typical for owners (the beneficiaries) to demand assurances of performance from contractors (the applicants), sometimes in the form of bonds, and often in the form of financial guarantees issued by third parties (the guarantors). To enjoin the beneficiary from calling on or encashing the demand guarantee, or the guarantor from executing the payment, the applicant could "sail" to national courts or to one or more emergency arbitrators (if there is an arbitration clause in the underlying contract and/or the guarantee agreement that directly or indirectly includes this option). In this triangle—between the applicant, the beneficiary, and the guarantor—stemming from at least two different contracts, each binding only two of the parties, the choice between, or for all, the potential fora requires careful analysis. Only by assessing the pros and cons of each of them against the specific circumstances of the case can the call (not on the demand guarantee, but for the competent forum, or for a parallel application for interim relief) be supported by a more propitious wind. This contribution will follow this route: first, consider on-demand guarantees in the construction industry—where they are more widely used—and second, assess the arguments for and against an injunction before an emergency arbitrator, national courts, or both simultaneously.

1 "Ignoranti quem portum petat nullus suus ventus est." in Lucius Annaeus Seneca, *Epistulae Morales ad Lucilium* (65), 71.

 | DOI:10.1163/9789004514874_013

2 On-Demand Guarantees in the Construction Industry: Knowing the Ropes

2.1 *On-Demand Guarantees: "Pay First, Argue Later"*

On-demand guarantees—the "life-blood of international commerce"[2] —are especially wide-used in the construction industry given their primary function of providing security.[3] The financial prowess of business partners is essential in long-term, technically complex, and expensive projects like the ones in construction and infrastructure.[4] The industry's main risks lie in the number of parties involved (the employer, the main contractor, the sub-contractor(s), the suppliers, the public authorities, where there is a public tender, ...). Time and cash-flow are of the essence, and any non-performance, lower, or delayed performance may cause a domino effect throughout the supply-chain.[5] Performance guarantees provide security precisely because the beneficiary can encash the amount guaranteed "on first demand," independently from any disputes under the underlying contract (principle of independence), by mere compliance with the formal conditions on the security (principle of documentary compliance).[6]

Merchants and bankers developed the practice of letters of credit (later evolving into on-demand guarantees) to meet the needs of international commerce for effective and secure instruments to the safeguard of their transactions.[7] The law recognizes this form of abstract payment and security (the "equivalent of cash in hand") that is indispensable in a sector like construction, where the need for cash-flow and the constant risk of under-capitalization or insolvency of any of the parties involved is immanent.[8] If the beneficiary

---

2 R.D. *Harbottle (Mercantile) Ltd. v. National Westminster Bank Ltd* [1977] 2 All ER 862, 870b.

3 They are widely used in construction contracts and often required in standard-form contracts; Karl Marxen, Demand Guarantees in the Construction Industry: A comparative legal study of their use and abuse from a South African, English and German perspective (Nomos, 2018), 51, 97.

4 *Id.*; Jurgita Petkute-Guriene, "Chapter 1: Access to Arbitral Justice in Construction Disputes (Dispute Board-Related Issues, Time Bar and Emergency Arbitration)," in *Construction Arbitration in Central and Eastern Europe: Contemporary Issues*, eds. Crina Baltag and Cosmin Vasile (Kluwer Law International, 2019), 1.

5 Todd Wetmore and Simon Elliot, "Chapter 12: COVID-19 and Construction Disputes," in *International Arbitration and the COVID-19 Revolution*, eds. Maxi Scherer, Niuscha Bassiri, and Mohamed S. Abdel Wahab (Kluwer Law International, 2020), 211; see *infra* Section 4., para. 1.

6 Marxen, *supra* note 3, at 74 et seq.; Nils Kleine-Möller: "Die Sicherung bauvertraglicher Ansprüche durch Bankbürgschaft und Bankgarantie," NZBau 2002, 590.

7 Marxen, *supra* note 3, at 74.

8 *Id.*, at 74, 99, 110; see also Wetmore and Elliot, *supra* note 5, at 211.

can encash the guarantee "on first demand" according to the adage "pay first, argue later,"[9] it is because of a trilateral relationship, or, rather, two separate contractual relationships between three parties. On one hand, the owner (or beneficiary) is entitled to call on the guarantee in case of non-performance or defective performance of the main contract by the applicant (or principal). On the other hand, the bank or another third financial institution, or, at times, the parent company of the applicant (the guarantor), issues the on-demand guarantee based on a separate agreement with the beneficiary (the guarantee agreement).[10] Due to the independence between these two contractual arrangements, the owner is secured against the principal's eventual failure to meet his obligations and obtains swift access to money. At the same time, the guarantor is not entangled in the dispute between the owner and the principal under the main contract.[11] The guarantor's obligation to pay solely arises from the on-demand guarantee, and he could be held liable by the owner if he does not comply. Therefore, whether the principal is effectively in breach of the main contract is immaterial. Nothing—or almost nothing—can stop the guarantor from paying on first demand.

2.2 *The Fraud Exception: Courts and Arbitral Tribunals' Case Law*

Today, the fraudulent call on a demand guarantee represents an internationally recognized exception to the principle of independence. Case law of national courts and arbitral tribunals applies the so-called fraud exception, though only in cases of forgery in the presented documents or absence beyond doubt of any right for the beneficiary to demand payment.[12]

English courts' case law, for example, first forbade the encashing of letters of credit in cases of document forgery, and then progressively extended its reach to on-demand guarantees and adopted a more liberal approach, shifting the attention away from the security to the overall transaction. By embracing a wider notion of "fraud," it sanctions the owner who has positive knowledge of his disentitlement to payment and justifies judicial intervention even when fraud "is situated in the *underlying transaction*."[13] However, the standard of proof on the applicant remains high. English courts:

---

9 Marxen, *supra* note 3, at 76.

10 *Id.* at 66, 98.

11 Christopher R. Seppala, "The ICC Uniform Rules for Demand Guarantees ('URDG') in Practice: A Decade of Experience," Presented at the ICC Conference, Paris (15 May 2001).

12 See Georges Affaki and Roy Goode, *Guide to ICC Uniform Rules for Demand Guarantees: URDG 758* (ICC, 2011), 5; Marxen, *supra* note 3, at 128; and *infra* Section 2.2., paras. 2 et seq.

13 Marxen, *supra* note 3, at 128, 131 (emphasis in the original); see also reference to *Deutsche Ruckversicherung AG v Walbrook Insurance Co Ltd* [1994] All ER 181 QBD, on appeal *Group*

> will generally grant an injunction where there is no dispute as to the formal validity of the demand only where it is established that the only realistic inference is that (a) the beneficiary could not honestly have believed that it was entitled to make a demand for payment and (b) the bank was aware that the demand was fraudulent.[14]

In the United States, case law has long been divided on the standard of fraud and relevance of the underlying transaction. More recent decisions seem to accept the notion of material fraud.[15] The official comment to the 1995 revised Article 5 of the Uniform Commercial Code (UCC) further provides that "this recodification makes clear that fraud must be found either in the documents or must have been committed by the beneficiary on the issuer or applicant." In *MID America Tire Inc v. PTZ Trading Ltd*, the Supreme Court of Ohio held that "material fraud committed by the beneficiary in either the letter of

---

Josi Re v Walbrook Insurance Co Ltd [1996] 1 WLR 1152 for letters of credit—although the injunction sought was eventually denied—and *TTI Team Telecom International Ltd v Hutchison 3G UK Ltd* [2003] 1 All ER (Comm) 914 ("*TTI Team Telecom*") for on-demand guarantees, 131–134. *TTI Team Telecom*, para. 31: "[o]nly if the issuer is about to make payment to the beneficiary in circumstances where fraud, dishonesty or bad faith in relation to the demand is shown to exist or where the original issue of the documentary credit was procured by fraud or, possibly, where the underlying transaction was itself procured by fraud will a court intervene to restrain payment by the issuer to a beneficiary."

14 *Shapoorji Pallonji & Company Private Limited v Yumn Ltd and Standard Chartered Bank* [2021] EWHC 862 (Comm), para. 19, referring to *Alternative Power Solution Ltd v Central Electricity Board* [2014] UKPC 31; see also Marxen, *supra* note 3, at 135.

15 In *Sztejn v. J Henry Schroder Banking Corp.* 177 Misc. 719, 31 N.Y.S.2d 631 (N.Y. Sup. Ct. 1941), the Supreme Court of New York explained that the independent principle applies "in cases concerning alleged breaches of warranty," but does not extend to a case "involving an intentional fraud on the part of the seller." *Id.* at 722. Until its revision in 1995, Article 5 of the Uniform Commercial Code ("UCC"), a codification of laws governing commercial transactions, entitled a court to enjoin honoring an on-demand guarantee only if there was forgery or fraud in the required document. In 1957, the text was amended to codify the *Sztejn* judgment by providing that a court may enjoin such honour where "a required document [...] is forged or fraudulent or there is fraud in the transaction." Yet, courts were split as to the standard of fraud and whether the "transaction" included the underlying contract; recapitulation at *MID America Tire Inc v. PTZ Trading Ltd*, 95 Ohio St. 3d 367, 768 N.E.2d 619 (2002), paras. 118–130; see also regarding various standards of fraud pre-1995 *Dynamics Corp. of America v. Citizens & Southern Nat'l Bank*, 356 F. Supp. 991 (N.D. Ga. 1973); *NMC Enterprises v. Columbia Broadcasting System, Inc*, 14 U.C.C. Rep. Serv. 1427 (N.Y. Sup. Ct. 1974); *American Bell International v. Islamic Republic of Iran*, 474 F. Supp. 420 (S.D.N.Y. 1979); *United Bank Ltd v. Cambridge Sporting Goods Corp.*, 392 N.Y.S.2d 265, 271 (N.Y. 1976); *Intraworld Industries v. Girard Trust Bank*, 336 A.2d 316 (Pa. 1975); *New York Life Insurance v. Hartford National Bank and Trust*, 173 Conn. 492, 378 A. 2d 562 (Conn. 1977).

credit transaction or the underlying sales transaction is sufficient to warrant injunctive relief."[16] Material fraud "means fraud that has so vitiated the entire transaction that the legitimate purposes of the independence of the issuer's obligation can no longer be served."[17]

German and Italian courts rely on the notion of *Rechtsmissbrauch* (abuse of rights, also referred to as *Rechtsmissbrauchsverbot*, or prohibition of abuse of rights)[18] and *exceptio doli* (defense to a claim on account of fraud), respectively. They also impose a high standard against the "pay first, argue later" principle (*"erst zahlen—dann prozessieren"*).[19] For German courts, the abuse of formal rights—the owner acting abusively because of clear lack of substantial entitlement[20]—should result from evident and immediately available proof (*"offensichtlich oder liquide beweisbar"*).[21] For example, performance under the underlying contract might have become clearly impossible,[22] or the event that would justify the calling on the demand guarantee clearly did not occur.[23]

For Italian courts, the principal of an on-demand guarantee waives all rights to raise any objections under the underlying transaction, except where (i) the underlying contract is null and void or (ii) the calling on the demand guarantee is abusive or fraudulent (*exceptio doli*).[24] The *exceptio doli*—a legacy of

---

16 MID *America Tire Inc.*, *supra* note 15, at para. 133.

17 *Id.* at para. 139.

18 Marxen, *supra* note 3, at 80, 150 et seq. German courts derived the notion from provisions of the German Civil Code (*Bürgerliches Gesetzbuch*, "BGB"), in particular §242 BGB on the principle of performance in "good faith" (*Leistung nach Treu und Glauben*), but also §138 BGB (*Sittenwidriges Rechtsgeschäft*; *Wucher*, or unethical legal transaction; usury), §158 BGB (*Aufschiebende und auflösende Bedingung*, or condition precedent and condition subsequent), §162 BGB (*Verhinderung oder Herbeiführung des Bedingungseintritts* or preventing or bringing about the occurrence of the condition), §226 BGB (*Schikaneverbot* or prohibition of harassment) and §826 BGB (*Sittenwidrige vorsätzliche Schädigung*, or unethical intentional damage); see also Holger Sutschet, "BGB § 242 Leistung nach Treu und Glauben," in *BeckOK BGB*, eds. Wolfgang Hau and Roman Poseck, 62nd ed. (München: C.H. Beck, 2022), para. 86; Markus Gehrlein, "BGB § 783 Rechte aus der Anweisung—Bankgarantie," in *BeckOK BGB*, eds. Wolfgang Hau and Roman Poseck, 62nd ed. (München: C.H. Beck, 2022), para. 22.

19 BGH BGHZ 101, 84, 91, in Marxen, *supra* note 3, at 152; see para. 0 for Italian case law.

20 "Ausbleiben des materiellen Garantiefalls," BGH BGHZ 90, 292, in Marxen, *supra* note 3, at 152 and fn. 142.

21 BGH 2011 WM 2216, OLG Stuttgart 10 U 102/14 (20.1.2015) (juris), paras. 30, 32; see also BGH BGHZ 145, 286, 291, BGH BGHZ 140, 49, 51–52, and BGH BGHZ 90, 287, 292, in Marxen, *supra* note 3, at 151–152; Kleine-Möller, *supra* note 6, at 591.

22 BGH BGHZ 90, 291–292, in Marxen, *supra* note 3, at 153.

23 OLG Oldenburg 2001 WM 732, 734, in Marxen, *supra* note 3, at 153.

24 Italian Cassation Court, decision No. 26262, 14 December 2007: "[i]n tema di contratto autonomo di garanzia, l'assunzione da parte del garante dell'impegno di effettuare il

Roman law—could materialize when the owner (i) omits the existence of circumstances that have modified or extinguished his underlying right to payment, (ii) exercises this right for a different purpose than provided by the law, or (iii) aims solely at damaging others.[25]

Arbitral practice similarly finds that the principle of independence of the on-demand guarantee does not prevent the intervention of arbitral tribunals competent to decide disputes arising out of the underlying contracts—when the calling is fraudulent or abusive.[26] Their judgment could extend to the fraudulent or abusive call on demand guarantees that had their "foundation in the [underlying] contracts."[27] If an arbitral tribunal finds, for example, that the underlying contract has been terminated,[28] or that the owner accepted the works with retroactive effect, the call on the demand guarantee would be abusive.[29]

---

pagamento a semplice richiesta del beneficiario della garanzia comporta la rinuncia ad opporre le eccezioni inerenti al rapporto principale, ivi comprese quelle relative all'invalidità del contratto da cui tale rapporto deriva, con il duplice limite dell'esecuzione fraudolenta o abusiva, a fronte della quale il garante può opporre l'*exceptio doli,* e del caso in cui le predette eccezioni siano fondate sulla nullità del contratto presupposto per contrarietà a norme imperative o per illiceità della sua causa, tendendo altrimenti il primo contratto ad assicurare il risultato che l'ordinamento vieta." (English: "[i]n the case of an independent guarantee contract, the undertaking by the guarantor to make payment upon the request of the beneficiary of the guarantee implies the waiver of the objections inherent in the principal relationship, including those relating to the invalidity of the contract from which that relationship derives, subject to the twofold limitation of fraudulent or abusive performance, in respect of which the guarantor may rely on the *exceptio doli*, and where such defences are based on the nullity of the underlying contract on the ground that it is contrary to mandatory rules or that its purpose is unlawful, the first contract otherwise tending to ensure the result which the law prohibits.") See also Italian Cassation Court, decision No. 15216, 12 September 2012, cited by Cassation Court, No. 20397, 25 August 2017 (*infra* note 25).

25 Italian Cassation Court, decision No. 20397, 25 August 2017.

26 Bernard Hanotiau, "Arbitration and Bank Guarantees: An Illustration of the Issue of Consent to Arbitration in Multicontract–Multiparty Disputes," *Journal of International Arbitration* 16, no. 2 (1999): 18.

27 *Id.* at 18–20, quoting ICC Case No. 5721/1990.

28 *Id.* at 20, quoting ICC Case No. 3896/1982. The arbitral tribunal proposed that (i) the claimant formally withdraw its submission that the calling on the guarantees had been abusive and fraudulent and (ii) the respondent formally renounce calling on the guarantees until the rendering of the final award. Once it had decided on whether the underlying contract had been terminated, among its consequences there would be the nullity of the guarantees and "it is a principle that any arbitral tribunal, when dealing with a disputed issue or a given question properly referred to it, has also jurisdiction to decide on the necessary effects or consequences arising from this point or this issue."

29 *Id.*; see also Hanotiau, *supra* note 26.

However, the ruling of the arbitral tribunal established only under the main contract would not be binding on the guarantor (a third party).[30] Yet, if the finding is part of the decision on the merits, and the guarantor is aware of the award, any payment would "engage their liability."[31] Before the final decision, the arbitral tribunal could enjoin the owner from encashing the guarantee if the principal seeks interim relief and meets the corresponding requirements.[32] The principal who needs urgent interim or conservatory relief that cannot await the constitution of an arbitral tribunal may make an application pursuant to the emergency arbitrator provisions of the agreed institutional rules—if they include this option—or the arbitration agreement if the parties specifically agreed on it. The decision of the emergency arbitrator would be binding upon the parties until the arbitral tribunal's final award, bearing in mind that the arbitral tribunal could confirm, modify, or reverse the decision of the emergency arbitrator.[33] Interim relief becomes necessary, because if the call is found to be invalid only at the end of the main arbitration proceedings, conditions could have potentially changed and repayment could have become impossible.

The applicant needing an injunction against the call on a demand guarantee before the constitution of an arbitral tribunal needs to assess the advantages and disadvantages of seeking interim relief before (i) the emergency arbitrator, (ii) domestic courts, or (iii) both fora.

3 Planning the Route: Interim Relief before Emergency Arbitrators and/or Domestic Courts

3.1 *Adjusting the Sail: Direction Emergency Arbitrator or State Courts?*

Due to the risks associated with construction projects,[34] interim relief is often necessary.[35] Construction and engineering disputes have historically

30 See *infra* Section 3.1., paras. 4 and 6 et seq. regarding the state courts' power to join third parties.

31 See Hanotiau, *supra* note 26. *Id.* at 20.

32 This contribution does not focus on the requirements of urgency and irreparable harm that are usually necessary to successfully request interim relief.

33 For examples, see the Rules of Arbitration of the International Chamber of Commerce, in force as from 1 January 2021, Appendix V: Emergency Arbitrator Rules, Article 6(6) ("ICC Rules"); Rules of the Milan Chamber of Arbitration, in force as from 1 March 2023, Article 44(8) ("CAM Rules"); Swiss Rules of International Arbitration, June 2021, Article 43(8) ("Swiss Rules"); see also *infra* Section 3.1., para. 7 regarding the finality of the decision.

34 See *supra* Section 2.1., paras. 1 et seq.

35 Interim relief likely to be requested in construction disputes includes: preventing the contractor from "walking off site"; applying or suspending the application of contractual

represented the bulk of the caseload of the International Chamber of Commerce (ICC)[36] and now of emergency arbitrator applications, according to statistics collected since the introduction of emergency arbitrator provisions in the ICC arbitration rules (ICC Rules) in 2012.[37] This should not be a surprise when it is "a fact of life in international construction" that guarantees callable on first demand must be paid, even when the beneficiary is wrong,[38] and this exposes them to abusive calls.[39] In the choice between emergency arbitration and domestic courts, the applicant seeking interim relief should be mindful of the pros and cons of each of these solutions. A parallel application before both fora requires further consideration.

All major institutional rules include emergency arbitrator provisions except the rules of the German Arbitration Institute (Deutsche Institution für Schiedsgerichtsbarkeit, DIS Rules).[40] Emergency arbitrators have ordered

---

penalties; enjoining a party from removing disputed equipment, disposing of spare parts, or terminating the contract; protecting rights under a technology transfer provision or sensitive information; preserving evidence or assets, provisions of security for costs or interim payments; and enjoining the calling of a performance bond. See Lisa Beisteiner, "Chapter 5: Provisional Measures Specific to Construction Arbitration: Focus on the Austrian Legal Framework and Jurisprudence," in *Construction Arbitration in Central and Eastern Europe: Contemporary Issues*, eds. Crina Baltag and Cosmin Vasile (Kluwer Law International, 2019), 64–65; Lars Markert and Raeesa Rawal, "Emergency Arbitration in Investment and Construction Disputes: An Uneasy Fit?," *Journal of International Arbitration* 37, no. 1 (2020): 138–139; Petkute-Guriene, *supra* note 4, at 15; Philip Norman and Leanie van de Merwe, "Interim Relief, Including Emergency Arbitrators in Construction Arbitration," in *The Guide to Construction Arbitration*, eds. Stavros Brekoulakis and David Brynmor Thomas (Law Business Research Ltd, 2021), 202; Jane Jenkins, *International Construction Arbitration Law*, 3rd ed., vol. 1 (Kluwer Law International, 2021), 197.

36 International Chamber of Commerce (ICC), "ICC Dispute Resolution Statistics: 2020," ICC, 17, accessed 28 August 2022, https://iccwbo.org/publication/icc-dispute-resolution-statistics-2020/.

37 *Id.* at 20: "[h]alf of the EA applications relate to the construction/engineering and energy sectors." While statistics for the years 2021 and 2022 were not yet available at the time this chapter was submitted for publication, preliminary statistical data revealed that in 2021, the Secretariat received 27 new requests under the emergency arbitrator provisions but provided no detail on the involved service sectors.

38 Seppala, *supra* note 11; see also Marxen, *supra* note 3, at 126, who considers on-demand guarantees a well-established feature in the construction sector.

39 Marxen, *supra* note 3, at 109.

40 For examples, see ICC Rules, *supra* note 33, at Article 29, Appendix V; Arbitration Rules of the London Court of International Arbitration, Article 9B ("LCIA Rules"); Swiss Rules, *supra* note 33, at Article 43; CAM Rules, *supra* note 33, at Article 44; Arbitration Rules of the International Centre for Dispute Resolution, in effect as from 1 March 2021, Article 7 ("ICDR Rules"); Arbitration Rules of the China International Economic and Trade Arbitration Commission, in effect as from 1 January 2015, Article 23, Appendix III ("CIETAC

various types of relief, some of which are particularly apt for construction disputes, including: anti-suit/anti-arbitration injunctions; measures aimed at maintaining the *status quo* and preserving assets or property; measures demanding the performance of contractual obligations; measures enjoining the enforcement of demand guarantees, and a declaratory order of the abusiveness of a potential enforcement of such guarantees; measures ordering security, as well as prohibiting the opposing party from drawing down on the demand guarantee.[41]

There are advantages associated with seeking interim relief before an emergency arbitrator as opposed to state courts: confidentiality, a front-loading approach, and a short deadline within which the main arbitration proceedings should start, to name a few.[42] Appendix V, Article 1(6) of the ICC Rules (Appendix V) and Article 43(3) of the Swiss Rules of Arbitration (Swiss Rules), for example, set a ten-day time limit from the receipt of the application for the commencement of the main arbitration proceedings—extendable in exceptional circumstances.[43] This tight deadline puts pressure on the applicant, who must sustain counsel costs in the preparation of two submissions on short

Rules"); Rules of the Arbitration Institute of the Stockholm Chamber of Commerce, in force as of 1 January 2017, Appendix II ("SCC Rules"); Arbitration Rules of the Singapore International Arbitration Centre, in force as of 1 August 2016, Article 30, Schedule 1 ("SIAC Rules").

41 ICC Commission on Arbitration and ADR, "Report on Emergency Arbitrator Proceedings," ICC, April 2019, accessed 28 August 2022, para. 179 https://iccwbo.org/news-publications/arbitration-adr-rules-and-tools/emergency-arbitrator-proceedings-icc-arbitration-and-adr-commission-report/ ("ICC Commission Report").

42 Beisteiner, *supra* note 35, at 78; Gustav Flecke-Giammarco, "An Interview with Gustav Flecke-Giammarco on Emergency Arbitration," in *Young Arbitration Review*, eds. Pedro Sousa Uva and Gonçalo Malheiro, 43rd ed. (Oct.-Dec. 2021), 102.

43 For example, under Appendix V, Article 1(6) of the ICC Rules, *supra* note 33, the President of the ICC International Court of Arbitration shall terminate the emergency arbitrator proceedings if a request for arbitration has not been received by the ICC Secretariat ("Secretariat") within ten days from the Secretariat's receipt of the application, unless the emergency arbitrator determines that a longer period of time is necessary. Article 43(3) of the Swiss Rules, *supra* note 33, sets the same time limit, extendable by the Court in exceptional circumstances. Under Article 44(9) of the CAM Rules, *supra* note 33, the term is 60 days and mirrors the time limit provided under Article 669-octies of the Italian Code of Civil Procedure regarding interim measures *ante causam* (*i.e.*, before the filing of the main case) before state courts. (With the same order with which the judge upholds the requested measures, he sets a peremptory time limit of no more than 60 days for the inception of the main proceedings). The emergency arbitrator can shorten the time limit, which should not be shorter than fifteen days from the filing of the application.

notice. In addition, registration fees could be high,[44] but so could court fees, especially if—as it is often the case—they are calculated based on the amount in dispute.[45]

However, courts can order interim relief against third parties—an emergency arbitrator cannot.[46] This is significant for on-demand guarantees, where the guarantor is a third party to the contractual relationship between the owner and the principal. Further, courts can order *ex parte* interim measures, which can be decisive in situations where the guarantor can execute the payment at any time. Yet, courts seldom use the instrument, because it temporarily hampers the responding party's right to be heard—restored through a hearing held in short order.[47] Nevertheless, a remote possibility could make a difference when institutional arbitration rules, except for the Swiss Rules and the Arbitration Rules of the Milan Chamber of Commerce (CAM Rules),[48] do not

44 This amounts, for example, to USD 40,000.00 for ICC emergency arbitrator proceedings and ranges from CHF 2,000.00 to 20,000.00 for emergency arbitrator proceedings under the Swiss Rules.

45 Before state courts, the court fees often depend on the amount in dispute, which could be comparatively more expensive or even prohibitive (especially for major construction and infrastructure projects). In some cases, there is a reduction in court fees; for example, in Italy, the amount of court fees for emergency proceedings is based on the amount in dispute according to specific thresholds, but the resulting amount is then divided by half. See Law Decree No. 132 of 12 September 2014, converted into Law No. 162 of 10 November 2014 (*Decreto Giustizia*).

46 Gustav Flecke-Giammarco and Martina Magnarelli, "Live and Learn: Emergency Arbitration in Post–M&A Disputes," in *Young Arbitration Review*, eds. Pedro Sousa Uva and Gonçalo Malheiro, 36th ed. (Jan. 2020), 10; Beisteiner, *supra* note 35, at 77–78; Simon Horn, Der Eilschiedsrichter im institutionellen Schiedsverfahren, Zeitschrift für Schiedsverfahren, no. 1 (2016): 22, 24.

47 Under Article 669-sexies of the Italian Code of Civil Procedure, for example, the judge may, through a reasoned decree, order *ex parte* interim relief when summoning the responding party to the hearing could jeopardize the execution of the order. In the same decree, the judge sets the date of the hearing within no later than fifteen days.

48 Article 29(3) of the Swiss Rules, *supra* note 33, provides that: "In exceptional circumstances, the arbitral tribunal may rule on a request for interim measures by way of a preliminary order before the request has been communicated to any other party, provided that such communication is made at the latest together with the preliminary order and that the other parties are immediately granted an opportunity to be heard." *Id.* at Article 43(6) provides that: "The emergency arbitrator may conduct the emergency relief proceedings in such a manner as the emergency arbitrator considers appropriate, taking into account the urgency inherent in such proceedings and ensuring that each party has a reasonable opportunity to be heard on the Application." Article 44(4) of the CAM Rules, *supra* note 33, provides that "the emergency arbitrator may issue the procedural order without notice to the other party, if such notice would seriously prejudice the applicant's interests. In this case, with the decision granting the application, the emergency arbitrator

provide for ex parte interim relief.[49] The ICC Arbitration and ADR Commission Report on Emergency Arbitrator Proceedings dated 2019 (ICC Commission Report), found an order issued by an emergency arbitrator prior to the notification of the application to the responding party incompatible with Appendix V, Article 1(5) (transmission of the application by the Secretariat to the responding party).[50] At least in one of the first 80 emergency arbitrator proceedings,[51] the emergency arbitrator ordered the *status quo* to be maintained by enjoining the responding party from calling on a bank guarantee before the filing of the response to the application.[52] Some members of the ICC task-force preparing the ICC Commission Report considered that, in some circumstances, the need to preserve the status quo could justify an *ex parte* order based on the parties' duty to "comply with any order of the emergency arbitrator" under Article 29(2) of the ICC Rules and the wide discretion granted to the emergency arbitrator by Appendix V, Article 5.[53] Several other members criticized the *ex parte*

schedules a hearing within 10 days of the decision to discuss the case with the parties and set deadlines for the submission of briefs, if any. At the hearing, or in any case within the following 5 days, the emergency arbitrator, having heard the parties, issues an order confirming, modifying or revoking the measure already granted." The Arbitration Rules of the German Institute of Arbitration, in force as of 1 March 2018, Article 25(2) ("DIS Rules"), also provides that "[i]n exceptional circumstances, the arbitral tribunal may rule on a request pursuant to Article 25.1 without giving prior notice to or receiving comments from the other party, if otherwise it would risk frustrating the purpose of the measure," but the DIS Rules do not include emergency arbitrator provisions. See *supra* Section 3.1., para. 2 and Christopher Boog and David Quinke, "Article 25: Interim Relief," in *The DIS Arbitration Rules: An Article-by-Article Commentary*, eds. Gustav Flecke-Giammarco et al. (Kluwer Law International, 2020), paras. 79 et seq.

49 See Flecke-Giammarco and Magnarelli, *supra* note 46, at 10.

50 ICC Commission Report, *supra* note 41, at paras. 24, 106–108; Appendix V, Article 1(5) of the ICC Rules, *supra* note 33, reads: "[i]f and to the extent that the President of the Court (the 'President') considers, on the basis of the information contained in the Application, that the Emergency Arbitrator Provisions apply with reference to Article 29(5) and Article 29(6) of the Rules, the Secretariat shall transmit a copy of the Application and the documents annexed thereto to the responding party. If and to the extent that the President considers otherwise, the Secretariat shall inform the parties that the emergency arbitrator proceedings shall not take place with respect to some or all of the parties and shall transmit a copy of the Application to them for information." See also Daniel Girsberger and Nathalie Voser, *International Arbitration: Comparative and Swiss Perspectives*, 4th ed. (Schulthess Juristische Medien AG, 2021), 307, 314–315.

51 The ICC Commission Report, *supra* note 41, examined the first 80 cases since the entry into force of the 2012 ICC Rules. The latest available ICC statistics, *supra* note 36, reported 154 emergency arbitrator proceedings through the end of 2020.

52 ICC Commission Report, *supra* note 41, at para. 113.

53 *Id.* at para. 115.

order and referred to Appendix V, Article 1(5) and Article 5(2) (the responding party's right to be heard).[54]

Yet, proceedings before state courts have their downsides, too. First, there is no confidentiality before domestic courts. Although some state courts may order the exclusion of the public, this only occurs in exceptional circumstances.[55] Second, the interim relief that courts can order is limited to the measures in the applicable domestic procedural law.[56] On the contrary, arbitral tribunals enjoy greater leeway, and can order measures other than those provided in the procedural legislation of a given country. For example, under German law (§1041 German code of civil procedure—*Zivilprozessordnung*, ZPO) an arbitral tribunal has the power to grant interim relief with respect to the subject matter as it considers necessary.[57] Third, the parties to proceedings before domestic courts need counsel who are admitted before those courts and that are familiar with court litigation in that jurisdiction. Besides, all documents not in the official language would need to be translated,[58] which is problematic when the clock is ticking, adding to the overall costs. Fourth, courts may not provide a neutral forum, and their service might not be speedy enough. Several institutional rules establish that the emergency arbitrator is appointed within two to five days from the receipt of the application[59] and should render the decision within fifteen days from the transmission of the file.[60]

However, courts have the coercive power ("imperium") that arbitrators lack.[61] Enforcement of the emergency arbitrator's decision always requires court intervention. In this respect, relevant factors are (i) the form of the decision, (ii) whether courts can intervene, and, if they can, (iii) whether their

54 *Id.* at para. 114. Moreover, the risk remains whether the *ex parte* order could be enforced by the courts of the jurisdiction where enforcement is sought. See *infra* Section 3.1., paras. 6 et seq. on enforcement of the emergency arbitrator's decision.

55 Beisteiner, *supra* note 35, at 78.

56 *Id.* at 78–79; see also *infra* note 57 and *infra* Section 3.1., para. 8.

57 Jan K. Schäfer, "Part II: Commentary on the German Arbitration Law (10th Book of the German Code of Civil Procedure), Chapter IV: Jurisdiction of Arbitral Tribunal, § 1041—Interim Measures of Protection," in *Arbitration in Germany: The Model Law in Practice*, eds. Karl-Heinz Bockstiegel, Stefan Kröll, and Patricia Nacimiento, 2nd ed. (Kluwer Law International, 2015), 215–237, para. 20.

58 See Beisteiner, *supra* note 35, at 79.

59 For example, Appendix V, Article 2(1) of the ICC Rules, *supra* note 33 (two days); Article 9.6 of the LCIA Rules, *supra* note 40 (three days); Article 44(2) of the CAM Rules, *supra* note 33 (five days).

60 For example, Appendix V, Article 6(4) of the ICC Rules, *supra* note 33; Article 43(7) of the Swiss Rules, *supra* note 33; Article 44(3) of the CAM Rules, *supra* note 33.

61 Girsberger and Voser, *supra* note 50, at 307–308.

power is limited to arbitrations seated in their own jurisdictions, and (iv) which measures they can order.

Some institutional rules bestow the emergency arbitrator with discretion as to whether to issue an order or an award;[62] other institutional rules only refer to an order.[63] Although with some discordant voices in the literature,[64] the prevailing position is that the New York Convention on the Recognition and Enforcement of Foreign Arbitral Awards (NY Convention) does not apply to interim orders.[65] The NY Convention does not refer to provisional measures and does not include a definition of "arbitral award," but finality is usually considered an essential characteristic.[66] Hence, emergency arbitrator's orders would not benefit from the greater recognition and circulation of arbitral awards as opposed to state court judgments.[67] However, the actual form of the emergency arbitrator's decision would be irrelevant, especially in a jurisdiction like France, where it would not be binding on French courts. Because of the substance-over-form approach, the finality of the decision is the sole crucial factor.[68] That said, some commentators propose that the decision of the emergency arbitrator be considered final as to the issue that is being decided.[69]

In any event, domestic courts usually provide their assistance to the enforcement of emergency arbitrator's orders through a declaration of enforceability or by confirming the order and exercising coercive power.[70] Swiss and German

---

62 For example, Article 9B of the LCIA Rules, *supra* note 40; Article 7 of the ICDR Rules, *supra* note 40; Article 23 of the CIETAC Rules, *supra* note 40; Schedule 1, para. 8 of the SIAC Rules, *supra* note 40; Sai Ramani Garimella and Poomintr Sooksripaisarnkit, "Chapter 5: Emergency Arbitrator Awards: Addressing Enforceability Concerns Through National Law and the New York Convention," in *60 Years of the New York Convention: Key Issues and Future Challenges*, eds. Katia Fach Gómez and Ana Mercedes López Rodríguez (Kluwer Law International, 2019), 70–72.

63 Article 29(2) and Appendix V, Article 6(1) of the ICC Rules, *supra* note 33; Article 44(3) of the CAM Rules, *supra* note 33.

64 Maxime Chevalier, "Enforcement of Emergency Arbitrator Decisions: Dream or Reality? The French Perspective," *Journal of International Arbitration* 38, no. 6 (2021): 837; see also Ank A. Santens and Jaroslav Kudrna, "The State of Play of Enforcement of Emergency Arbitrator Decisions," *Journal of International Arbitration* 34, no. 1 (2017): 11.

65 Flecke-Giammarco and Magnarelli, *supra* note 46, at 10–11.

66 See Andrea Carlevaris, "Towards a New Arbitration Law in Italy: Arbitrators' Power to Order Interim Relief Finally Recognized?," *Cahiers de l'arbitrage*, no. 1 (2002): 7.

67 *Id.*; see also Santens and Kudrna, *supra* note 64, at 10–11.

68 Chevalier, *supra* note 64, at 842, 844, 846.

69 *Id.* at 848–849; Jakob Horn, "Kapitel 8 Vollstreckung ausländischer Emergency-Anordnungen," in Jakob Horn, *Der Emergency Arbitrator und die ZPO* (Mohr Siebeck, 2019), 173.

70 Chevalier, *supra* note 64, at 840–841 and Carlevaris, *supra* note 66, referring, *inter alia*, to Dutch courts for the "*exequatur* model" and to Swiss courts for the "court assistance"

courts, as well as courts of countries that adopted the UNCITRAL Model Law as amended in 2006 (Model Law, see Article 17(H)(1)), enjoy this power, even if the seat of the arbitration is in a country other than the one where enforcement is sought.[71] In Germany, the order of the emergency arbitrator should be enforceable like a decision on interim measures and regardless of the seat.[72]

---

model. German law adopts a "hybrid" model or a variation of the court assistance model: under §1041(2) ZPO, a party can apply to German courts for the enforcement of an interim measure, provided that an application for a corresponding measure of temporary relief has not already been filed with a court. German courts, however, can also recast the order to adapt its content based on the types of measures envisaged by German law. Since this provision is not mentioned under §1025(2) ZPO, which identifies those that also apply to foreign-seated arbitrations, the prevailing view considers a declaration of enforceability to not be a requirement for a foreign interim order (*cf.* Hans-Joachim Musielak and Wolfgang Voit, "ZPO § 1061 Ausländische Schiedssprüche," in Hans-Joachim Musielak and Wolfgang Voit, *Zivilprozessordnung mit Gerichtsverfassungsgesetz Kommentar*, 20th ed. (Franz Vahlen, 2023), para. 3). Others think that, based on the jurisdictional rule under §1062(2) ZPO that concerns foreign-seated arbitration and which identifies the competent higher regional court for enforcement purposes, this provision would be meaningless if §1041(2) ZPO were not to apply to foreign arbitration proceedings (*cf.* Horn, *supra* note 69, at 198). In any event, on 18 April 2023, the German Federal Ministry of Justice released its "Eckpunkte [...] zur Modernisierung des deutschen Schiedsverfahrensrechts" ("Eckpunkte des Bundesministeriums der Justiz," or its "cornerstones" on the "modernisation of German Arbitration Law"), which, under point 9, foresees the explicit inclusion of the possibility for German courts to grant leave for enforcement of interim measures even when the seat of arbitration is abroad, enabling courts to make admission for enforcement dependant on the provision of security ("Ordnet ein Schiedsgericht Maßnahmen des einstweiligen Rechtsschutzes an, wollen wir die gerichtliche Zulassung der Vollziehung dieser Maßnahmen im Inland auch dann ermöglichen, wenn der Schiedsort im Ausland liegt. Hierdurch stärken wir die Verkehrsfähigkeit von Entscheidungen im schiedsrichterlichen einstweiligen Rechtsschutz. Gerichten ermöglichen wir, die Zulassung der Vollziehung von einer Sicherheitsleistung abhängig zu machen."); see also the Statement Opinion No. 21 of the German Bar Association, released in May 2023, 6–8 ("Stellungnahme Nr. 21," Bundesrechtsanwaltskammer, 2023 May), accessed 27 June 2023, https://www.brak.de/fileadmin/05_zur_rechtspolitik/stellungnahmen-pdf/stellungnahmen-deutschland/2023/stellungnahme-der-brak-2023-21.pdf ("Statement Opinion No. 21 of the German Bar Association").

71 Girsberger and Voser, *supra* note 50, at 319, referring to Article 185a of the Swiss Private International Law Act ("PILA") and §1062(2) of the Swiss Civil Code ("ZGB"). Under Article 17H(1) of the UNCITRAL Model Law, as amended in 2006, "[a]n interim measure issued by an arbitral tribunal shall be recognised as binding and, unless otherwise provided by the arbitral tribunal, enforced upon application to the competent court, irrespective of the country where it was issued, subject to the provisions of Article 17I [grounds for refusing recognition and enforcement]"; Santens and Kudrna, *supra* note 64.

72 Schäfer, *supra* note 57, at 226–237; Klaus-Albrecht Gerstenmaier, "Die Vollziehbarkeit von Entscheidungen des Eilschiedsrichters," in *Festschrift für Siegfried H. Elsing zum 65. Geburtstag*, eds. Werner F. Ebke, Dirk Olzen, and Otto Sandrock (Fachmedien Recht und

English courts, instead, can only intervene if the seat is in the United Kingdom or, if it has not yet been established, if there is an appropriate connection to the United Kingdom.[73]

The tendency is generally towards greater recognition of arbitrators' orders, not only in jurisdictions notoriously in favor of arbitration, but also in jurisdictions where the enforcement of interim orders was, until now, dubious. The Singapore International Arbitration Act as amended in 2012 and the Hong Kong Arbitration Ordinance as modified in 2013, provide that all orders and directions, including of an emergency arbitrator, are enforceable as if they were orders or directions of their courts.[74] By contrast, until recently, according to the wording of Article 818 of the Italian code of civil procedure (c.p.c.), arbitrators could not order interim relief, except in the limited cases provided by the law (as established by a 2006 amendment).[75] However, even before a reform of Italian arbitration law that started with the law on the guiding principles to the government for the reform of civil justice, including arbitration (Law 206/21), transfused in Legislative Decree No. 149 of 10 October 2022 (Decree 149/2022) that amended the corresponding c.p.c. provisions, a systematic interpretation of the law led to the position that if the parties agreed on institutional arbitration rules giving the arbitral tribunal the power to order interim relief, party autonomy should be respected.[76] The new CAM Rules released in

Wirtschaft, dfv Mediengruppe, 2015), 153, 157; Horn, *supra* note 69, at 171–204; see also the Eckpunkte des Bundesministeriums der Justiz, *supra* note 70, at 5, which include specific proposals for reform for interim measures; note that under Section IV, point 1, with regard to emergency arbitration, it should also be considered whether to include an explicit provision in the ZPO and, as part of the same analysis, whether measures adopted by an emergency arbitrator with a foreign seat should also be explicitly admitted for enforcement by German courts, a position supported by the Statement Opinion No. 21 of the German Bar Association, *supra* note 70, at 6–7.

73 Girsberger and Voser, *supra* note 50, at 319–320, referring to Section 2(1) and (4) in conjunction with Section 42 of the English Arbitration Act 1996.

74 Santens and Kudrna, *supra* note 64, at 12.

75 Legislative Decree No. 40 of 2 February 2006; see also Martina Magnarelli, "'Do You Know the Land Where Lemon Blossom Grows?'—Journey into the Italian Arbitration Rules on Interim Measures," Kluwer Arbitration Blog, 26 February 2020, http://arbitrationblog.kluwerarbitration.com/2020/02/26/do-you-know-the-land-where-lemon-blossom-grows-journey-into-the-italian-arbitration-rules-on-interim-measures/; Paolo Biavati, "Spunti critici sui poteri cautelari degli arbitri," *Rivista dell'Arbitrato*, no. 2 (2013): 329–346; Carlevaris, *supra* note 66; Alessio Carosi, "Arbitrato e tutela cautelare: limiti di possibile derogabilità dell'art. 818 c.p.c. e relativi effetti," *Rivista dell'Arbitrato*, no. 1 (2021): 43, 53.

76 *Id.* Under Article 832 of the Italian Code of Civil Procedure, when the parties agree on institutional arbitration and the institution declines to administer the arbitration proceedings, the provisions on arbitration under the Code of Civil Procedure apply. When read *a contrario*, this was considered to entail that the provisions of the Code of Civil

2019 (before their latest revision in 2023) already followed these footsteps and provided for interim relief by arbitral tribunals and emergency arbitrators.[77] Now, reformed Italian law provides for the arbitral tribunals' power to order interim relief, if the parties so agree, even through a reference to administrative rules—but it says nothing specific on emergency arbitration.[78] In India, the Delhi High Court rendered a pivotal decision on August 6, 2021. It held that in India-seated arbitrations, an emergency arbitrator is an "arbitral tribunal" within the meaning of the Arbitration and Conciliation Act 1996 and any order by the emergency arbitrator is like any other order of an arbitral tribunal to which state courts should give effect. If the parties agreed on the application of institutional rules that include emergency arbitrator provisions, the context requires interpreting the definition of arbitral tribunal to encompass the emergency arbitrator. Party autonomy—"the backbone of arbitrations"—should be respected.[79]

One should also consider, however, that state courts will apply their own procedural law. If the order envisages measures that are unknown in that jurisdiction, it could become a problem, unless the courts enforce the measures to the extent possible without modifying its substance—which is what the Model Law provides.[80]

In any event, parties usually comply spontaneously with emergency arbitrators' decisions. Non-compliance gives rise to contractual responsibility under

---

Procedure on arbitration, including Article 818, should not apply to an administered arbitration. See now Articles 818 to 818-ter c.p.c. as recently amended or introduced.

77 Articles 26 and 44 of the CAM Rules, *supra* note 33; a new version of the CAM Rules has entered into force on 1 March 2023 with amendments, including to Articles 26 and 44, taking into account and mirroring those to the c.p.c. entered into force on the same day.

78 Legislative Decree No. 149 of 10 October 2022 (Official Gazette, No. 243, 17 October 2022), Law No. 206 of 26 November 2021 (Official Gazette, No. 292, 9 December 2021), see also *infra* Section 3.2., para. 1. The reformed provisions apply to proceedings instituted after 28 February 2023.

79 *Amazon.com NV Investment Holding LLC v. Future Retail Limited & Ors.*, Civil Appeal Nos. 4494–4495 and Civil Appeal Nos. 4496–4497, 6 August 2021; Vikas Mahendra, "Emergency Arbitration Orders Declares Enforceable in India-seated Arbitration," *ICC Dispute Resolution Bulletin*, no. 3 (2021): 22–24; see also Chevalier, *supra* note 64, at 837.

80 Girsberger and Voser, *supra* note 50, at 320, referring to Article 17I(1)(b)(i) of the UNCITRAL Model Law that explicitly provides that: "[r]ecognition or enforcement of an interim measure may be refused only: [...] (b) [i]f the court finds that: (i) [t]he interim measure is incompatible with the powers conferred upon the court unless the court decides to reformulate the interim measure to the extent necessary to adapt it to its own powers and procedures for the purposes of enforcing that interim measure and without modifying its substance; or." See also Article 183(2) of the PILA and §1041(2) of the ZPO; see also Schäfer, *supra* note 57, at paras. 3, 22 regarding German law.

the arbitration agreement (where the parties agreed that their proceedings be governed by institutional rules, including emergency arbitrator provisions, without opting out).[81] Once again, the applicant can seek support from local courts, although not for enforcement, but for breach of contract.[82] In addition, non-compliance risks giving a bad impression to the would-be arbitral tribunal[83] and could have repercussions on costs allocation.[84] Importantly, the emergency arbitrator's preliminary assessment could incentivize the parties to find an early settlement of their dispute, not only solving up-front any enforcement issues, but also offering the best solution for all the parties involved.[85] Besides, emergency arbitrator's decisions could influence domestic courts. The ICC Commission Report, for example, refers to at least one case of an order not to draw on performance bonds not respected by the responding party. Following payment by the guarantor, who was not a party to the emergency arbitrator proceedings, the applicant successfully sought before courts that the counter-guarantor be ordered not to pay the guarantor.[86]

Therefore, a party can rely on state courts for enforcement or directly for interim relief,[87] with emergency arbitration often representing a valid alternative to state courts. Most institutional rules now include provisions on emergency arbitrator proceedings and parties rarely opt out.[88]

3.2 *Parallel Application before an Emergency Arbitrator and State Courts*

Depending on the circumstances of the case, parties could also choose to apply in parallel before an emergency arbitrator and state courts. Article 29(7) of the ICC Rules explicitly provides that the emergency arbitrator provisions are not intended to prevent a party from seeking urgent interim or conservatory measures from the competent courts before an application, and, in appropriate circumstances, even thereafter. Parties are only required to notify any such application to the ICC Secretariat without delay.[89] Interestingly, after the

81 Flecke-Giammarco and Magnarelli, *supra* note 46, at 11.

82 ICC Commission Report, *supra* note 41, at para. 204; see also *id.* at paras. 17 and 22, respectively.

83 Flecke-Giammarco, *supra* note 42, at 102; see also Santens and Kudrna, *supra* note 64, at 14–15.

84 See Carosi, *supra* note 75.

85 Flecke-Giammarco and Magnarelli, *supra* note 46, at 11.

86 ICC Commission Report, *supra* note 41, at para. 207.

87 Santens and Kudrna, *supra* note 64, at 15.

88 Flecke-Giammarco, *supra* note 42, at 100.

89 Article 29(7) of the ICC Rules, *supra* note 33, provides that: "[t]he Emergency Arbitrator Provisions are not intended to prevent any party from seeking urgent interim or

reform entered into force on 1 March 2023, Italian law provides that,[90] not only should just arbitral tribunals have the power to order interim relief if the parties so agreed,[91] but also that this power remains with judges "only in cases" ("*nei soli casi*") of application prior to the appointment of the arbitral tribunal. Hence, the Italian legislator aims at extending the power to order interim relief to arbitral tribunals only, and seemingly not to emergency arbitrators[92]—but for constituted arbitral tribunals, it goes as far as to render the power almost exclusive.[93] It remains to be seen how case-law and practice will interpret and apply these provisions.

In any case, a parallel application before an emergency arbitrator and state courts unleashes "a race to the finish line" between the two adjudicative bodies.[94] It further increases costs and the time-pressure on both parties. It is a race against time especially for the applicant, who needs to file two interim relief applications as soon as possible after the (threat to) call on the demand guarantee and a request for arbitration in short order. Sometimes more counsel would be involved, as procedures before state courts require not only knowledge of the applicable procedural law, but also lawyer(s) authorized to appear before those courts. Yet, in some circumstances it could be advisable. For example, the applicant may seek to obtain interim relief by an emergency arbitrator within the tight deadline provided by institutional rules, while in the meantime requesting an *ex parte* order from domestic courts.[95] The applicant

conservatory measures from a competent judicial authority at any time prior to making an application for such measures, and in appropriate circumstances even thereafter, pursuant to the Rules. Any application for such measures from a competent judicial authority shall not be deemed to be an infringement or a waiver of the arbitration agreement. Any such application and any measures taken by the judicial authority must be notified without delay to the Secretariat."

90 See *supra* Section 3.1., para. 9.

91 Articles 818 to 818-ter c.p.c. post Decree 149/2022; see *supra* note 78.

92 At least, Law 206/2021 contains no explicit guidelines and so Decree 149/2022 does not rule expressly in this respect. But see Carlevaris, *supra* note 66: "[i]t is likely that the jurisdiction of state courts will be excluded as of the emergency arbitrator's acceptance of his/her appointment (or as of the moment any other procedural requirement under the applicable rules is satisfied)."

93 See *supra* note 90. The reform maintains state courts having the power to order interim relief before the constitution of the arbitral tribunal, to hear challenges (*reclamo cautelare*) on the interim order, and to grant enforcement; see Carlevaris, *supra* note 66. With regard to the exclusion of the courts' power to order interim relief after the constitution of the arbitral tribunal, it remains unclear how the new Article 818(1) c.p.c. ensures harmonization with the fundamental principle that no one shall be deprived of his natural judge (Article 25 of the Italian Constitution).

94 Flecke-Giammarco, *supra* note 42, at 102.

95 See *supra* Section 3.1., para. 4.

could seek to enjoin (a) the owner from encashing the demand guarantee he had already called on through the emergency arbitrator, and (b) the guarantor from executing the payment through state courts. In the same court proceedings, the applicant could also seek both measures, as courts can order the joinder of, and issue orders against, third parties.[96] Reasons for a parallel application might be manifold. Maybe the competent state courts have a record of mostly unsuccessful requests, or they can only issue certain measures,[97] or they are known for not reacting fast enough;[98] while the applicant does not expect the opposing party or the guarantor to spontaneously comply with the order of an emergency arbitrator (especially when certain jurisdictions would be involved in the enforcement).[99] Another risk to bear in mind, though, is that the opposing party may file a counterapplication and seek an anti-suit injunction. Lastly, despite the internationally recognized position on the fraud exception in case law across jurisdictions, it is not unlikely that in a specific case, an emergency arbitrator and state courts reach different decisions. The two could be seized based on different agreements governed by different substantive rules, or they could simply rely on different case law and principles. But they could also reach comparable decisions or be influenced by the decision of the one that decides first.[100] Differently from state courts, arbitrators do not belong to a specific jurisdiction. Therefore,

> it is realistically arguable that such an arbitrator will apply procedural rules and principles that are different from and independent of those applied by a state court, that does not lead necessarily to the conclusion that the emergency arbitrator will grant the order sought by [the applicant] when a court in England would not.[101]

96 See *supra* Section 3.1., para. 4.

97 See *supra* Section 3.1., para. 10.

98 See *supra* Section 3.1., para. 5.

99 See *supra* Section 3.1., para. 9.

100 See *id.* On a parallel application triggering a race between the two adjudicating authorities.

101 *Shapoorji Pallonji & Company Private Limited*, *supra* note 14, at para. 29. The quote continues: "[t]he principles that I have outlined above, to the extent they are principles of substantive English law, will apply irrespective of whether the issues are being considered by a court in England or by an international arbitrator required to apply substantive English law to the dispute between the parties. However, that said, this is not in any sense a pre-emptive challenge to the decision-making of the emergency arbitrator, and he must be left to do his work as he considers appropriate."

4 When Further Risks Loom: Construction Industry in the Age of COVID-19

The experience of the recent pandemic has made it even more apparent how much the construction industry is prone to risks and strengthens the consideration that bearing in mind some fundamentals on injunctive relief for on-demand guarantees could be a game-changer. COVID-19 has hit the sector hard. Day to day, companies faced severe manpower and materials shortages, as well as stringent restriction requirements on site. These exposed companies to rising costs to progress in the execution of projects and thereby reduced cash-flow. In a vicious circle, financial distress amplified delays, too. If milestones are not reached, payment do not follow, and penalties usually apply (with increasing difficulties in invoking force majeure as the time passed from February 2020).[102] At the same time, suppliers and subcontractors on "pay when paid" arrangements were not paid.[103] Delay and disruption occurred at every level of the supply chain, and each level had an impact on the next, so that "the more varied and lengthy the supply chain, the greater the exposure."[104] Even in countries where the spreading of the virus was, to a certain extent, less critical, and health and safety requirements were comparatively lower, hindrances came from travel restrictions and quarantine measures for the imported labour force.[105] Compulsory testing and distancing obligations reduced the number of workers on site and slowed down activities.[106] Considering the magnitude of the impact on all industry sectors, especially with the construction sector among the most exposed,[107] governments enacted

102 See Wetmore and Elliot, *supra* note 5, at 219–222.

103 *Id.* at 214.

104 *Id.* at 212; see also *supra* Section 2.1., para. 1.

105 *Id.* at 211–212.

106 *Id.* at 212–213.

107 *Id.*: for example, a study on seventy medium-sized UK construction projects concluded that: "[a] GBP 20 million commercial real estate project with an eighty-one-week programme will likely suffer productivity losses in the order of 15% as a result of labour and materials shortages, remote-working arrangements and site-based social distancing restrictions, with delays to project completion of up to thirty-two weeks and increases of around GBP 600,000 in preliminaries costs alone." In Italy, the pandemic is estimated to have caused a 10.1% reduction in investments in the construction sector and to have contracted Italian GDP by-9.2% in 2020, see Marco Padovan et al., "Construction and Projects in Italy: Overview," Thomson Reuters: Practical Law, 2021, accessed 28 August 2022, 2, https://uk.practicallaw.thomsonreuters.com/3-520-0016?transitionType=Default&contextData=(sc.Default)&firstPage=true#co_anchor_a463889. A report prepared by a Dutch engineering and management consulting firm in 2021 states that 60% of the consulted respondents reported that COVID-19 had had some impact on their projects.

temporary special measures and moratoria suspending payments to banks and other financial institutions[108] or the enforcement of rights, claims for liquidated damages, and the calls on performance bonds, in particular in the case of Singapore.[109] While these measures are temporary, any disruptions could have lasting effects.

5 Conclusions: Unfurling the Sails and Heading for the Destination

The specific characteristics of on-demand guarantees,[110] the independence between the main contract and the guarantee agreement,[111] the limited application of the fraud exception,[112] in some cases unsettled case law,[113] and the pros and cons of an application for injunctive relief before an emergency arbitrator or state courts, are all factors to consider when a principal seeks to enjoin the owner from calling on or encashing the demand guarantee or the guarantor from executing the payment. The risks inherent in construction projects have made on-demand guarantees an immanent reality.[114] But the principle of independence on which they rest, also exposes them to abuses.[115] Therefore, carefully evaluating all the factors that weigh in favor of applying before an emergency arbitrator, or state courts,[116] or both,[117] is pivotal.

See Arcadis, "2021 Global Construction Disputes Report: The road to early resolution," Arcadis, 2021, accessed 28 August 2022, 5, https://media.arcadis.com/-/media/project/arcadiscom/com/perspectives/north-america/united-states/2021/global-construction-disputes-report/2021-global-construction-disputes-report.pdf.

108 For example, Article 56 of the Italian Decree No. 18 of 17 March 2020 (*Decreto Cura Italia*) suspended repayments on loans and other financial services for small and medium-size enterprises.

109 Article 6 of the COVID-19 (Temporary Measures) Act 2020 (No. 14 of 2020) passed by the Parliament in Singapore on 7 April 2020 and assented to by the President on 7 April 2020, introduced a moratorium for businesses, including in the construction sector, unable to meet their contractual obligations due to the pandemic. It suspended for six months the enforcement of rights, claims for liquidated damages, and the calls on performance bonds and equivalent guarantees relating to contracts entered into before 25 March 2020; see also Wetmore and Elliot, *supra* note 5, at 207.

110 See *supra* Section 2.1., paras. 1 et seq.

111 *Id.*

112 See *supra* Section 2.2., paras. 1 et seq.

113 See *supra* Section 2.2., paras. 2 et seq.

114 See *supra* Section 2.1., paras. 1 et seq.

115 See *supra* Section 2.1., paras. 1 et seq.; and Section 2.2., paras. 2 et seq.

116 See *supra* Section 3.1., paras. 1 et seq.

117 See *supra* Section 3.2., paras. 1 et seq.

The pandemic has revealed once more how the construction industry is prone to risks, with the sector facing shortages of personnel, materials, and cash-flow overnight. Any shock exacerbates the already precarious situation, especially when a lack of liquidity is the sword of Damocles in the construction sector. Data are not yet available, but if already before the pandemic construction disputes represented the majority of the ICC caseload and half of the applications for emergency arbitrator proceedings,[118] it can be expected that this trend at least continued, if not increased. In any event, the pandemic exposed even more the risks of the industry and the importance of an informed call when seeking interim relief.

Only by knowing to which port to sail, one can find the more favorable wind.

118 See *supra* Section 3.1., paras. 1 et seq.

CHAPTER 11

COVID and Construction Disputes: Lessons Learnt and the Future Outlook

Oluwaseun Oloruntimehin

1 Introduction

Globally, construction is an over USD 11 trillion industry, with construction-related spending representing approximately 13% of the world's GDP[1] and an estimated 7–8% of global workforce employment.[2] However, with the decline from USD 11,217.4 billion in 2019 to USD 10,741.2 billion in 2020,[3] and forecasted low investment in global construction throughout 2021,[4] the industry was not immune to the COVID-19 pandemic and its macroeconomic impact. Companies struggled with financial pressures and tried to reduce expenditure to stave off insolvency, while contractors faced supply chain disruptions, material shortages, labor inefficiencies, unprecedented government restrictions, shutdowns, and delay costs. Inevitably, the consequence to these problems has been a rise in construction disputes.

However, the pandemic did not have the same effect on every region of the world. The impact of the COVID-19 pandemic on the European and African construction sectors was different. Therefore, a comparative analysis which explores the English common law and Continental Europe civil law dichotomy on excusatory doctrines, such as *force majeure* and frustration, which

1 Smiljanic Stasha, "30+ Fascinating Construction Industry Statistics (2022)," Policy Advice, last modified March 5, 2022, https://policyadvice.net/insurance/insights/construction-industry-statistics/.

2 "Construction Sector Employment in Low-Income Countries: Size of the Sector," Infrastructure and Cities for Economic Development ("ICED"), accessed March 30, 2022, http://icedfacility.org/resource/construction-sector-employment-low-income-countries-size-sector/.

3 "Impact of COVID-19 on Construction Industry Market by Type (Residential, Non-Residential and Heavy & Civil Engineering) and Region (North America, Europe, Asia Pacific, Middle East & Africa, South America) – Global Forecast to 2024," Markets and Markets, accessed March 30, 2022, https://www.lawdepot.com/force-majeure/#.YM8SvG6xX-Y. https://www.marketsandmarkets.com/Market-Reports/covid-19-impact-on-construction-market-65270035.html.

4 Stasha, *supra* note 1.

 | DOI:10.1163/9789004514874_014

discharges liability for non-performance but not improper performance, is warranted. Also relevant are possible claims for Extension of Time ("EOT"), suspension or termination of works, and financial entitlement to delay/increased costs or reimbursement of losses and expenses within the context of standard industry contracts, Joint Contracts Tribunal ("JCT") contracts,[5] and Fédération Internationale des Ingénieurs-Conseils ("FIDIC") contracts.[6]

The argument should also be made that industry standard contracts, as drafted, are inadequate and largely ambiguous in addressing the increasingly interconnected world and the ripple effect of potential disruptions in any one or more continents. Vague provisions and ambiguous catch-all phrases should be avoided, and a greater focus should be on specific terms that anticipate disruptive circumstances, allocate risk for non-performance, and clearly define excusatory doctrines with their consequences, thereby making resolutions easier and more predictable.

2 Force Majeure

The term "*force majeure*" is French for "superior, greater or irresistible force."[7] The concept of *force majeure*, which originates from French jurisprudence, is the alteration of contractual obligations and liabilities due to the occurrence of extraordinary circumstance(s) beyond the control of parties after the contract formation. This extraordinary circumstance(s) prevents, hinders, or delays a party from performing its obligations. As a source of liability exemption, *force majeure* protects defaulting parties from a claim for increased cost/losses and breach of contract liability by entitling the termination or suspension of performance, allowing non-performance or an extension of time for performance.

5 JCT suite of contracts are a range of standard form building and construction contracts formulated by the Joint Contracts Tribunal Limited, registered in the United Kingdom ("UK"). Thus, these standard contracts are mostly used for commercial developments in the UK but may be adapted by parties in other jurisdictions. "Our History," JCT, accessed March 30, 2022, https://corporate.jctltd.co.uk/about-us/our-history/.

6 FIDIC contracts are standard form contracts for the consulting engineering industry and includes contracts for works, clients, consultants, sub-consultants, joint ventures and representatives. These contracts are formulated by FIDIC, a global organization with members from over 100 countries. "About Us" FIDIC, accessed March 30, 2022, https://fidic.org/about-us.

7 "Using Force Majeure in a Contract," LawDepot, accessed March 30, 2022, https://www.lawdepot.com/force-majeure/#.YM8SvG6xX-Y.

In *Lebeaupin v. Crispin*,[8] the King's Bench in the United Kingdom ("UK") further defined *force majeure*:

> This term is used with reference to all circumstances independent of the will of man, and which it is not in his power to control ... [t]hus war, inundations and epidemics are cases of *force majeure*, it has even been decided that a strike of workmen constitutes a case of *force majeure*.[9]

Force majeure is recognized in common and civil law jurisdictions; however, the premise for its enforcement differs in each system. Its required elements are provided in most civil law codes, while it must be defined in contractual terms for common law jurisdictions.

2.1 *Continental Europe Civil Law and Francophone Africa*

As a civil law concept, *force majeure* or similar provisions are codified in civil law jurisdictions in Europe (France,[10] the Netherlands,[11] and Germany)[12] and Francophone and North Africa (such as Senegal[13] and Egypt).[14] In these jurisdictions, *force majeure* need not be contractually provided, as statutory provisions would apply automatically to all contracts.

These statutory provisions provide avoidance of liability for breach of contract if an external, unavoidable, unforeseeable, unanticipated, or unpredictable event occurs post-contract formation that prevents or renders performance impossible and is beyond the control of, or not attributable to, the non-performing party.

There is an emphasis on the causal link and absence of fault or non-attribution to the non-performing party for the breach because the impediment (*force majeure* event) is unavoidable and outside the sphere of risk for the party. The Dutch Civil Code in Article 6:75 requires that the non-performing

8 *Lebeaupin v. Crispin* [1920] 2 K.B 714.

9 *Id.* at 719; Stephen Furst et al., *Keating on Construction Contracts*, 9th ed. (London: Sweet & Maxwell Ltd, 2012), 893, 20–118.

10 French Civil Code 2016, Article 1218.

11 Dutch Civil Code 1992, Book 6 (The Law of Obligations), Article 6:75.

12 German Civil Code, Section 275.

13 Senegalese Civil and Commercial Obligations Code, Article 129.

14 Egyptian Civil Code, Article 165.

party must not be responsible for the breach by law, juridical act, or generally accepted principles (common opinion).[15]

Except as contractually provided, financial incapacity, increased cost, or illness of personnel are not valid reasons for the invocation of *force majeure*. The non-performing party is required to notify the other party of the circumstances and must implement measures to mitigate the impact of the impediment.

The typical remedy to a *force majeure* breach is to suspend performance or set aside the contract.[16] In Article 1218 of the French Civil Code, if the impediment is temporary, the obligation is suspended; however, if it is permanent, the contract is automatically terminated and the parties are free from their obligations.[17] Usually, specific performance or monetary damages are not available remedies.

Over time, French courts have treated the consequence of epidemics differently, as minor epidemics are not considered to be *force majeure* events, while other wide-spread epidemics such as the Ebola epidemic are treated as *force majeure* events.[18] It was therefore debatable whether this pandemic would be found to be an epidemic that warranted a declaration of *force majeure*. However, given its wide-spread impact and the declaration by the World Health Organization that COVID-19 was a pandemic,[19] it was likely to justify a declaration of *force majeure*.

While these civil law jurisdictions allow parties to add *force majeure* clauses in their contract, the parties are not allowed to use these clauses to derogate from mandatory laws and principles.[20]

15 Dutch Civil Code 1992, *supra* note 11; "Corona And Contracts In The Netherlands," Dutch Law Institute, accessed March 30, 2022, https://dutch-law.com/corona-contract-netherlands.html.

16 French Civil Code 2016, Article 1351.

17 *Id.* at Article 1218; Arnaud Belisaire, "France: Construction *force majeure* and alternative relief: *Force majeure* and alternative relief under standard form construction contracts and local law," Norton Rose Fulbright, May 2020, https://www.nortonrosefulbright.com/en-fr/knowledge/publications/02e4f9bd/france-relief-provisions-in-construction-contract-suites.

18 French Courts in CA Paris, 25 September, 1998, 1996/08159 and CA Basse-Terre, 17 December, 2018, 17/00739 held that minor plague epidemics and the chikungunya virus epidemic are not *force majeure* events, but held in CA Paris, 17 March, 2016, 15/04263 that the 2013 Ebola epidemic was a *force majeure* event.

19 "WHO Director-General's opening remarks at the media briefing on COVID-19 – 11 March 2020," World Health Organization, accessed March 30, 2022, https://www.who.int/director-general/speeches/detail/who-director-general-s-opening-remarks-at-the-media-briefing-on-covid-19---11-march-2020.

20 Principles of reasonableness and fairness under Dutch Civil Code 1992 and abusive clauses under French law, Article L212–1. of the Consumer Code.

2.2 *Swiss Jurisprudence*

Force majeure is not defined under the Swiss Code of Obligations ("SCO").[21] Thus, there is no statutory definition of *force majeure*, and its enforcement will depend on the existence of contractual provisions. When a *force majeure* clause is provided for in a contract but not defined, the Swiss courts have recognized that *force majeure* occurs when an extraordinary and unforeseeable external event renders performance objectively impossible.[22]

In the absence of a *force majeure* clause, the legal consequences will depend on whether the impossibility to fulfill a contract exists only for a limited period of time, or whether the impossibility to perform is permanent.[23] If the impossibility to perform is for a limited time, the non-defaulting party may extend the time for performance, but if performance is still not rendered by the end of the extended time limit, the contract may be terminated.[24] The non-defaulting party who withdraws from the contract may refuse the promised consideration, demand the return of any performance already made, and claim damages. Damages will be recoverable unless the defaulting party can prove absence of fault.[25]

When the impossibility to perform is permanent and the circumstances causing this default is not attributable to the defaulting party, the obligation to perform is discharged.[26] In such instances, Swiss law applies restitution for unjust enrichment; therefore, consideration already received must be returned.[27] However, in cases where the risk passes to the non-defaulting party prior to performance by virtue of law or the contract, this may not be applicable.[28]

In addition, because contractual liability for non-performance of obligations under the Swiss Code of Obligations is based upon fault,[29] the non-performing party may be released from liability by proving the absence of fault if non-performance is caused by *force majeure*.

---

21 Federal Act on the Amendment of the Swiss Civil Code (Part Five: Code of Obligations) of 30 March 1911 (hereafter "SCO").

22 Swiss Federal Supreme Court case, BGE (1976) 102 Ib 257, 262.

23 Philipp J. Dickenmann, "Q&A: Force Majeure Under Swiss Law – Requirements and Consequences," CMS: Law, Tax, Future, accessed 30 March 2022, https://cms.law/en/che/publication/q-a-force-majeure-under-swiss-law-requirements-and-consequences.

24 SCO, *supra* note 21, at Article 107(1) and (2); Dickenmann, *supra* note 23.

25 SCO, *supra* note 21, at Article 109.

26 *Id.* at Article 119 (1).

27 *Id.* at Article 119 (2).

28 *Id.* at Article 119 (3).

29 *Id.* at Article 97 (1).

2.3 *English Common Law and Anglophone Africa*

A creation of civil law, *force majeure* is not a term of art under common law and has no statutory definition. Therefore, in common law jurisdictions like the UK, the United States of America ("USA"), Nigeria, and Ghana, the presence of a *force majeure* clause is vital to the enforceability of this doctrine because the contract terms determine its scope.

To successfully sustain a declaration of *force majeure*, a *force majeure* event must have occurred after the contract formation, the event must be unforeseeable and the sole cause of non-performance, steps must have been taken to mitigate the consequences, and notice must have been given within the specified time frame (notice requirements).

In construction disputes, the COVID-19 pandemic may be deemed a *force majeure* event if not specified in the contract clause. As far back as 1920,[30] English courts have declared pandemics to be a *force majeure* event, and given the declaration by the World Health Organization on March 11, 2020[31] that COVID-19 was a pandemic, this shifts in favor of a *force majeure* declaration. However, the affected contract must have been formed pre-COVID-19 because the *force majeure* event must be unforeseeable.

The *force majeure* event must "prevent," "delay," or "hinder" performance.[32] It is not enough that the event increased costs or made performance more expensive or difficult to fulfil; it must have prevented performance.[33] If the clause states that the event must make performance impossible, this sets a high bar for its invocation.

Further, the event must be the sole cause of non-performance. The English court in *Classic Maritime Inc. v. Limbungan Makmur SDN BHD*[34] applied the "but for" test for causation and held that there was no *force majeure* because there were competing causes for non-performance, one of which was not a *force majeure* event. This test was also upheld in *Seadrill Ghana Operations Limited vs Tullow Ghana Limited.*[35]

The non-performing party is typically required to serve notice declaring that a *force majeure* event has occurred and detailing the effect of the event on performance. It is important that the notice requirements (form, substance of

30 *Lebeaupin*, *supra* note 8.

31 World Health Organization, *supra* note 19.

32 *Tennants (Lancashire) Limited v. CS Wilson & Co. Ltd* [1917] UKHL 523.

33 *Thames Valley Power Limited v. Total Gas & Power Limited* [2006] 1 Lloyd's Rep. 668.

34 *Classic Maritime Inc. v Limbungan Makmur SDN BHD* [2018] EWHC 2389 (Comm).

35 *Seadrill Ghana Operations Limited vs Tullow Ghana Limited* [2018] EWHC 1640 (Comm).

notice, and time limits) are adhered to, because failure to do so may render the claim or extension request void.[36]

Finally, the non-performing party must have taken steps to mitigate the effect of the event. If it is the failure to take mitigating steps instead of the event itself that causes the inability to perform, there may be no entitlement to relief.

The available remedies are usually provided in the *force majeure* clause. A typical relief would be extension of time for performance, resulting in the suspension of performance and discharge of liability, with the option to terminate the contract if the *force majeure* event persists for a certain period or beyond a specified deadline. Some clauses may also provide for financial entitlement for costs or losses. If the clause is silent as to the allocation of costs already incurred or payments made by either party, they are usually not recoverable. In such instances, businesses may need to look to available insurance claims or consider the doctrine of frustration.

3 Frustration, Impossibility, and Impracticability of Performance

Where *force majeure* is not available, the affected party may rely on the English common law doctrine of frustration. As a serious limitation of the principle *pacta sunt servanda*,[37] frustration applies where an unforeseeable and unavoidable event occurs after the contract has been entered into, which is not due to the fault of either party, and which renders further performance "impossible," "illegal," "unlawful," or "makes the parties' obligations radically different from those contemplated when the contract was entered into." In addition, non-performance must not be preventable or mitigatable by alternative measures. However, notices are not required to be sent for enforcement.

This defense presents difficulties in proving the unforeseeability of the event and the impossibility of, illegality of, or radical change to, performance with no possible alternatives. Like *force majeure*, the mere fact that performance has become more difficult, expensive, or commercially unviable does not suffice in establishing frustration. However, frustration goes a step further, requiring that performance must be impossible (subject matter of contract destroyed), illegal (against new mandatory laws), or something radically different from the

36 *GPP Big Field LLP v Solar EPC Solutions* [2018] EWHC 2866.

37 The principle *pacta sunt servanda* means "agreements must be kept."

contemplation of parties at contract formation (changed circumstances). The event need not be the sole cause of non-performance.[38]

A successful defense of frustration renders the contract void by operation of law, and all contractual obligations cease to exist. Parties revert to the position they were in prior to contract formation, as if the contract never took place.

The presence of a *force majeure* clause does not automatically exclude the operation of frustration. However, frustration applies to unforeseen events, and if parties addressed a particular event under the *force majeure* clause of their contract, it may be argued that parties foresaw that event, and the party must pursue relief under the *force majeure* clause and not assert frustration.

3.1 *English Common Law and Anglophone Africa*

Frustration of purpose is one borne from general precepts of English common law. Recognized as far back as 1903 in *Krell v. Henry*,[39] and formulated by the House of Lords Appellate Committee's decision in *National Carriers Ltd v. Panalpina (Northern) Ltd*,[40] frustration is applicable in common law jurisdictions, like the UK and Anglophone Africa (such as Nigeria, Ghana), even in the absence of contractual provisions.

A contract can be rescinded where a supervening event takes place, the occurrence and impact of which is without fault of either party, and for which the contract makes no sufficient provision. This event must render further performance of the contract impossible (doctrine of impossibility), illegal, or transform the nature of the parties' rights and obligations to such an extent that it would be unjust for the parties to be held to their original bargain.

The UK Law Reform (Frustrated Contracts) Act 1943, Section 1, provides the legal consequences of frustration, so that when contracts governed by English law have become impossible to perform or frustrated, parties are discharged from further performance. Contract sums, costs, expenses, and benefits conferred are recoverable except in limited circumstances.

In the USA, frustration of purpose is embodied in Section 265 of the Restatement (Second) of Contracts when the event causing the party's performance to be impracticable was not the party's fault. The doctrine of

38 *Bremer Handelsgesellschaft mbH. v Vanden Avenne-Izegem PVBA* [1978] 2 Lloyd's Rep. 109.

39 *Krell v. Henry* [1903] 2 KB 740.

40 *National Carriers Ltd v. Panalpina (Northern) Ltd* [1981] 1 AC 675; Quinn Emanuel Urquhart & Sullivan, "Managing the Growing Fallout from the Coronavirus – Contractual Non-Performance Defenses Around the World," The International Comparative Legal Guides, May 15, 2020, https://iclg.com/briefing/12346-managing-the-growing-fallout-from-the-coronavirus-contractual-non-performance-defenses-around-the-world.

commercial impracticability is also recognized in Article 2–615(a) of the Uniform Commercial Code 1951,[41] wherein a seller is protected from breach of contractual duty (obligations) when performance is impracticable due to unforeseen circumstances.

Frustration is difficult to establish, but if successful, brings the contract to an end.

3.2 *Continental Europe Civil Law and Francophone Africa*

The doctrine of frustration is not recognized under civil law codes, but there are statutory provisions that provide for such circumstances where performance is impossible, onerous, or excessively difficult.[42] A right of recission is recognized, and courts may either discharge the contract or reduce the obligation of the promisor by a reasonable extent.

Article 1195 of the French Civil Code 2016 introduced the principle of *imprévision* (hardship), allowing for renegotiation of the contract if performance becomes excessively onerous for a party who did not accept the risk of the change. If renegotiation is rejected or fails, the contract may be terminated, subject to judicial review.[43]

Section 313 of the German Civil Code[44] contains the principle of *clausula rebus sic stantibus* (changed circumstances), giving parties the right to renegotiate, revoke, or terminate a contract if circumstances have significantly changed, the change was unforeseeable, and a party cannot reasonably be expected to uphold the contract without an alteration. This is based on the principle of reasonableness and fairness in most civil codes. Section 275 of the German Civil Code provides for the discharge of liability for impossibility of performance.[45]

3.3 *Swiss Jurisprudence*

The doctrine of hardship due to a radical or extraordinary change in the contract is not regulated in the Swiss Code of Obligations but is recognized under Swiss law and by Swiss courts as a matter of the general principles of good faith and fair dealing.[46]

41 "Uniform Commercial Code: Summary," Uniform Law Commission, accessed March 30, 2022, https://www.uniformlaws.org/acts/ucc.

42 Pan. J. Zepos, "Frustration of Contract in Comparative Law and in the New Greek Civil Code of 1945 (Article 388)," *The Modern Law Review* 11, no. 1 (January 1948): 36.

43 French Civil Code 2016, Article 1195.

44 German Civil Code, Section 313.

45 *Id.* at Section 275.

46 Swiss Civil Code of 10 December 1907, Article 2.

Additionally, Article 119 of the Swiss Code of Obligations[47] provides that contractual obligations are deemed extinguished where performance is impossible by circumstances not attributable to the obligor. The Swiss Federal Supreme Court has held that the event must be unexpected, unavoidable, unforeseeable, and beyond the control of parties.[48] The event must cause the permanent and objective impossibility of performance. The parties must be put back to the same position that they were in before the contract was made.

4 Defenses and Claims in Industry Standard Construction Contracts

4.1 *JCT 2016: Relevant Events, Termination and Relevant Matters*

Force majeure, albeit not defined in the JCT's *Design and Build Contract 2016*,[49] is categorized as a relevant event in Clause 2.26.14,[50] entitling the contractor to an extension of time for the period in which completion of the works was delayed because of a *force majeure* event. This raises the issue of enforceability of this clause, because it is dependent on the definition or interpretation of *force majeure* in the governing jurisdiction, which creates uncertainties.[51]

The contractor must give notice to the employer of material circumstances (a *force majeure* event) causing delays when it becomes reasonably apparent that the progress of the work is, or is likely to be, delayed. The notice should include the expected effect(s) of the event, including an estimate of the delay to the completion date.[52] The contractor must attempt to prevent or mitigate the delay.[53] Once accepted, an extension of time extends the period before

47 Swiss Code of Obligations, Article 119; see also *supra* Section 2.2., which delves into the considerations and legal consequences when the impossibility to perform is permanent.

48 ATF 111 II 352; Luc Thévenoz and Franz Werro, *Code des obligations I. Commentaire romand*, 2nd ed (Basel: Helbing Lichtenhahn Verlag, 2012), article 119 para. 7; Konstantin Christie, Charis Tan, and Mino Han, "When circumstances change: a comparative view of the law and ICC model clauses," International Bar Association, accessed March 30, 2022, https://www.ibanet.org/article/776f5fed-b7ff-4320-a246-7b52770fcd7a.

49 Joint Contract Tribunal, *Design and Build Contract 2016* (London: Sweet & Maxwell Ltd, 2016) ("JCT Contract 2016").

50 Any reference to "Clause" in Section 4.1. refers to the corresponding Clause in the JCT Contract 2016.

51 In *British Electrical and Associated Industries (Cardiff) Limited v. Patley Pressings Limited* [1953] 1 WLF 280, the court held that a clause which stated "the usual *force majeure* conditions shall apply" was too uncertain, as *force majeure* clauses came in too many different varieties.

52 JCT Contract 2016, *supra* note 49, at Clause 2.24.1 and 2.24.2.

53 To prevent or mitigate delay, the contractor would typically be expected to use best endeavors. The English court in *Sheffield District Railway v. Great Central Railway* [1911]

which the contractor is liable to pay liquidated and ascertained damages for failing to complete the work by the completion date.

Either party may terminate the contract if the uncompleted work is suspended for a continuous period of 2 months or such other time agreed by the parties in the contract because of a *force majeure* event under Clause 8.11.1 or due to the exercise of governmental statutory power under Clause 8.11.5. At the end of the 2-month period, the terminating party must serve a 7 days' notice of impending termination and then a notice of termination at the end of the 7-day period. Upon termination, the contractor is required to vacate the site and issue a final account on the value of works carried out, losses, expenses, and the costs of demobilization, materials, and goods ordered.

If *force majeure* cannot be established, Clause 2.26 provides other circumstances in which a contractor may be entitled to additional time. These include: a delay caused by a change (Clause 2.26.1); an employer's instruction to postpone any work (Clause 2.26.2); a deferment of giving possession of the site (Clause 2.26.3); an employer's impediment, prevention, or default (Clause 2.26.6); carrying out of works by a statutory undertaker (Clause 2.26.7); labor issues caused by civil commotion or union action, strike or lock-out (Clause 2.26.11); the exercise of statutory powers by the UK government or any local or public authority after the base date[54] that is not caused by a contractor's default and which directly affects the works (Clause 2.26.12); and/or a delay in receiving permissions from statutory bodies (Clause 2.26.13).

In contrast to FIDIC Contracts, there is no entitlement to compensation under Clause 4.19 for the resulting losses and expenses unless the relevant event is also a relevant matter. Unfortunately, neither a pandemic, a *force majeure* event, a change in law, nor a governmental exercise of statutory power are listed as relevant matters under Clause 4.21. Therefore, under Clause 4.21, a successful claim for costs is unlikely. However, if the delays are caused by

---

27 TLR 451 held that "best endeavours means what it says – it does not mean second best endeavours." However, Anthony May et al., *Keating on Building Contracts* 6th ed. (London: Sweet & Maxwell Ltd, 1995), 642 and Stephen Furst, Vivian Ramsey and Donald Keating, *Keating on Construction Contracts* 10th ed. (London: Sweet & Maxwell Ltd, 2016), 20–152, 791, clarifies that how a contractor should go about exercising best endeavors depends on the circumstances of each case, but "it does not contemplate the expenditure of substantial sums of money." Nicholas Downing and Emma Schaafsma, "Managing Delay Under JCT Contracts Due to COVID-19," Herbert Smith Freehills, March 12, 2020, https://hsfnotes.com/construction/2020/03/12/managing-delay-under-jct-contracts-due-to-covid-19/.

54 The base date is the date of tender submitted by the contractor. This date is usually stipulated in the contract as some days prior to the latest submission date of tenders.

changes instructed by the employer (Clause 4.21.1), an express suspension or postponing of work by the employer (Clause 4.21.2.1), or any impediment, prevention, or default by the employer (Clause 4.21.5), additional costs may be given.

4.2 *FIDIC Contracts 1999 & 2017*

4.2.1 Force Majeure: Exceptional Events

Force Majeure is defined in Sub-Clause ("SC")[55] 19.1 of the Red Book 1999 (RB1999),[56] Yellow Book 1999 (YB1999),[57] and Silver Book 1999 (SB1999)[58] as an event or circumstance: (a) which is beyond a Party's control; (b) which such party could not reasonably have provided against before entering into the Contract (*unforeseeable*); (c) which, having arisen, such party could not reasonably have avoided or overcome (*unavoidable*); and (d) which is not substantially attributable to the other party (*absence of fault*). The non-performing party must use all reasonable endeavors to minimize the impact, delay, and additional cost of a *force majeure* event.

In the Red Book 2017 (RB2017),[59] Yellow Book 2017 (YB2017),[60] and Silver Book 2017 (SB2017)[61] (2017 Edition),[62] the title "*Force Majeure*" was changed to "Exceptional Events" in SC 18.1, but they are in effect the same provisions.

While war, hostilities, strikes, lockouts, and natural catastrophes (earthquakes and hurricanes, among others) are *force majeure* events under SC 19.1, 1999 Edition and SC 18.1, 2017 Edition, a pandemic or epidemic is not listed. However, the list is non-exhaustive. Therefore, COVID-19-related claims are subject to different factors in different jurisdictions. A claim's success may depend on the severity of government restrictions or whether COVID-19 was deemed a natural catastrophe within the jurisdiction.

---

55 Any reference to "Sub-Clause" or "SC" in Section 4.2. refers to the corresponding subclause in the referenced FIDIC Contract/Book.

56 FIDIC, *Conditions of Contract for Construction*, 1st ed. (1999).

57 FIDIC, *Conditions of Contract for Plant and Design-Build*, 1st ed. (1999).

58 FIDIC, *Conditions of Contract for EPC/Turnkey Projects*, 1st ed. (1999).

59 FIDIC, *Conditions of Contract for Construction*, 2nd ed. (2017).

60 FIDIC, *Conditions of Contract for Plant and Design-Build*, 2nd ed. (2017).

61 FIDIC, *Conditions of Contract for EPC/Turnkey Projects*, 2nd ed. (2017).

62 The 1999 and 2017 Editions have uniform clauses and definitions. This analysis is on the corresponding provisions of 1999 and 2017 Editions and the "FIDIC COVID-19 Guidance Memorandum to Users of FIDIC Standard Forms of Works Contract," FIDIC, accessed March 30, 2022, https://fidic.org/sites/default/files/COVID%2019%20Guidance%20Memorandum%20-%20PDF.pdf.

There must be a causal link between the event and non-performance. The event must have prevented performance; difficulty in performance does not suffice. With the implementation of relevant health and safety policies responding to COVID-19 (restricted movement, social distancing, use of masks, personal protection equipment ("PPE") and sanitizers, additional health and safety training for employees, COVID-testing, contact tracing and isolation for employees that tested positive, among others), one challenge was to show that the policies actually prevented performance. This is because, in some instances, it was arguable that these policies only made it more difficult or expensive to perform contractual obligations.

If difficulty in performance is encountered, extension of time may be sought under SC 8.4(d), 1999 Edition and SC 8.5(d), 2017 Edition for unforeseeable shortages in availability of personnel, goods, or employer-supplied materials[63] caused by an epidemic or governmental action. A contractor may also be entitled under SC 8.5 1999 Edition and SC 8.6 2017 Edition to an extension of time if they suffered from delays caused by authorities or government measures.

Under SC 19.2 RB1999 and SC 18.2 RB2017, the party in default is required to give notice within 14 days of the date the party became aware or should have become aware of the *force majeure* or exceptional event. The notice must stipulate the event or circumstances constituting *force majeure* and the obligations which it is or will be prevented from performing. If the notice is received by the other party after the 14-day period, then the defaulting party is excused from performance of any prevented obligations only from the date on which the notice is received by the non-defaulting party.

If successful, the contractor will be entitled to an extension of time for any resulting delays and excused from performance of the prevented obligations under SC 19, 1999 Edition and SC 18, 2017 Edition. In addition, the continuation of a *force majeure* event for a continuous period of 84 days or multiple periods totaling 140 days would entitle either party to terminate the contract, with the value of any completed work and relevant costs being recoverable.

If the consequence of an event renders performance impossible or unlawful for one or both parties, or the governing law of the contract releases the parties from further performance of the contract, then either party has the right to be released from its contractual obligations.[64] Financial entitlements are unlikely, as these arise from non-performance caused by man-made changes or changes in laws or legislation.

63 Wording in RB2017.

64 SC 19.7 in RB1999.

4.2.2 Change in Laws or Legislation

The FIDIC contracts in SC 13.7 RB1999 and SC 13.6 RB2017 envisage an "adjustment to the execution of works" caused by a change in legislation[65] or laws,[66] or under SC 5.4 YB and SB as "changed or new applicable standards constituted by a change in legislation/laws."

The 2017 Edition gives a broad definition of laws in SC 1.1.49 to mean "all national (or state or provincial) legislation, statutes, acts, decrees, rules, ordinances, orders, treaties, international law and other laws, and regulations and by-laws of any legally constituted public authority." This definition covers a wide range of legislation and regulatory actions from any legally constituted public authority, including parliamentary acts, down to state-wide action and local levels, such as municipality orders.[67]

Once established that the inability to perform is caused by local authorities or local governments in what is considered to be changes in laws of the country, then the contractor may seek remedies under SC 13.7 1999 Edition or SC 13.6 2017 Edition. The rationale for entitlement to increased costs, reimbursement of losses, and an extension of time is that the contractor has an obligation to comply with applicable laws under SC 1.13, 1999 Edition and SC 1.12, SB2017. Parties are also entitled to terminate the contract if the governmental order or change in applicable law makes contract performance impracticable or impossible.

5 Practical Considerations

Parties seeking protection or relief should carefully review contractual provisions, relevant facts, judicial interpretation and precedents, and/or governmental or industry guidance in order to establish *force majeure* or frustration. Relevant parties should timely serve procedural notices, execute site preservation strategies, record specific COVID-19 impacts on the project, and any measures taken to mitigate that impact. Consultation with a Dispute Adjudication Board for JCT contracts or Dispute Avoidance/Adjudication Board for FIDIC contracts is prudent, as they provide tailored advice on COVID-19 impact based on the contract terms and relevant facts.

Finally, parties are advised to shy away from a literal, strict, or rigid application of contract terms and instead value the importance of social responsibility

65 RB1999.

66 RB2017.

67 FIDIC, *supra* note 62.

and long-term interests in preserving business activities and cooperation. Thus, negotiation and compromise through early dispute resolution and mutual agreement is favored.

6 Recommendations and Conclusion

There is a need for industry standard contracts to provide a clear and comprehensive definition of *force majeure* and frustration, with an identification of diverse events that can disrupt performance. While *force majeure* should prevent performance, frustration should render performance impossible, unlawful, or radically different from the contemplation of parties.

Events such as pandemics, epidemics, economic embargoes, sanctions, travel restrictions, and/or depression or recession, amongst others, should entitle the affected party to an extension of time, the suspension or termination of work, and/or price adjustment. Catch-all phrases, like "any other cause beyond the parties' control," should be avoided, as there may be a conflict between the *ejusdem generis* rule and the parties' intentions.

The causal link between the inability to perform and the event must also be clear, as the use of certain phrases should not be the only deciding factor. This is especially useful in common law jurisdictions, where, unlike in civil law jurisdictions, parol (external) evidence is generally prohibited.

The timing and effect of procedural notices should also be clarified in the contract, because while the event may have occurred, ascertaining when and how it affects performance may not immediately be clear. Thus, compliance with notice requirements should not be interpreted to preclude or delay entitlement to relief to prevent the issuance of premature notices that may lead to more disruptions.

While contractors are required to mitigate or use any reasonable or best endeavors to reduce delays, specific drafting or legal guidance is likely required to define best endeavors.

The disruptions that continue once the *force majeure* event has ended should also be addressed, as this will become an issue post-COVID-19. Provided that such disruptions directly stem from the pandemic, the legal consequences of the *force majeure* event should remain available to parties, and/or parties should be open to renegotiations and early dispute resolution.

The consequences of the COVID-19 pandemic are that careful attention must be given to the drafting of future *force majeure* clauses and similar provisions, especially regarding the type of events that would constitute *force majeure*, its consequences, and the allocation of risk between the parties. Contract drafters should utilize the inherent flexibility of *force majeure* clauses by effectively adapting them to include possible events that could disrupt performance and clearly identifying the legal consequences of the occurrence of such event(s).

While there are no general provisions applicable to every contract, it is recommended that the guiding principles on the enforcement of *force majeure*, frustration, and similar provisions are put into consideration when negotiating contracts. Based on the lessons learned from the pandemic, amendments to JCT and FIDIC contracts are also encouraged.

Conclusion

Steven G. Shapiro

This book was imagined in the early arc of the pandemic, when those first months were filled with tragic news, uncertainty, dramatic decisions, and the days were dominated with profound feelings of panic and upheaval. We selected the hospitality and construction industries based on their roles as international economic drivers, the complexity of relationships in these sectors, and legal issues that were uprooted in the crisis. We first invited topic suggestions from experts in international arbitration with portfolios as arbitrators, litigants, academics, and representatives of arbitral institutions.

We were oversubscribed with submissions across topics, with our publisher first assigning peer reviewers to assess and approve the title and chapter proposals, then we finally selected the topics and authors. The authors wrote and delivered the chapters while vaccines were first being administered, along with comments from independent experts in the fields, and a conference to deliver the topics, with audience feedback.

We deliver this book in the next era that follows the pandemic. As this book moves to publication, we have started to refer to time as pre-COVID, COVID, and post-COVID. Our authors have sorted through the many cases and experiences during the pandemic, and have identified pertinent topics, including key contract provisions, and the impact of the COVID pandemic on arbitration.

There were few historical comparisons to prepare for the chaos created when the COVID-19 pandemic swept across the globe. It is hard to identify analogous situations. Times of war are similar in terms of scope and the need for a drastic response, yet armed battle among nations differs from a mysterious and deadly global infectious disease with, at the time, no cure. In any event, unlike topics that emerge out of the regular cycles of the time, the COVID-19 pandemic created complete havoc for healthcare and public policy, as well as a crushing impact on commerce, law, and disputes.

Cases and rulings are not static and live along a continuum in time, movement, and context. The evolution of legal agreements, the tools of technology, and disputes in hospitality and construction are, of course, not confined to any sort of strict schedule. Certainly, there are eras of rapid change and eras when progress is methodical. In most economic cycles, there are shifts and subtle changes over time and there are rare times of collapse. COVID-19, in a matter of weeks and days, created a global crisis in international commerce.

 | DOI:10.1163/9789004514874_015

It has been our guiding intent that this book should carry academic merit and scholarly rigor, while at the same time the book should be a valuable text and reference in practice and procedure. It is our hope that readers gather insight, are able to incorporate material for their work, and are able to make future decisions informed with an analysis of the COVID era. A thoughtful review of this era should include, in our view, a look ahead and if not predictions, then at least hints of direction. The work of the international economy demands a semblance of order and consistency of the ground rules.

Our authors have distinguished themselves in offering important cases and facts and especially their expert wisdom in context with the issues. While most readers likely proceeded through this book in the linear order of the chapters or by specific topic interest, the chapters can also be regrouped by theme. As a general matter, the topics can be classified into: (i) arbitration procedures and arbitrators; (ii) changes needed, if any, to the terms and conditions of underlying legal agreements, most notably the expectation and allocation of risk; (iii) government actions and impact on investment treaties; and (iv) collateral financial instruments of the industries such as lending and performance bonds.

Part 1. Hospitality

Dating back to ancient stories of lodging, hospitality, at its most essential description, is an industry to house and feed itinerant travelers. Of course, the global hotel sector now includes multinational hotel brands, convention hotels, and resorts at a massive scale, plus countless hotels ranging from small independent inns to boutique hotels to luxury properties.

The economic relationships in hospitality are legally defined in the governing legal agreements. Like other contracts, those provisions certainly shift over time, express the details of the relationships, anticipate fact scenarios, and allocate legal and economic risk. In the current economic structure of the industry, there may be three or four disparate parties connected by legal agreements, including franchise agreements and hotel management agreements. These agreements often have a stated term of years that far exceed typical commercial relationships. While a lease for a large real estate tenant may be set at 10 years, hotel management agreements often have a stated term of 40 or 50 years and franchise relationships may be in place for 20 years, with rights to renew.

In the lodging industry, like other types of real estate asset types, the function of the lender is critical to create growth. The model, in general, is that the hotel owner seeks funding for a project, then makes payments for principal and interest until the debt is satisfied. The lender holds a right to the property to secure its debt, but its fundamental plan is to receive funds and then find the next projects.

With these topics in mind, we launched this book with the chapter examining the funding of arbitration matters, applicable to disputes of all types, including hospitality and construction. Funding legal cases has quickly altered the economics of clashes: it is an area that will continue to become highly specialized. There are characteristics of complex financial analysis, legal underwriting, and pressures on the relationships among lawyers, clients, and funders.

Other chapters in the hospitality section examine the direct impact of COVID on hotel development and agreements. In the sudden change in hotel revenue and profitability, banks were forced to make decisions to foreclose or abstain on hotel portfolios. In Chapter 2, our author offers the tenets of game theory to consider the decisions to foreclose.

In the bedlam of making health decisions, political leaders, legislatures, agencies, and regulators also made critical health policy and economic policy decisions. Governments made necessary decisions that impacted investment treaties. These decisions are discussed in Chapter 6.

In the relationships in the industry, there are times when outside forces cause an event beyond the control of the parties and forces that defy reasonable expectations of the parties. The agreements typically allocate and assign the party that will absorb this risk. By way of example, a catastrophic weather event that is well beyond expected and the average is certainly a risk to operations. The question for the parties and their counsel, then, is which party bears that risk. In many ways, the pandemic was a risk unforeseen by parties, which generated an impact on the industry. The pandemic suddenly tested these traditional contract provisions in agreements. In Chapters 3 and 4, the authors examine the notion that major events may excuse contract performance.

Part 2. Construction Matters

At its core, construction starts with design and engineering, then moves along a logical path to erecting structures. Design and construction date back at least to building the pyramids. Incredibly, the process to make and use concrete remains fundamentally the same as used for structures built in the Roman Empire, some still in place today. It is a stark juxtaposition when construction superintendents use laptops or computer tablets to review construction drawings while at the same time workers mix and place concrete with the formula of water, cement, and aggregate that was used in the days of aqueducts.

A construction project is a swarm of activities that is managed and logical, with the process that includes design, engineering, management, and of course, workers across trades in a highly dangerous project environment. Incredibly, the disparate parties that are enmeshed in a construction project often do not have a direct legal link when there is a dispute. Put differently, the partners and key participants in the construction industry are typically not legally connected by contracts. The property developers legally engage the architects and engineers; the property developers legally engage the general contractors. The general contractors legally engage the subcontractors; the property developers rely on government agencies to permit construction and sometimes receive economic incentives from public entities.

In the path of design and construction, especially internationally, the projects continue to be complex and costly. There are tools of technology in design and engineering, notably software, that help to solve complex tasks. There are improvements in the construction process and teams that test the limits of productivity and scale.

By its nature, construction is an industry of necessary confusion that needs constant clarifications and resolutions, most often without delay. In many cases, the quick resolution of construction disputes or clarifications is a key part of the process of design and construction. In fact, clarifications are incorporated into the process of design and construction. In Chapter 9, the authors discuss the crucial role of expedited arbitration and the need for efficient resolution of disputes. An important question, explored in Part 2, is whether legal process and procedures are meeting this task. In this environment, the arbitrators, dispute boards, mediators, or others are placed in key roles along the critical path of a project.

In construction, when a party fails in its performance, financial bonds and surety are critical to continue operations and move toward project completion. In Chapter 10, the author offers a deep look at the need for performance bonds and the use of injunctions in the process.

Again, political leaders and government agencies made important decisions during the pandemic that were identified in the chapters on hospitality. Like issues discussed in Chapter 5 on investment treaty claims in hospitality, Chapter 8 reviews investor-state arbitration in the construction industry. In parallel with hospitality issues, Chapter 7 again looks at the terms and conditions of the underlying legal agreements to adapt to the drastic changes taken in the pandemic.

Part 3. A Look, Perhaps, to the Future

The conclusion, by title and placement, is reserved to consider, reflect, and perhaps make an overarching sense of the content of the chapters. Of course, the pace of the construction industry and the hotel industry continues to push ahead, but will inevitably face timeless challenges, like delays and *force majeure*, and new challenges, like the pandemic or topics that we cannot yet imagine.

The authors have alerted us to contract provisions that need to be reconsidered and redrafted, and the impact on investment treaties when a government makes a public policy decision. At the same time, arbitrators and the process of arbitration will need to adapt procedures to meet these challenges and will need to somehow weave precedent and practical solutions to facts and scenarios that are unanticipated.

The authors have, in sum, shown that legal agreements, treaties, and arbitration were severely stressed and tested during the pandemic. The conclusion, we believe, is that we saw a deep flexing of traditions and ideas and that, as we have now hopefully emerged fully from the crisis, the systems were fair, adaptable, and permitted continued success.

We could clearly have been editors of a book on the collapse of the international hospitality and construction industries, and the failure of arbitration. Instead, we see healthy industries that were a bit battered, and yet ultimately strengthened in the work of thoughtful arbitrators and arbitration. We congratulate our authors on their work, thank our commentators for improving each chapter, and send our best wishes to our readers for the next era ahead of us.

Index

www.ingramcontent.com/pod-product-compliance
Lightning Source LLC
LaVergne TN
LVHW010625300926
849162LV00001B/69